Lecture Notes in Computer Science 2550

Edited by G. Goos, J. Hartmanis, and J. van Leeuwen

Springer
Berlin
Heidelberg
New York
Barcelona
Hong Kong
London
Milan
Paris
Tokyo

Alain Jean-Marie (Ed.)

Advances in Computing Science – ASIAN 2002

Internet Computing and Modeling, Grid Computing, Peer-to-Peer Computing, and Cluster Computing

7th Asian Computing Science Conference
Hanoi, Vietnam, December 4-6, 2002
Proceedings

 Springer

Series Editors

Gerhard Goos, Karlsruhe University, Germany
Juris Hartmanis, Cornell University, NY, USA
Jan van Leeuwen, Utrecht University, The Netherlands

Volume Editor

Alain Jean-Marie
Université de Montpellier 2
Laboratoire d'Informatique, de Robotique et de Microélectronique
161 Rue ADA, 34392 Montpellier Cedex 5, France
E-mail: ajm@lirmm.fr

Cataloging-in-Publication Data applied for

A catalog record for this book is available form the Library of Congress.

Bibliographic information published by Die Deutsche Bibliothek
Die Deutsche Bibliothek lists this publication in the Deutsche Nationalbibliografie;
detailed bibliographic data is available in the Internet at <http://dnb.ddb.de>.

CR Subject Classification (1998): C.2, D.1.3, D.2.7, D.2.12, D.4, H.3-4, I.2.3, F.2

ISSN 0302-9743
ISBN 3-540-00195-6 Springer-Verlag Berlin Heidelberg New York

Springer-Verlag Berlin Heidelberg New York
a member of BertelsmannSpringer Science+Business Media GmbH

http://www.springer.de

© Springer-Verlag Berlin Heidelberg 2002
Printed in Germany

Typesetting: Camera-ready by author, data conversion by PTP- Berlin, Stefan Sossna e. K.
Printed on acid-free paper   SPIN: 10871704   06/3142   5 4 3 2 1 0

Preface

The series of annual Asian Computing Science Conferences (ASIAN) was initiated in 1995 by AIT, INRIA, and UNU/IIST to provide a forum for researchers in computer science from the Asian region and to promote interaction with researchers from other regions. The first six conferences were held, respectively, in Bangkok, Singapore, Katmandu, Manila, Phuket, and Penang. The proceedings have been published in the Lecture Notes in Computer Science Series of Springer-Verlag.

This year, the main themes chosen for ASIAN 2002 were:

- Internet Computing and Modeling,
- Grid, Peer-to-Peer, and Cluster Computing.

The program committee selected 17 papers out of 30 submissions, and these papers show very well the richness of this field of scientific investigations. We have indeed papers on topics ranging from scientific cluster computing to advanced networking applications for the general public, and from network protocol design and evaluation to the architecture of the Grid.

The invited speakers of ASIAN 2002 were Alessandro Bassi (University of Tennessee), Brigitte Plateau (Institut Polytechnique de Grenoble), and Shinji Shimojo (Osaka University). The program committee thanks them for accepting its invitation.

The conference was held in Hanoi, Vietnam. We are much obliged to the Asian Institute of Technology of Hanoi, and its director Prof. Nguyen Cong Thanh, for coordinating the local arrangements.

Many thanks are due to our sponsoring institutions: the Asian Institute of Technology (Thailand), INRIA (France), and Waseda University (Japan).

Finally, I wish to thank warmly the program committee and the additional referees, for their efficient handling of the papers under unusual time constraints.

October 2002   Alain Jean-Marie

Program Committee

Chadi Barakat (INRIA, France)
Denis Caromel (University Nice Sophia/INRIA/CNRS-I3S/IUF, France)
Frederic Desprez (ENS Lyon, France)
Alain Jean-Marie (University Montpellier 2, France), Chair
Kanchana Kanchanasut (AIT, Thailand)
Zhen Liu (IBM Yorktown Heights, USA)
Phong Nguyen (ENS Paris, France)
CongDuc Pham (INRIA/University Lyon 1, France)
Brigitte Plateau (IMAG Grenoble, France)
Shinji Shimojo (Osaka University, Japan)
Kian-Lee Tan (NUS, Singapore)
Yong-Meng Teo (NUS, Singapore)
Putchong Uthayopas (Kasetsart University, Thailand)
Kenichi Yoshida (University Tsukuba, Japan)
Li Zhang (IBM Yorktown Heights, USA)

General Chairs

Kanchana Kanchanasut (AIT, Thailand)
Kazunori Ueda (Waseda University, Japan)

Local Organization Chair

Prof. Nguyen Cong Thanh (Director, Asian Institute of Technology, Vietnam)

Local Organization Committee

Nguyen Thi Bich Hoa (AIT, Vietnam)
Patcharee Basu (AIT, Thailand)
Natchana Poonthaweelap (AIT, Thailand)

Steering Committee

Shigeki Goto (Waseda University, Japan)
Stéphane Grumbach (INRIA, France)
Joxan Jaffar (NUS, Singapore)
R.K. Shyamasundar (TIFR Bombay, India)
Gilles Kahn (INRIA, France)
Kazunori Ueda (Waseda University, Japan)
Kanchana Kanchanasut (AIT, Thailand)
Zhou Chaochen (UNU/IIST, Macau)

Referees

Tigist Alemu
Rabea Boulifa
Yvan Calas
Eddy Caron
Serge Chaumette
Philippe Chrétienne
Arnaud Contes
Mongkol Ekpanyapong
Eric Fleury
Kazutoshi Fujikawa
Jerôme Galtier
Kaname Harumoto
Ludovic Henrio
Fabrice Huet

Junzo Kamahara
Frédéric Koriche
Eric Madelaine
Yutaka Nakamura
Martin Quinson
Yves Roudier
Abhik Roychoudhurey
P.S. Thiagarajan
Mabel Tidball
Julien Vayssiere
Marie-Catherine Vilarem
Roland Yap Hock Chuan
Leong Hon Wai

Table of Contents

The Logistical Backbone: Scalable Infrastructure for Global Data Grids

Alessandro Bassi, Micah Beck, Terry Moore, and James S. Plank

LoCI Laboratory - University of Tennessee
203 Claxton Building - 37996-3450 Knoxville, TN, USA
{abassi, mbeck, tmoore, plank}@cs.utk.edu

Abstract. Logistical Networking [1] can be defined as the global optimisation and scheduling of data storage, data movement, and computation. It is a technology for shared network storage that allows an easy scaling in terms of the size of the user community, the aggregate quantity of storage that can be allocated, and the distribution breadth of service nodes across network borders.
After describing the base concepts of Logistical Networking, we will introduce the Internet Backplane Protocol, a middleware for managing and using remote storage through allocation of primitive "byte arrays", showing a semantic in between buffer block and common files. As this characteristic can be too limiting for a large number of applications, we developed the exNode, that can be defined, in two words, as an inode for the for network distributed files. We will introduce then the Logistical Backbone, or L-Bone, is a distributed set of facilities that aim to provide high-performance, location- and application-independent access to storage for network and Grid applications of all kind.

Keywords: Logistical Networking, IBP, storage-enable Internet.

1 Introduction

While explosive growth in the use of compute and data intensive simulation continues to transform the practice of scientific investigation across every field, a parallel transformation is also revolutionizing the ability of researchers to collaborate across geographic and disciplinary barriers. The vision of a new era of science, produced by the convergence and maturation of these two powerful trends in scientific computing, is shared broadly within the research community. An indispensable key to realizing this vision, though, is the development of advanced network and middleware services that can provide reliable, fast, flexible, scalable, and cost-effective delivery of data to support distributed and high performance applications of all types.

[1] This work is supported by the National Science Foundation under Grants ACI-9876895, EIA-9975015, EIA-9972889, ANI-9980203, the Department of Energy under the SciDAC/ASCR program, and the University of Tennessee Center for Information Technology Research.

A. Jean-Marie (Ed.): ASIAN 2002, LNCS 2550, pp. 1–12, 2002.

At the base of the Logistical Networking project [10] is a richer view of the use of storage in communication. Most current approaches to advanced network services rely on the standard end-to-end model of communication where the state of network flows is to be maintained at the end nodes and not in the network. On this view, the network itself offers no model of storage; so it is not surprising that there is no current service that makes storage available for general use "in the network", i.e. available in the sense that it is easily and flexibly usable by a broad community without individual authorization or per-transaction billing. There is no shared distributed storage infrastructure for the support of asynchronous communication generally.

By contrast, our concept of Logistical Networking represents a more radical approach, trying to get maximum leverage out of the ongoing, exponential growth in all types of computing resources - processing power, communication bandwidth, and storage. Logistical Networking can thus be defined as the global scheduling and optimization of data movement, storage and computation based on a model that takes into account all the network's underlying physical resources, including storage and computation.

By adding a uniform model of storage to the definition of the network, and thereby exposing such embedded storage for direct scheduling, it is possible for application designers, and in particular grid appliction designers, to make much stronger assumptions about the ability of next generation applications to manage distributed state and engage in asynchronous communications of all types. Logistical Networking offers a general way of using the rising flood of computing resources to create a common distributed storage infrastructure that can share out the rapidly growing bounty of storage (and computation) the way the current network shares out bandwidth for synchronous communication (i.e. the sender and receiver are simultaneously connected to the network.)

A common reaction to the storage-enabled Internet idea is that many of these functions could be served by using individually owned resources accessed by various protocols already established. Examples are mail and news servers, Web caches, and distributed file and database systems. While it is true that each of these cases works without the use of common storage resources, the result is a balkanization of resources dedicated to specific applications and a lack of interoperability between similar applications. Today, objects shared during collaboration are held in private storage. But this approach gives out when, for instance, an average user decides to bring a data set into a collaborative session that is so large it cannot be held in private storage owned by the participants in the session, or when different collaborative applications fail to interoperate because there is no private storage that is jointly accessible to them at the time required. In that case, the community may be willing to provision massive storage for time-limited use and to make it freely available. Although the community is unlikely to take such a step for a particular application, it may be willing to do so if, as in the case of provisioning IP networks, all users can share it for a wide range of applications. High degrees of interoperability tend to enable ambitious community investment.

This paper is organized as follows: section 2 descroibes the the Internet Backplane Protocol, which can be considered the basic mechanism for any work in the Logistical Networkinging area. Section 3 presents a file abstraction for storage in the wide area, called the exNode, a necessary brick to build in the robustness, ease of use, and scalability that the storage-enabled Internet will require. Section 4 describes the Logistical Backbone, while Section 5 presents some applications and projects that already use the Logistical Networking conceps and the IBP software in particular.

2   The Internet Backplane Protocol

IBP [8] is middleware for managing and using remote storage. Invented as part of LoCI to support Logistical Networking in large scale, distributed systems and applications, it acquired its name because it was designed to enable applications to treat the Internet as if it were a processor backplane. Whereas on a typical backplane, the user has access to memory and peripherals and can direct communication between them with DMA, IBP gives the user access to remote storage and standard Internet resources (e.g. content servers implemented with standard sockets) and can direct communication between them with the IBP API. By providing a uniform, application-independent interface to storage in the network, IBP makes it possible for applications of all kinds to use Logistical Networking to exploit data locality and more effectively manage buffer resources. We believe it represents the kind of middleware needed to overcome the current balkanization of state management capabilities on the Internet. IBP allows any application that needs to manage distributed state to benefit from the kind of standardization, interoperability, and scalability that have made the Internet into such a powerful communication tool.

Since IBP draws on elements from different traditional designs, it does not fit comfortably into the usual categories of mechanisms for state management: IBP can be viewed as a mechanism to manage either communication buffers or remote files. Both characterizations are equally valid and useful in different situations. If, in order to use a neutral terminology, we simply refer to the units of data that IBP manages as byte arrays, then these different views of IBP can be presented as follows:

- **IBP as buffer management:** Communication between nodes on the Internet is built upon the basic operation of delivering packets from sender to receiver, where each packet is buffered at intermediate nodes. Because the capacity of even large storage systems is tiny compared with the amount of data that flows through the Internet, allocation of communication buffers must be time limited. In current routers and switches, time-limited allocation is implemented by use of FIFO buffers, serviced under the constraints of fair queuing. Against this background, IBP byte arrays can be viewed as application-managed communication buffers in the network. IBP supports time-limited allocation and FIFO disciplines to constrain the use of storage. With such constraints in place, applications that use these buffers can improve communication and network utilization by way of application-driven staging and course-grained routing of data.

- **IBP as file management:** Since high-end Internet applications often transfer gigabytes of data, the systems to manage storage resources for such applications are often on the scale of gigabytes or terabytes in size. Storage on this scale is usually managed using highly structured file systems or databases with complex naming, protection, and robustness semantics. Normally such storage resources are treated as part of a host system and therefore as more or less private. From this point of view IBP byte arrays can be viewed as files that live in the network. IBP allows an application to read and write data stored at remote sites, as well as direct the movement of data among storage sites and to multiple receivers. In this way IBP creates a network of shareable storage in the same way that standard networks provide shareable bandwidth for file transfer.

This characterization of IBP as a mechanism for managing state in the network supplies an operational understanding of our approach to the problem of Logistical Networking for storage. The usual view is that routing of packets through a network is a series of spatial choices that allows control of only one aspect of data movement. An incoming packet is sent out on one of several alternative links, but any particular packet is held in communication buffers for as short a time as possible. But Logistical Networking with storage makes it possible to route packets in two dimensions, not just one: IBP allows for data to be stored at one location while en route from sender to receiver, adding the ability to control data movement temporally as well as spatially. This is a key aspect of Logistical Networking, but to see how IBP implements this concept we need to examine its API in detail.

2.1 IBP Structure and Client API

IBP has been designed to be a minimal abstraction of storage to serve the needs of Logistical Networking. Its fundamental operations are:

1. Allocating a byte array for storing data.
2. Moving data from a sender to a byte array.
3. Delivering data from a byte array to a receiver (either another byte array or a client).

We have defined and implemented a client API for IBP that consists of seven procedure calls and server daemon software that makes local storage available for remote management. Connections between clients and servers are made through TCP/IP sockets, but we are testing the integration of other network protocols (i.e. UDP) and various other means to improve the communication performance as much as possible. IBP client calls may be made by anyone who can attach to an IBP server (which we also call an IBP depot to emphasize its logistical functionality). IBP depots require only storage and networking resources, and running one does not necessarily require supervisory privileges. These servers implement policies that allow an initiating user some control over how IBP makes use of storage. An IBP server may be restricted to use only idle physical memory and disk resources, or to enforce a time-limit on all allocations, ensuring that the host machine is either not impacted or that encourage users to experiment with logistical networking without over-committing server resources.

Logically speaking, the IBP client sees a depot's storage resources as a collection of append-only byte arrays. There are no directory structures or client-assigned file names. Clients initially gain access to byte arrays by allocating storage on an IBP server. If the allocation is successful, the server returns three cryptographically secure URLs, called   to the client: one for reading, one for writing, and one for management. Currently, each capability is a text string encoded with the IP identity of the IBP server, plus other information to be interpreted only by the server. This approach enables applications to pass IBP capabilities among themselves without registering these operations with IBP, thus supporting high-performance without sacrificing the correctness of applications.

The IBP client API consists of seven procedure calls, broken into three groups, as shown in Table 1 below. For clarity, we omit error handling and security considerations. Each call does include a timeout so that network failures may be tolerated gracefully. The full API is described separately [7] and is available at http://loci.cs.utk.edu/ibp/documents.

Table 1. IBP API calls

Storage Management	Data Transfer	Depot Management
IBP_allocate	IBP_store	IBP_status
IBP_manage	IBP_load	
	IBP_copy	
	IBP_mcopy	

The heart of IBP's innovative storage model is its approach to allocation. Storage resources that are part of the network, as logistical networking intends them to be, cannot be allocated in the same way as they are on a host system. To understand how IBP needs to treat allocation of storage for the purposes of logistical networking, it is helpful to consider the problem of sharing resources in the Internet, and how that situation compares with the allocation of storage on host systems. In the Internet, the basic shared resources are data transmission and routing. The greatest impediment to sharing these resources is the risk that their owners will be denied the use of them. The reason that the Internet can function in the face of the possibility of denial-of-use attacks is that it is not possible for the attacker to profit in proportion to their own effort, expense and risk. When other resources, such as disk space in spool directories, are shared, we tend to find administrative mechanisms that limit their use by restricting either the size of allocations or the amount of time for which data will be held.

By contrast, a user of a host storage system is usually an authenticated member of some community that has the right to allocate certain resources and to use them indefinitely. Consequently, sharing of resources allocated in this way cannot extend to an arbitrary community. For example, an anonymous FTP server with open write permissions is an invitation for someone to monopolize those resources; such servers must be allowed to delete stored material at will. In order to make it possible to treat storage as a shared network resource, IBP supports some of these administrative limits on allocation, while at the same time seeking to provide guarantees for the client that are as strong as possible. So, for example, under IBP allocation can be restricted to a certain length of time, or specified in a way that permits the server to revoke the allocation at will. Clients who want to find the maximum resources available to them must choose the weakest form of allocation that their application can use. To allocate storage at a remote IBP depot, the client calls IBP_allocate(). The maximum storage requirements of the byte array are noted in the size parameter, and additional attributes are included in the attr parameter. If the allocation is successful, a trio of capabilities is returned.

All reading and writing to IBP byte arrays is done through the four reading/writing calls in Table 1. These calls allow clients to read from and write to IBP buffers. IBP_store() and IBP_load() allow clients to write from and read to their own memory. The IBP_copy() call allows a client to copy an IBP buffer from one depot to another. IBP_mcopy() is a more complex operation, which utilises a Data Mover plug-in module to move data to a number of end points, using different underlying protocols (TCP, UDP). The syntax of this call provides a great flexibility, allowing the research of new and non-standard ways to transfer data. Note that both IBP_copy() and IBP_mcopy() allow a client to direct an interaction between two or more other remote entities. The support that these two calls provide for third party transfers are an important part of what makes IBP different from, for example, typical distributed file systems. The semantics of IBP_store(), IBP_copy(), and IBP_mcopy() are append-only. Additionally, all IBP calls allow portions of IBP buffers to be read by the client or third party. If an IBP server has removed a buffer (due to a time-limit expiration or volatility), these client calls simply fail, encoding the reason for failure in an IBP_errno variable. Management of IBP byte arrays and depots is performed through the IBP_manage() and IBP_statue() calls. With these calls clients may manipulate reference counts, modify allocation attributes, and query the state of depots. Additionally, authenticated clients may alter the storage parameters of an IBP depot.

2.2   IBP Implementation

Depot. The main IBP depot architecture goals were identified as flexibility, reliability and performance. The software architecture of the current IBP depot implementation (1.2) is a multi-threaded one, with a pool of threads created at boot time, in order to have good performance results. The code base is shared between Unix/Linux/OS X and Win32 versions, and between file system and

RAM based depot. The I/O calls are encapsulated, and two different libraries (for the File System and for pinned RAM memory) have been created; this strategy allows us to concentrate on the general design of the implementation, and to have always versions on sync.

Client Library. The IBP Client Library, offered in a few different versions and systems, was designed to be flexible, to ease the implementation of future changes to both the API and the protocol, to be very maintainable code and to be extremely robust and fault-tolerant. In order to satisfy these three goals we decided to separate our client library into two different modules: the API2P Module and the Communication Module.

The first module translates the API command into Communication Units, which are abstract data types that specify the communication and its characteristics (direction, semantics of the message, the message itself or the expected message). Then, the ComModule allows the execution of the communication. No analysis of the message is made at this level, the API2P module being responsible to interpret the message and to take the appropriate action. This design allows easy changes to the API (as it's seen as a sequence of communication units) and to the protocol.

Protocol. The version 1.0 of the protocol is currently on a final draft phase. We intend to publish the specification in the comiong months within organisations such as the Global Grid Forum [3] or IETF [4]. The protocol had to be designed from scratch as there was no current framework that allowed, explicitly or implicitely, the allocation of space at remote network appliances.

3   The exNode: Aggregating IBP Storage Resources to Provide File Services

Our approach to creating a strong file abstraction on the weak model of storage offered by IBP continues to parallel the design paradigm of the traditional network stack. In the world of end-to-end packet delivery, it has long been understood that TCP, a protocol with strong semantic properties, such as reliability and in-order delivery, can be layered on top of IP, a weak datagram delivery mechanism. Retransmission controlled by a higher layer protocol, combined with protocol state maintained at the endpoints, overcomes non-delivery of packets. All non-transient conditions that interrupt the reliable, in-order flow of packets can then be reduced to non-delivery. We view retransmission as an aggregation of weak IP datagram delivery services to implement a stronger TCP connection. The same principle of aggregation can be applied in order to layer a storage service with strong semantic properties on top of a weak underlying storage resource that does not generally provide them, such as an IBP depot. Examples of aggregating weaker storage services in order to implement stronger ones include the following:

- **Reliability:** Redundant storage of information on resources that fail independently can implement reliability (e.g. RAID, backups).
- **Fast access:** Redundant storage of information on resources in different localities can implement high performance access through proximity (e.g. caching) or through the use of multiple data paths (e.g. RAID [17]).
- **Unbounded allocation:** Fragmentation of a large allocation across multiple storage resources can implement allocations of unbounded size (e.g. files built out of distributed disk blocks, databases split across disks).
- **Unbounded duration:** Movement of data between resources as allocations expire can implement allocations of unbounded duration (e.g. migration of data between generations of tape archive).

In this exposed-resource paradigm, implementing a file abstraction with strong properties involves creating a construct at a higher layer that aggregates more primitive IBP byte-arrays below it. To apply the principle of aggregation to exposed storage services, however, it is necessary to maintain state that represents such an aggregation of storage allocations, just as sequence numbers and timers are maintained to keep track of the state of a TCP session. Fortunately we have a traditional, well-understood model to follow in representing the state of aggregate storage allocations. In the Unix file system, the data structure used to implement aggregation of underlying disk blocks is the inode (intermediate node). Under Unix, a file is implemented as a tree of disk blocks with data blocks at the leaves. The intermediate nodes of this tree are the inodes, which are themselves stored on disk. The Unix inode implements only the aggregation of disk blocks within a single disk volume to create large files; other strong properties are sometimes implemented through aggregation at a lower level (e.g. RAID) or through modifications to the file system or additional software layers that make redundant allocations and maintain additional state (e.g. AFS [16], HPSS [15])

Following the example of the inode, we have chosen to implement a single generalized data structure, which we call an external node, or exNode, in order to manage of aggregate allocations that can be used in implementing network storage with many different strong semantic properties. Rather than aggregating blocks on a single disk volume, the exNode aggregates storage allocations on the Internet, and the exposed nature of IBP makes IBP byte-arrays exceptionally well adapted to such aggregations. In the present context the key point about the design of the exNode is that it has allowed us to create an abstraction of a network file to layer over IBP-based storage in a way that is completely consistent with the exposed resource approach. The exNode is the basis for a set of generic tools for implementing files with a range of characteristics. Because the exNode must provide interoperability between heterogeneous nodes on a diverse Internet, we have chosen not to specify it as a language-specific data structure, but as an abstract data type with an XML serialization. The basis of the exNode is a single allocation, represented by an Internet resource, which initially will be either an IBP capability or a URL. Other classes of underlying storage resources can be added for extensibility and interoperability.

Despite our emphasis on using an exposed-resource approach, it is natural to have the exNode support access to storage resources via URLs, both for the sake of backward compatibility and because the Internet is so prodigiously supplied with it. It is important to note, however, that the flexibility of a file implemented by the exNode is a function of the flexibility of the underlying storage resources. The value of IBP does not consist in the fact that it is the only storage resource that can be aggregated in an exNode, but rather that it is by far the most flexible and most easily deployed.

4   The Logistical Backbone: Deployment of Logistical Networking

IBP models the fundamental structure of the Internet at the level of network locality. In order to be of maximum use, it must be deployed across a variety of localities, allowing it to be used for management of stored data and computational state among those localities. We are following the usual deployment strategy, which is to make open source software freely available to the Internet community. We are also following a second strategy: we are establishing IBP depots on the servers being deployed in a number of institutions, with particular regards to the Internet2 Distributed Storage Infrastructure (I2-DSI) project [1], creating the first nodes of an experimental testbed for logistical network that we call the Logistical Backbone (L-Bone). This aggressive deployment strategy will put IBP services into people's hands as soon as they obtain the client software, much as the early Web was available to anyone with a Web browser, except the resources served up by IBP are writable and can be used in flexible and powerful ways.

The logistical networking capabilities supported on this infrastructure will include NWS sensing [18] of the storage and network resources, IBP caches, and state management for IBP Mail inclusions.

4.1   The Implementation

In its current stage, it is based on a LDAP directory of IBP depots, and informations such as network proximity to any Internet access point can be calculated in real-time. The L-Bone client library allows users to query for depots that satisfy user-specified criteria, such as available space, network or geographical proximity. The server replies with a depots set, the size of which can be chosen by the user in his request.

5   Experience and Applications

5.1   e-Toile

The e-Toile project [5] aims to build a grid for experimental applications. This grid is intended to be modular: it is built by dedicated servers, provisioned by the partners, servers that might be added to the e-Toile grid permanently or just temporarely. Other servers and other partners can be freely added to the original topology.

After a set-up time, when the Globus [2] middleware has been intensively used, this project aims to explore new middlewares and new concepts for the grid, such as active networking and logistical networking, with the deployment of both active routers, able to run services, and IBP depots, to value the local environment and to allow easy integration between purposely made and more generic tools.

5.2   Tamanoir

Tamanoir [14] is a project developed by the RESO team of the Ecole Normale Sup/'erieure of Lyon, France, in the in the field of Active Networking. It is composed by a complete framework that allows users to easily deploy and maintain distributed active routers on wide area networks. IBP is not only a part of the set of distributed tools provided, such as routing manager and stream monitoring tool, but it is currently used as a caching tool to improve performance [9]. Any Tamanoir Active Node (TAN) is able to process the data according to a certain service; when the service is not available, the receiver sends a message to the sender asking to provide the service needed. After the deployment of the service, the data can be treated. In such a situation, the IBP depot stores the data while the service is not active yet, therefore improving performance by avoiding the retransmission of the first packets.

IBP depots are also used by a Tamanoir node in a reliable multicast situation. There are three major benefits of performing storage in the network for a reliable multicast application. First of all, we can look at the TAN with its depot as a kind of mirror for data distribution, to download them from the geographically (or network) closest point to the consumers. Another advantage is that clients can consume data with their own processing speed capabilities without disturbing the server where data come from, and finally, a TAN can retransmit lost data without uselessly overloading the network between the server and the TAN.

5.3   IBP-Mail

IBP-Mail [13] is a project developed by the University of Tennessee that uses IBP to transmit and deliver mail attachments that require storage resources beyond the capacity of standard mail servers. After successfully testing its potential with a prototype, we are now focusing on a more robust and scalable architecture. IBP-mail allows a mail attachment to be passed between users by storing it first into a suitable IBP server; then, the Sender forwards the exNode holding the capabilities to the Receiver in a MIME attachment. Upon receiving the attachment, the receiver user's mailer launches a program that downloads the file from the IBP server. File deallocation at the IBP server may be performed either via the time-limited allocation feature, or by sending the receiver the management capability, and having him deallocate the file. Using the information provided by the L-Bone, a very simple form of file routing has been already implemented in IBP-Mail, allowing the sender to insert the file into an IBP buffer on a depot close to his system, and moving the buffer asynchronously to an IBP buffer close to the receiver, and therefore allowing fast insertion for the sender and fast delivery to the receiver.

5.4   Netsolve

NetSolve [12] is a widely known project whose aim is to provide remote access to computational resources, both hardware and software. When implementing distributed computation in a wide area network, data can be produced at any location and consumed at any other, and it might be difficult to find the ideal location for the producer of the data, its consumer, and the buffer where the data are stored. To implement a system where globally distributed caches cooperate to move data near consuming resources, IBP was chosen as a natural solution. IBP is now integrated in Netsolve since the version 1.4 (august 2001), and results from testing and normal use show a much-improved efficiency.

6   Related Works

IBP occupies an architectural niche similar to network file systems such as AFS[16] and Network Attached Storage appliances, but its model of storage is more primitive, making it similar in some ways to Storage Area Networking (SAN) technologies developed for local networks. In the Grid community, projects such as GASS [11] and the SDSC Storage Resource Broker [6] are file system overlays that implement a uniform file access interface and also impose uniform directory, authentication and access control frameworks on their users.

7   Conclusion and Future Works

While some ways of engineering for resource sharing focus on optimizing the use of scarce resources within selected communities, the exponential growth in all areas of computing resources has created the opportunity to explore a different problem, viz. designing new architectures that can take more meaningful advantage of this bounty. The approach presented in this paper is based on the Internet model of resource sharing and represents one general way of using the rising flood of storage resources to create a common distributed infrastructure that can share the growing surplus of storage in a way analogous to the way the current network shares communication bandwidth. It uses the Internet Backplane Protocol (IBP), which is designed on the model of IP, to allow storage resources to be shared by users and applications in a way that is as open and as easy to use as possible while maintaining a necessary minimum of security and protection from abuse. IBP lays the foundation for the intermediate resource management components, accessible to every end-system, which must be introduced to govern the way that applications access and utilise this common pool in a fully storage-enabled Internet

References

1. http://dsi.internet2.edu.
2. http://www.globus.org.
3. http://www.gridforum.org.
4. http://www.ietf.org.
5. http://www.urec.cnrs.fr/etoile.
6. C. Baru, R. Moore, A. Rajasekar, and M. Wan. The SDSC Storage Ressource Broker. In *CASCON'98*, Toronto, Canada, 1998.
7. A. Bassi, M. Beck, J. Plank, and R. Wolski. The internet backplane protocol: Api 1.0. Technical Report ut-cs-01-455, University of Tennessee, 2001.
8. A. Bassi, M. Beck G. Fagg, T. Moore, J. Plank, M. Swany, and R. Wolski. The internet backplane protocol: A study in resource sharing. In *Proceedings of the IEEE/ACM International Symposium on Cluster Computing and the Grid*. IEEE/ACM, may 2002.
9. A. Bassi, J.-P. Gelas, and L. Lefèvre. Tamanoir-ibp: Adding storage to active networks. In *Active Middleware Services*, pages 27–34, Edinburgh, Scotland, July 2002. IEEE computer society. ISBN: 0-7695-1721-8.
10. M. Beck, T. Moore, and J. Plank. An end-to-end approach to globally scalable network storage. In *ACM SIGCOMM 20002 Conference, Pittsburgh, PA, USA*, August 2002.
11. J. Bester, I. Foster, C. Kesselman, J. Tedesco, and S. Tuecke. Gass: A data movement and access service for wide area computing systems. In *Sixth Workshop on I/O in Parallel and Distributed Systems*, may 1999.
12. H. Casanova and J. Dongarra. Applying netsolve's network enabled server. *IEEE Computational Science and Engineering*, 5(3), 1998.
13. W. Elwasif, J. Plank, M. Beck, and R. Wolski. Ibp-mail: Controlled delivery of large mail files. In *NetStore 99, Seattle, WA, USA*, 1999.
14. Jean-Patrick Gelas and Laurent Lefèvre. Tamanoir: A high performance active network framework. In C. S. Raghavendra S. Hariri, C. A. Lee, editor, *Active Middleware Services, Ninth IEEE International Symposium on High Performance Distributed Computing*, pages 105–114, Pittsburgh, Pennsylvania, USA, August 2000. Kluwer Academic Publishers. ISBN 0-7923-7973-X.
15. H. Hulen, O. Graf, K. Fitzgerald, and R. Watson. Storage area network and the high performance storage system. In *Tenth NASA Goddard Conference on Mass Storage Systems*, April 2002.
16. J.H. Morris, M. Satyanarayan, M.H. Conner, J.H. Howard, D.S.H. Rosenthal, and F.D. Smith. Andrew: A Distributed Personal Computing Environment. *Communication of the ACM*, 29(3):184–201, 1986.
17. D. Patterson, G. Gibson, and M. Satyanarayanan. A case for redundant arrays of inexpensive disks(raid). In *Proc "eedings of the 1988 ACM Conference on Management of Data (SIGMOD), Chicago, IL, USA*, pages 81–94, June 1988.
18. R. Wolski. Forecasting network performance to support dynamic scheduling using the network weather service. In IEEE Press, editor, *6th IEEE Symp. on High Performance Distributed Computing, Portland, Oregon*, 1997.

The Grid: Challenges and Research Issues

Brigitte Plateau

Institut National Polytechnique de Grenoble, Laboratoire ID-IMAG
Grenoble, France
http://www-ide.imag.fr

Abstract. The purpose of this talk is to give an introduction to the
main challenges to achieve the integration of computing and data services
across distributed and disparate computing, storage and visualization
resources. It also describes a set of research actions which are undertaken
in France with a funding of the French governement "the ACI GRID".

1 The Grid

Grid computing is one example of distributed systems. As such it relies on standard networking and system technology. Its popularity comes from the fact that
it is an area of potentially big impact on many application domains: physical
sciences, biology, environment, medical services,,... It is also an area where the
academic world can impact societal problems by bringing the possibility to solve
larger and more complex problems. This input of the academic community can
be of major importance at different levels: at the infrastructure level (how to
interconnect efficiently distributed, heterogeneous, numerous, and volatile computing devices), at the software level (how to integrate, and ease the use of a
large number of software services), at the application level (how to couple existing applications in order to solve multiphysics problems or to bridge the gap
between data in different social areas).

The issues in computer science are numerous and the following are examples
of research topics:

- sofware architecture for grid computing and peer-to-peer services
- grid infrastructure, security and accountability
- adaptative middleware with scalability, reliability and responsiveness properties (including naming services and group membership)
- network efficient middleware
- computation models for large scale and distributed systems
- application algorithms suited to large-scale GRID or Peer-to-Peer systems
  (adaptable and self-configurable) and to to be integrated in large systems
- novel applications

To cope with these issues, it is necessary to engage collaboratives actions on:
the reliable and fast connection distributed sites, a vertical cooperation between
disciplines (computer science, mathematics, physical sciences) and the connection between societal domains (e.g. environment and urbanism, education and
simulation, finance and commerce, etc). A recent and evolving document can be
found at http://www.globus.org/research/papers/ogsa.pdf).

A. Jean-Marie (Ed.): ASIAN 2002, LNCS 2550, pp. 13–14, 2002.

2   Research Actions in France

To design, implement and use efficiently GRID or Peer-To-Peer infrastructures, it is fondamental to develop research projects in an international context which is already highly competitive. The software for these infrastructures relies more and more on the ability to integrate complementary approaches involving different disciplines. The French governement has launched in 2001 an action to amplify both research activities in computer science and multi-disciplinary platforms in order to be able to face these emerging technologies.

These projects[1] cover the major issues of the grid and Peer to Peer technologies. Some of these projects have the objectives of building and offering a grid infrastructure for experimentation, others are dedicated to network issues. Many projects are dedicated to software issues and to multi-disciplinary actions. This talk wil detail some of these actions and open on new initiatives.

---

[1] A complete list can be found on
http://www-sop.inria.fr/aci/grid/public/acigriduk.html.

Personalized Video for Contents Delivery Network

Shinji Shimojo[1], Junzo Kamahara[2], Takahiro Nishizawa[1], and Hideo Miyahara[1]

[1] Graduate School of Information Science and Technology Osaka University
1-3 Machikaneyama Toyonaka, Japan 560-8531
{shimojo, miyahara, nishizawa}@ist.osaka-u.ac.jp
[2] Information Processing Center, Kobe University of Mercantile Marine
5-1-1 Fukaeminami-cho, Higashinada-ku, Kobe, Japan 658-0022
kamahara@cc.kshosen.ac.jp

Abstract. By the introduction of Contents Delivery Network, more personalized program is required for satisfying with various users' request. For achieving the variety of programs, we proposed a new architecture for contents delivery. By this architecture, the chunk of the video stored at the database is selected and edited based on the profile of metadata and a viewer on his side. Not only connecting the chunk of the merely chosen video, we propose the method of giving a scenario, and the method of introducing movie grammar for editing the chunks of video.

1 Introduction

In digital multi-channel era, although the opportunity where we can broadcast programs through a satellite and the Internet increases, it is required to provide various programs according to the demand of various users at low cost. Especially, it is important how the demand of individual user is met. This tendency is accelerated by existence of Contents Delivery Network (CDN).

In CDN, one important change has taken place in distribution of contents. It is shown in Fig. 1. Fig. 1-a represents a former type of contents distribution.

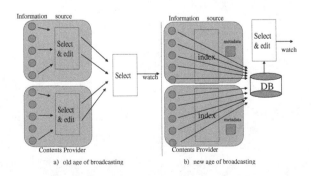

Fig. 1. Contents Delivery Architecture

A. Jean-Marie (Ed.): ASIAN 2002, LNCS 2550, pp. 15–18, 2002.

Selection and edit of information is performed from various information sources in Information Provider such as broadcast station and the program is delivered to the viewers. Therefore, when it comes to a viewer, choice of information has already been performed. Now, the demand of various viewers cannot be met. Then, the new architecture in CDN is shown in Fig. 1-b. In order to meet the demand of various viewers, information is sent to a viewer as it is, and choice and edit are performed according to the taste and demand by the viewer side. Instead of selection and editing, metadata which describes the information contents is put by the Information Provider with the contents itself for the sake of CDN. A viewer is provided with the various contents according to his taste by this architecture. In this paper, the generation method of contents based on such a new contents distribution architecture is proposed.

In this architecture, the chunk of the video stored at the database will be selected and edited based on the profile of metadata and a user on the viewer side. However, it never becomes a legible program only by connecting the chunk of the merely chosen video. In this paper, we propose the method of giving a scenario, and the method of introducing movie grammar for editing the chunks of video.

2   A Scenario for Personalized Video

)   We have proposed the recommendation system for TV news with automatic recomposition[1] based on the proposed architecture. For personalized browsing of TV news articles on the viewer side, we propose three modes of presentation, the digest mode, the relaxed mode, and the normal mode, where each presentation length is different. To make these presentations, TV news articles are decomposed, analyzed, and stored in the database scene by scene with metadata. Then, the system selects desired items and synthesizes these scenes into a presentation based on a user's profile. For the profile of the user, we use a keyword vector and a category vector of news articles retrieved from its metadata. The system is designed so that user's control to the system becomes minimum operations (See Fig. 2). Therefore, a user only plays, skips, plays previous, and rewinds news articles in the system as same as an ordinary TV. However, different from an ordinary TV, the system collects user's behavior while he uses the system. Based on this information, the system updates the user's profile. The scenario for news digest editing is rather simple. It just retrieves the sound of the first summery dialog by an anchorperson and puts it over the selected video scenes.

)   Our second example is rather complicated one. We have proposed personalized sports digest composition system with scenario templates[2]. We apply an automatic editing mechanism to a baseball game. While our news example only selects and shows important events in a simple series, this system is capable to produce a direction to them with considering a story of a whole game such as a one-sided game or shut out game. Selection of the events to

Fig. 2. News on Demand system (News courtesy of ABC)

be displayed in the digest is made by the importance value of events, which is evaluated by a weight in the scenario template and user's preference. Event information is carried by the metadata. When user's preference is specified, scoring events made by the preferred team can obtain higher weight value. A scenario template is selected from prepared templates by the decision tree produced by the machine learning program, C4.5. The decision tree selects a template by feature values of a game such as the score of a team or the number of strikeouts. Our system needs real-time recording by the electric scorebook subsystem for structured indexing which forms metadata. The scorebook subsystem and the presentation of the digest in SMIL format is shown in Fig. 3.

3 Movie Grammar for Personalized Video

In the conventional techniques for editing video automatically, they just combine selected scenes. Therefore, the produced video is often hard to watch because they break some rules called movie grammar. For example, continuous close-up scenes in the digest movie are disgraceful to appreciate. We have collected a set of rules as movie grammar through interviewing from video specialists in a broadcast company. In our method, each scene have group of cut which can be chosen next, and appropriate next cut is chosen using video syntax from them. This method looks-ahead a list of cuts which can be chosen as a next cut in order to find a suitable one. In implementing this method, specific scene type and playout-time of a generated series of video can be dynamically chosen according to video metadata. Comparing our method with the method without movie grammar shows that the generated series of video is evaluated as smoother than one generated by the conventional method by video specialists in a broadcast company[3].

4 Conclusion

In this paper, we propose a new architecture for contents generation on CDN. By this architecture, the chunk of the video stored at the database is selected

18   S. Shimojo et al.

Fig. 3. Electric Scorebook Subsystem and the presentation of SMIL of a baseball game digest (News courtesy of ABC).

and edited based on the profile of metadata and a user on the viewer side. We propose the method of giving a scenario, and the method of introducing movie grammar for editing the chunks of video.

In contents delivery network, it is possible to deliver contents with their metadata at the same time. Also, viewer's profile for watching such as favorite genre of programs could be collected on a STB or a PC. Therefore, edit and select the contents by the metadata on the viewer's side is very effective for personalization.

Acknowledgement. This work was partly supported by Special Coordination Funds for promoting Science and Technology of the Ministry of Education, Culture, Sports, Science and Technology of Japan under the project "Establishment of a Peer-to-Peer Information Sharing Platform for Mobile Computing Environment."

References

1. Kamahara, J., Nomura, Y., Ueda, K., Kandori, K., Shimojo, S., Miyahara, H.: TV news Recommendation System with Automatic Recomposition, Proceedings of 1st International Conference on Advanced Multimedia Content Processing, (1998) 225–239

2. Okamoto, M., Kamahara, J., Shimojo, S., Miyahara, H.: An Architecture of Personalized Sports Digest System with Scenario Templates, Proceedings of the 7th Int'l Conf. on Database Systems for Advanced Applications (DASFAA2001), (2001) 170-171

3. Nishizawa, T., Kamahara, J., Shunto, K., Tsukada, K., Ariki, Y., Uehara, K., Shimojo, S., Miyahara, H.: Automatic Digest Generation System with Look-Ahead Mechanism for Video Syntax, (In Japanese) Proceedings of IEICE 13th Data Engineering Workshop (DEWS2002), ISSN1347-4413 (2002)
   http://www.ieice.org/iss/de/DEWS/proc/2002/papers/B4-2.pdf

Distributed Checkpointing on Clusters with Dynamic Striping and Staggering

Hai Jin[1] and Kai Hwang[2]

[1] Huazhong University of Science and Technology, Wuhan, 430074, China
[2] University of Southern California, Los Angeles, 90007, USA
hjin@hust.edu.cn

Abstract. This paper presents a new striped and staggered checkpointing (SSC) scheme for multicomputer clusters. We consider serverless clusters, where local disks attached to cluster nodes collectively form a distributed RAID (redundant array of inexpensive disks) with a single I/O space. The distributed RAID is used to save the checkpoint files periodically. Striping enables parallel I/O on distributed disks. Staggering avoids network bottleneck in distributed disk I/O operations. With a fixed cluster size, we reveal the tradeoffs between these two speedup techniques. Our SSC approach allows dynamical reconfiguration to minimize message-logging requirements among concurrent software processes. We demonstrate how to reduce the checkpointing overhead by striping and staggering dynamically. For communication-intensive programs, our SCC scheme can significantly reduce the checkpointing overhead. Benchmark results prove the benefits of trading between stripe parallelism and distributed staggering. These results are useful to design efficient checkpointing schemes for fast rollback recovery from any single node (disk) failure in a cluster of computers.

1 Introduction

In a cluster of computers, concurrent software processes executing on different cluster nodes communicate with each other through message passing. Therefore, global consistency among the nodes should be maintained at checkpointing time. Coordinated checkpointing requires freezing all cluster processes taking the checkpoints simultaneously. The purpose is to yield a consistent recovery globally in case of any failure. The drawback of conventional coordinated checkpointing is in the loss of freeze time and heavy network traffic created by synchronized checkpointing. Simultaneous writing of checkpoint files into local disks may cause a problem of heavy network contention and disk I/O bottlenecks.

To alleviate the problem, much of previous works have attempted to reduce the synchronization overhead [13] and to remove the bottleneck in writing a centralized stable storage simultaneously. To solve the disk contention problem, Plank and Li introduced a diskless checkpointing scheme [14][19]. This scheme can greatly reduce the checkpoint overhead. However, the fault coverage is rather limited in a diskless checkpointing scheme. Therefore, two-level checkpointing scheme was introduced by Vaidya [22]. Subsequently, he introduced the staggered writing into a central stable storage [23].

A. Jean-Marie (Ed.): ASIAN 2002, LNCS 2550, pp. 19-33, 2002.
© Springer-Verlag Berlin Heidelberg 2002

Although staggered writes reduce the storage contention to some extent, the method introduces inconsistent states among cluster nodes. Additional overhead is introduced by message logging to achieve correct rollback recovery. Therefore, if the number of nodes in a cluster increases, the staggering method suffers from logging a large number of messages, which cause the overheads in both time delay, and in memory space. The time lag in staggering can reduce the contention problem.

Based on striping and staggering, a distributed RAID system [11] is suggested for use in distributed checkpointing on a cluster of computers. Distributed checkpoint files are saved simultaneously in disks attached to cluster nodes. This *striped and staggered checkpointing* (SSC) scheme results in two fundamental advantages: (1) Simultaneous distribution of the checkpoint files greatly alleviates the network and I/O contention problems. (2) Rollback recovery latency is reduced on a distributed checkpointing RAID subsystem. Increased I/O bandwidth from the dispersed disks enables faster rollback recovery. Therefore, the mean time to repair of the cluster is reduced and higher cluster availability is achievable.

To take advantage of parallel disk I/O, the staggering is combined with striping across all disks in the software RAID. Only a subset of disks constitutes a stripe group to take the checkpoints simultaneously. After a stripe group finishes checkpointing, another stripe starts checkpointing in a staggered manner. Such distributed staggering benefits in two areas: (1) When the I/O contention is more serious a problem, staggering helps lessening the problem. (2) If network contention dominates, staggering enables pipelined accesses of disks attached to the same I/O bus or the same host.

A shortcoming of staggering is caused by inconsistency among checkpoints taken at different cluster nodes. This requires additional message logging to guarantee proper rollback recovery. The tradeoffs between striped parallelism and staggering will be discussed with message logging in mind.

The rest of the paper is organized as follows: Section 2 covers the concept of striping and staggering in distributed checkpointing. Section 3 presents a mathematical analysis of message logging overhead. Section 4 presents the experimental cluster architecture and basic features of the distributed RAID configurations. Section 5 presents the two benchmark results to reveal the effects of striping and staggering in checkpoint overhead. Section 6 discusses the research findings and related application issues. Finally, we conclude with some key messages and suggest meaningful work for future research.

2 Striping and Staggering in Distributed Checkpointing

As suggested by Vaidya [23], staggered writing of the checkpoints taken at different nodes reduces the contention of coordinated checkpointing. The original concept of staggered checkpointing allows only one process to store the checkpoint at a time. A token is passed around to determine the timing of staggering. When a node receives the token, the node starts to store the checkpoint. After finishing, the node passes the token to the next node.

Fig. 1 shows the timing diagram of Vaidya's staggered checkpointing. *Checkpointing overhead* is the time for one node to take a checkpoint. The checkpoint iteration is the time duration from the first node to the last node. Although

Vaidya's scheme may reduce the checkpoint overhead, different checkpoint times between nodes cause an inconsistency problem among nodes. Essentially, Vaidya adopted the Chandy-Lamport algorithm using a non-blocking strategy to ensure the consistency [23].

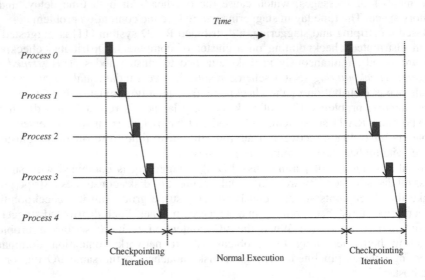

Fig. 1. Timing diagram of staggered checkpointing on a centralized stable storage

Vaidya scheme introduces non-blocking, staggered writing. The scheme suffers from message logging overhead and many control messages. The messages during each checkpointing iteration, the whole cluster files should be saved in a stable storage to guarantee global consistency. Therefore, checkpoint overhead increases dramatically with the cluster size. For an example, all messages between the first node and the last node during each iteration should be logged. Vaidya scheme introduces a logical checkpointing concept to recover from a consistent state. All messages must be logged to a stable storage in this case.

Fig. 2 depicts the need of message logging during staggering. To have a proper rollback, any crossing message should be handled properly. Without this assumption, the global snapshot results in inconsistent state. For example, Message 2 in Fig. 2 results in an inconsistent state. The need of message logging is a major drawback of staggered checkpointing. Because all nodes take checkpoints at different times, the messages must be logged to prevent from losing them when needed.

The overhead for message logging also causes the traffic for the stable storage. The stable storage bottleneck caused by message logging degrades the overall performance. Another possible drawback of the staggered checkpointing is blocking of process caused by the checkpointing of the other processes. The checkpointing of a certain node may cause the computation blocking of the other nodes. The delay of the response from the other node, which is taking checkpoints, may increase.

Simultaneous writing of multiple processes in coordinated checkpointing may cause a network contention and I/O bottleneck problem to a central stable storage. As suggested by Vaidya [23], staggered writing of the checkpoints taken by different nodes reduces the above contentions. The time lag between staggered checkpoints can alleviate the I/O bottleneck problem associated with a central stable storage.

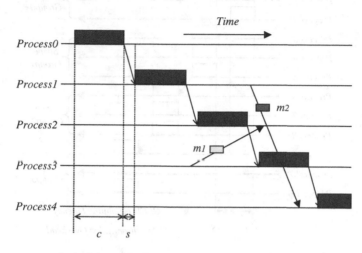

C: checkpointing overhead   s: synchronization overhead   m1,m2: messages

Fig. 2. The problem of inconsistency in staggered checkpointing

Staggered checkpointing allows only one process to store the checkpoint at a time. A token is passed around to determine the timing. When a node receives the token, the node starts to store the checkpoint. After finishing checkpointing, the node passes the token to the next node. A major drawback of staggered checkpointing is the low utilization of network capability, especially true in saving small checkpoint files in a large cluster system.

Parallel I/O capability of a distributed RAID is applied to achieve fast checkpointing in a cluster system. Our idea of *striped checkpointing* is to save the checkpoint files over distributed disks that forming a stripe group. A *stripe group* is defined as a subset of p disks that can be accessed in parallel. Only the disks in the same stripe group are used to save the checkpoints simultaneously. To alleviate the network contention, staggered writing is combined with striped checkpointing.

Fig. 3 combines the above ideas to yield a distributed SSC scheme using striping and staggering. Here, coordinated checkpointing on 12 disks is illustrated. Three software processes constitute a stripe group. Each stripe group takes its checkpoints one after another. The stripe group leads to parallelism and staggering avoids I/O contention. This SSC scheme can enhance both network utilization and I/O performance.

There exists a tradeoff between stripe parallelism p and the staggering depth q. For example, one can reconfigure the layout in Fig.3 into a 6×2 scheme, if a particular application can benefit from it. Higher parallelism leads to higher aggregate disk bandwidth. Higher staggering degree can cope better the contention problem at the cost of inconsistency.

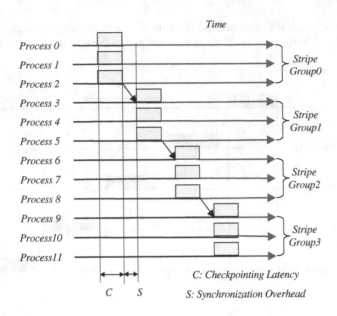

Fig. 3. Combined striping and staggering in our distributed checkpointing

In general, we denote a distributed checkpointing configuration as $p \times q$, where $n = p \times q$ is the number of processes, if there is only one disk attached to each node host. In particular, the conventional coordinated checkpointing scheme corresponds to the extreme $n \times 1$ configuration, where all disks form a single stripe group and no staggering is applied. Vaidya scheme assumes the other extreme denoted as a $1 \times n$ configuration, in which no striping is allowed and staggering reached it upper bound. Our SSC scheme covers the checkpointing configurations, by which $1 < p, q < n$.

3 Analysis of Message Logging Overhead

Although Vaidya's staggered checkpointing reduces the contention problem, it suffers from the message logging problem due to time difference in taking the successive checkpoints on cluster nodes. To guarantee proper rollback recovery, the messages between two nodes that take checkpointing at a different time should be logged. In this section, the number of messages that should be logged is analyzed for a given checkpointing configuration.

Let s be the total number of cluster nodes. Each checkpoint configuration is denoted by the direct product $p \times q$, where p is the number of processes in a stripe group and q is the number of stripe groups in the disk array. This implies that q stripe groups take their checkpoints in a staggered manner. Let C_p be the average checkpoint overhead per stripe group. We denote $I_s = C_p \times q$ as the total time from the first group checkpoint to the last group checkpoint.

Simultaneous writes may cause disk I/O and network contentions. In general, the product $p \times q$ is a constant for a fixed cluster size. Thus tradeoff exists between these two parameters. This implies that the higher the parallelism p, the shorter is staggering depth q and thus longer the overhead C_p per stripe group. On the contrary, deeper staggering q means lower parallelism number and thus lower overhead for the group.

The basic idea of striping and staggering technique is that the parallelism reduces the duration of inconsistent state at the cost of higher demand on network bandwidth. To decide the optimal values of p and q, two factors must be considered. One is the *checkpoint file size* and the other is the *message logging* needed. The file size adds to the checkpoint overhead. The larger the checkpoint file, the longer will be the inconsistent state. Therefore, the message logging overhead increases accordingly.

If the RAID bandwidth can afford grouping the staggered disks, striping can be more amenable than pure staggered writing. The number of messages logged is decided by the communication pattern in application code. However, the ratio of messages being logged out of the total messages is derived below for given p and q.

The message logging of Vaidya scheme is analyzed in Fig.4. The messages crossing the global recovery line in Fig.4 causes an inconsistent state. The duration of the inconsistent state between group 0 and group 1 is C_p. The inconsistent state between group 0 and group 2 is $2C_p$ and between group 0 and group 3 is $3C_p$. The duration of inconsistent state between checkpoints affects the amount of message logging needed.

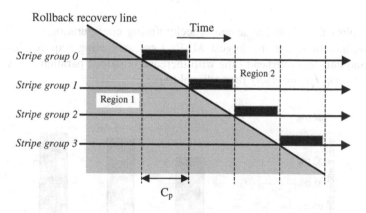

Fig. 4. Snapshot of an inconsistency state in staggered writes

Region 1 in Fig. 4 shows the steps before checkpointing procedure and region 2 shows the steps after checkpointing each staggered group. Therefore, the recovery to the global snapshot lost all the messages between the two regions. Therefore, all messages crossing the snapshot should be logged to guarantee a global consistency. The *message logging ratio* is the number of messages logged over the total number of message for the entire duration.

The number of messages to be logged equals the number of messages between two inconsistent regions. The number of messages logged equals the product of the *message frequency* λ and the inconsistent interval. Consider a $p \times q$ SCC configuration. We calculate the number of logged messages by:

$$M_{p \times q} = \lambda \times p^2 \times C_p \times \sum_{k=1}^{q-1}(k \times (k+1)) = \lambda \times \left(\frac{s}{q}\right)^2 \times C_p \times \sum_{k=1}^{q-1}(k \times (k+1)) = \tag{1}$$

$$\frac{\lambda \times s^2 \times C_p}{3} \times \frac{(q-1) \times q \times (q+1)}{q^2}$$

The total number of messages during the checkpointing iteration is:

$$M_{total} = s \times \lambda \times (s-1) \times C_P \times q \tag{2}$$

The *message logging ratio* (MLR) is thus obtained below:

$$\text{MLR} = \frac{M_{P \times S}}{M_{total}} = \tag{3}$$

$$\frac{\lambda \times s^2 \times C_p}{3} \times \frac{(q-1) \times q \times (q+1)}{q^2} \times \frac{1}{s \times \lambda \times (s-1) \times C_p \times q} =$$

$$\frac{(q-1) \times q \times (q+1) \times s}{3q^3 \times (s-1)}$$

Fig. 5 plots the MLR for several checkpointing configurations. Vaidya scheme (1×16 configuration) has the largest MLR. Less staggering requires less message logging and thus less overhead time with increase in striped parallelism. Although C_p increases with q, I_q is inversely proportional to p.

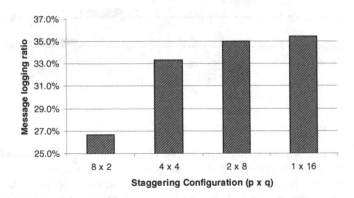

Fig. 5. Effects of checkpointing configuration on message logging ratio for a 16-node cluster

4 Experimental Cluster Configuration

Our experimental environment is a cluster with 16 Pentium PCs running the Linux Redhat Linux 7.2. The cluster nodes are connected by a 100 Mbps Fast Ethernet switch. Each node is attached with a 10-GB disk. With 16 nodes, the total capacity of the disk array is 160 GB. All 16 disks form a distributed RAID (*redundant array of independent disks*) [10].

The concept of distributed checkpointing on a distributed RAID is shown in Fig.6. Checkpoint files spread over the distributed disks. Striped checkpointing saves checkpoint files over the distributed RAID subsystem. Previous experimental result shows that distributed RAID system provides better I/O bandwidth compared to the use of NFS for the same purpose [10]. In the serverless cluster system, all local disks can be used to save the checkpoint files.

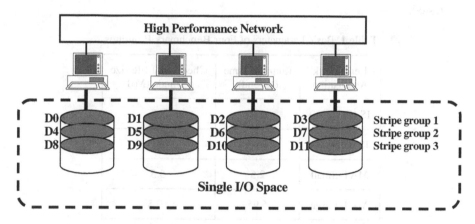

Fig. 6. Single I/O space for a distributed RAID in a cluster of computers

The distributed RAID system provides highly reliable and scalable secondary storage for fault tolerant clusters. Most checkpointing experiments were performed over a network-attached stable storage [7][19][23] or the memory of neighboring node [14]. Although diskless checkpointing shows lower checkpoint overhead and faster recovery, it suffers from the lack of scalability with a high memory demand.

Coordinated checkpointing is attracted to using a distributed RAID embedded in the cluster. In many cases, checkpointing files are large, and all cluster nodes must take checkpoints at the same time. Therefore, the coordinated checkpointing is an I/O- and communication-intensive procedure. Moreover, if the checkpointing file is spread over a distributed RAID, the recovery latency can be reduced using parallel I/O capabilities.

5   Benchmark Performance Results

Two benchmark programs, the IS and MAT, are inserted with checkpointing codes to carry out the cluster experiments. We use the checkpoint program Libckpt from [18] to implement a full-state, non-incremental checkpoints without using any fork system calls in the Linux cluster environment. Four benchmark experiments are performed on two benchmark programs. The performance is directly indicated by the checkpoint overhead measured in these experiments.

Table 1 presents the basic parameters of the benchmark experiments. Three checkpointing schemes are conducted on each benchmark program. The n × 1 coordinated checkpoint scheme forces all processes to take checkpoints at the same time. Vaidya's scheme allows only one node takes checkpoint at a time. To show our SSC scheme on a 16-node cluster, three SSC configurations: 2 × 8, 4 × 4 and 8 × 2 were tested.

Table 1. Basic Parameters of Four Benchmark Programs

Benchmark Application	Running Time (second)	Checkpoint file size per node (MB)
IS (Class W)	2.4	1.5
IS (Class A)	16.5	13.5
MAT-Small	2.5	5.5
MAT-Large	5.95	10.5

5.1   IS Benchmark Results

Integer sort (IS) is one of the NAS parallel benchmark programs [16]. The IS is communication-intensive to perform parallel sorting in the cluster environment. Randomly generated integer numbers are sorted by a parallel bucket sorting algorithm, based on a partitioning method [24]. In this parallel sorting algorithm, each processor works as one bucket. The IS can be tested with 5 problem sizes.

For checkpointing purpose, Class W and Class A of the IS code are tested in our benchmark experiments. For Class A test, the problem size is given as to sort 2^{23} integers. That means the number of keys to be sorted is 2^{23}. The problem size of Class W is 2^{20}. Class A needs to save 13.5 MB of checkpoint file and Class W saves 1.5 MB of checkpointing file per node. Normal execution time without checkpointing is 16.5 sec and 2.4 sec for the two IS classes.

Using MPI, the checkpointing codes are inserted inside of the source application code. Each iteration performs one checkpoint. Ten checkpoints are measured in these benchmarks. The message logging for IS benchmark is limited to a small numbers. Fig. 7 shows the checkpoint overhead for IS Class W and Class A on the NFS platform and over 6 disks and 12 disks, respectively.

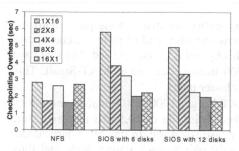 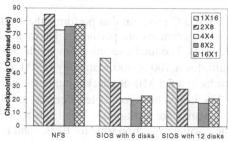

(a) CLASS W (checkpointing file size 1.5 MB)   (b) CLASS A (checkpointing file size 13.5 MB)

Fig. 7. Checkpointing overhead for the IS benchmark in two problem sizes

For benchmark IS with C and W, Vaiyda scheme always cause highest checkpointing overhead compared to striping and staggering checkpointing scheme and coordinate checkpointing scheme. This is due to the large amount of message should be logged to keep the consistency during each checkpointing duration. Our scheme is superior to other coordinated checkpointing for NFS and SIOS with 6 disks as storage platform. This is due to that in these cases, coordinate checkpointing will cause serious I/O contention.

By using 12 disks, the checkpoint overhead of our SCC scheme is higher than the coordinated checkpoint scheme. This is due to two reasons. First, the checkpoint size for IS Class W benchmark is quite small. I/O contention is lessened in our cluster platform for coordinated checkpointing. Second, messages need to be logged in the SCC scheme, while no message logging is needed in the coordinated checkpointing.

For benchmark IS with Class A, the overhead of staggered checkpointing scheme is the highest one among three checkpointing schemes. For the case of using NFS, coordinated checkpointing performs worse than Vaidya scheme due to much increased communication and I/O contentions. The checkpoint file size of this benchmark is the largest among all the four benchmark experiments.

Network and I/O contentions dominate the checkpoint overhead. Our SSC scheme performs the best in using a distributed RAID with kernel support of the SIOS. But when using the NFS, the 2×8 configuration performs the worst. This is due to added message logging overhead. From Fig. 7, the MLR for the 2×8 configuration is not much different from the Vaidya scheme with the 1 x 16 configuration. Two times more contention are observed on the 2×8 configuration.

For the SSC schemes, the checkpointing overhead of 8×2 configuration is the smallest. This is due to two reasons: (1). Parallel I/O accesses to the configuration provide higher I/O bandwidth. Therefore can serve more I/O requests at the same time. (2). The network latency for Fast Ethernet is short enough to server 8 I/O requests at the same time, no matter how large is the checkpoint file size.

5.2 MAT Benchmark Results

MAT is a C program that performs the multiplication for two floating-point matrices. Two experiments are performed below to show the overhead of different checkpoint file sizes. The total execution time without checkpoint is given 5.95 sec. The first case multiples a 700×300 matrix by a 300×300 matrix, denoted as MAT-Small. This results in a 5.5 MB of checkpointing file per cluster node.

For large checkpoint files, denoted as MAT-Large, 1000×400 matrix and 400×400 matrix are multiplied. This leads to a checkpoint file of 10.5 MB per processor. The normal execution time for the second test case is 2.4 sec. In this MAT-large code, the main program distributes a matrix multiply pair to each cluster node and thus heavier workload being executed.

To see the message-logging overhead, checkpointing is done at the last step when the results are gathered at a node. Therefore, the time lag of the checkpointing results in a large overhead for message logging. This corresponds to a case where the communication is intensive in the application code. Therefore, the message size is larger than that of the IS benchmark. The heights of the bars correspond to the overheads for MAT-Small and MAT-Large benchmarks on a NFS platform, on a distributed RAID with 6 disks, and on a 12-disk RAID with SIOS, respectively.

Fig. 8 shows the checkpoint overheads for two MAT workloads. Using the NFS checkpointing to execute the MAT-Small, the checkpoint overhead of the 16×1 configuration is the worst one due to heavy network and I/O contentions encountered. This is caused by large checkpoint file to be saved. The Vaidya scheme (1×16) will always cause the highest overhead due to a large number of messages that were logged.

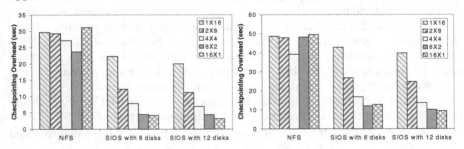

(a) MAT-Small (checkpoint file size = 5.5MB) (b) MAT-Large (checkpoint file size = 10.5MB)

Fig. 8. Checkpointing overhead in running the MAT benchmark

Using our distributed RAID platforms, the 16×1 checkpointing without staggering is the best for no need of message logging. Compared with the IS Class W benchmark where striped and staggered checkpointing is still better than coordinate checkpointing on 6 disks, the checkpointing overhead of coordinate checkpointing is less than our SSC scheme. This is due to more massages logged for MAT benchmark compared to that for IS benchmark.

MAT-Small and MAT-Large differ in the case of using 6 disks. For MAT-Large benchmark, large checkpoint files and more contentions are observed for coordinated checkpointing. Our SSC scheme is the best among all schemes tested in this case.

Specifically, the checkpoint overhead for the 8×2 configuration is the lowest. The only exception is for MAT-Large benchmark using the NFS scheme. In this case, the 4×4 configuration performs the best, because the 8×2 configuration causes more contentions due to the saving of even larger checkpoint files.

6 Discussions of the Experimental Results

The percentage of checkpoint overhead within total time of program execution is summarized in Table 2. All data are based on using the cluster platform of 12 disks forming a SIOS. The first row shows the results on a coordinated checkpoint scheme, while the last row shows those for Vaiyda scheme. The three middle rows are the results of our distributed SSC scheme under different configurations.

Table 2. Percentage of Checkpoint Overhead in Total Execution Time

Configurations		IS Class W	IS Class A	MAT-Small	MAT-Large
Coordinated checkpoint (16×1)		41%	56%	56%	62%
SSC Scheme	8×2	45%	52%	64%	63%
	4×4	48%	53%	73%	70%
	2×8	57%	63%	82%	81%
Vaiyda Scheme (1×16)		67%	67%	89%	87%

Among four experiments, the average checkpoint overhead runs from 41% to 89% of the total execution time. This overhead is rather high for efficient program execution. Vaidya scheme ends with the highest overhead. For light workload like IS Class W and MAT-Small, the coordinated scheme has the lowest overhead. For medium workload like MAT-Large, our SSC scheme performs similarly as the coordinated scheme. For heavy workload like IS Class A, our SSC scheme clearly outperforms all other checkpointing schemes.

In summary, Table 3 compares our distributed SCC scheme with the coordinated scheme and the Vaidya pure staggering scheme. Our SCC scheme applies better with large checkpoint files, scales better with larger clusters, and results in better use of network bandwidth. The dynamic reconfiguration capability of our scheme appeals better to variable checkpointing workload. The NFS and Vaidya schemes appeals better in saving small checkpoint files on small clusters. They do not scale well with large clusters.

Table 3. Comparison of Three Distributed Checkpointing Schemes

Checkpointing Scheme	Advantages	Shortcomings	Suitable applications
Coordinated scheme using (The 16×1 config. in Figs. 7 and 8)	Simple to implement, inconsistency does not exists	Network and I/O contentions, NFS is a single point of failure	Small checkpoint files, small clusters, and low I/O operations
Vaidya scheme with staggering (The 1×16 config. in Figs. 7 and 8)	Eliminate the network and I/O contentions	Wasted network bandwidth, NFS is a single point of failure	Medium checkpoint files, small clusters, low I/O operations
Our SCC scheme using the RAID (The 2×8, 8×2, 4×4 configs. in Figs. 7 and 8)	Eliminate network and I/O contentions, lower checkpoint overhead, tolerate multiple failures	Can not tolerate multiple node failures within the same stripe group	Large checkpoint files, large clusters, I/O intensive applications

7 Conclusions and Future Research

The proposed SSC scheme has been demonstrated effective to perform distributed checkpointing on clusters of computers. Striping exploits parallelism across multiple disks. Staggering alleviates the I/O bottleneck problem on each disk. In practice, staggering can be implemented with pipelined accesses to a string of disks attached to the same cluster node. The experimental results reported did not apply pipelining, because our Trojans cluster is implemented with only one disk per PC node.

The tradeoff between striping and staggering should be applied dynamically for different applications. The tradeoff results can be applied to yield the lowest SCC configuration for a given application. Higher stripe parallelism leads to higher aggregate disk bandwidth. Higher staggering depth copes better with the network contention problem. The results on message logging suggest that staggering should be discouraged in communication-intensive applications.

The checkpoint file size is another important factor in the selection of the optimal checkpointing configuration. This optimization process is evidenced by the overhead analysis given in section 6. Our SSC scheme is non-blocking in nature. That is why it can result in better resource utilization. In the case of a blocking scheme, staggered writing may introduce additional synchronization overhead. Blocking scheme is simpler to implement on a cluster than non-blocking scheme. However, blocking scheme suffers from large message passing overhead introduced.

We did not choose the blocking scheme, because every cluster node must be blocked during the checkpointing process. The basic idea is to shut down all processes temporarily to yield a globally consistent state. After all processes are blocked and all messages are clearly delivered, the global checkpoints are saved. In the staggered writing case, the blocked time increases with the cluster size. For this reason, we feel that the non-blocking SSC scheme is more scalable for large cluster applications.

For future research, we suggest that much longer benchmark programs should be selected to test the real performance of periodic checkpointing. In the extended benchmark experiments, all important system parameters: the *checkpoint interval, disk failure rate, checkpoint file sizes, stripe parallelism, staggering depth, and recovery latency* will come into play.

References

1. G. Cao and M. Singhal, "On coordinated Checkpointing in Distributed Systems", *IEEE Transactions on Parallel and Distributed Systems*, Vol.9, No.12, pp.1213-1225, Dec.1998.
2. G. Cao and N. Rishe, "A Nonblocking Consistent Checkpointing Algorithm for Distributed Systems", *Proceedings of the 8th International Conference on Parallel and Distributed Computing and Systems*, Chicago, pp.302-307, October 1997.
3. K. M. Chandy and L. Lamport, "Distributed Snapshots: Determining Global States of Distributed Systems", *ACM Trans. Computer Systems*, pp.63-75, Feb. 1985.
4. Y. Deng and E. K. Park, "Checkpointing and Rollback-Recovery Algorithms in Distributed Systems", *Journal of Systems and Software*, pp.59-71, Apr. 1994.
5. E. N. Elnozahy and W. Zwaenepoel, "Manetho: Transparent Rollback-Recovery with Low Overhead, Limited Rollback and Fast Output Commit", *IEEE Transactions on Computers*, Special Issue on Fault-Tolerant Computing, pp.526-531, May 1992.
6. E. N. Elnozahy, D. B. Johnson and Y. M. Wang, "A Survey of Rollback-Recovery Protocols in Message-Passing Systems", *Technical Report CMU-CS-96-181*, Department of Computer Science, Carnegie Mellon University, Sept. 1996.
7. E. N. Elnozahy and W. Zwaenepoel, "On the Use and Implementation of Message Logging", *Proceedings of the 24th Int'l Sym. on Fault-Tolerant Computing*, pp.298-307, June 1994.
8. G. A. Gibson and D. A. Patterson, "Designing Disk Arrays for High Data Reliability", *Journal of Parallel and Distributed Computing*, Vol.17, Jan. 1993, pp 4-27.
9. K. Hwang, H. Jin, E. Chow, C. L. Wang, and Z. Xu. "Designing SSI Clusters with Hierarchical Checkpointing and Single I/O Space", *IEEE Concurrency Magazine*, March 1999, pp.60-69.
10. K. Hwang, H. Jin, and R. S. C. Ho, "Orthogonal Striping and Mirroring in Distributed RAID for I/O-Centric Cluster Computing", *IEEE Transactions on Parallel and Distributed Systems*, Vol.13, No.1, January 2002, pp.26-44.
11. K. Hwang, H. Jin, R. Ho and W. Ro, "Reliable Cluster Computing with a New Checkpointing RAID-x Architecture", *Proceedings of 9-th Workshop on Heterogeneous Computing (HCW-2000)*, Cancun, Mexico, May 1, 2000, pp.171-184.
12. J. L. Kim and T. Park, "An efficient protocol for checkpointing recovery in distributed systems", *IEEE Transactions on Parallel and Distributed Systems*, Aug. 1993, pp.955 – 960.
13. R. Koo and S. Toueg, "Checkpointing and Rollback-Recovery for Distributed Systems", *IEEE Trans. on Parallel and Distributed Systems*, Vol.5. No.8, pp.955-960, Aug. 1993.
14. K. Li, J. Naughton and J. Plank, "Low-Latency Concurrent Checkpoint for Parallel Programs", *IEEE Trans. on Parallel and Dist. Computing*, Vol.5, No.8, 1994, pp.874-879.
15. M. Malhotra and K. Trivedi, "Reliability Analysis of Redundant Arrays of Inexpensive Disks", *Journal of Parallel and Distributed Computing*, 1993.
16. NAS Parallel Benchmarks. http://www.nas.nasa.gov/Software/NPB/

17. R. H. Netzer and J. Xu, "Necessary and Sufficient Conditions for Consistent Global Snapshots", *IEEE Trans. on Parallel and Distributed System*, pp.165-169, Feb. 1995.
18. J. S. Plank, M. Beck, G. Kingsley, and K. Li, "Libckpt: Transparent Checkpointing Under Unix", *Proceedings of Usenix Winter 1995 Technical Conference*, pp.213-223, Jan. 1995.
19. J. S. Plank, K. Li, and M. A. Puening, "Diskless Checkpointing", *IEEE Transactions on Parallel and Distributed Systems*, 1998, pp.972-986.
20. R. Prakash and M. Singhal, "Low-Cost Checkpointing and Failure Recovery in Mobile Computing Systems", *IEEE Trans. on Parallel and Distributed Systems*, pp.1035-1048, Oct. 1996.
21. L. M. Silva and J. G. Silva, "Global Checkpointing for Distributed Programs", *Proceedings of 11th Symposium Reliable Distributed Systems*, pp.155-162, Oct. 1992.
22. N. H. Vaidya, "A Case for Two-Level Distributed Recovery Schemes", *Proceedings of the ACM In'l Conf. On Meas. and Modeling of Computer Systems (Sigmetrics'95)*, pp.64-73.
23. N. H. Vaidya, "Staggered Consistent Checkpointing", *IEEE Transactions on Parallel and Distributed Systems*, 1999, Vol.10, No.7, pp.694-702.
24. B. Wilkinson and M. Allen, *Parallel Programming: Techniques and Applications Using Networked Workstations and Parallel Computers*, Prentice Hall, New Jersey, 1999.
25. J. Xu and R. H. B. Netzer, "Adaptive Independent Checkpointing for Reducing Rollback Propagation", *Proc. of the 5th IEEE Symposium on Parallel and Distributed Processing*, Dec. 1993.

Shortcut Replay: A Replay Technique for Debugging Long-Running Parallel Programs

Nam Thoai, Dieter Kranzlmüller, and Jens Volkert

GUP Linz
Johannes Kepler University Linz
Altenbergerstraße 69, A-4040 Linz, Austria/Europe
nam.thoai@gup.jku.at

Abstract. Applications running on HPC Platforms, PC clusters, or computational grids are often long-running parallel programs. Debugging these programs is a challenge due to the lack of efficient debugging tools and the inherent possibility of nondeterminism in parallel programs. To overcome the problem of nondeterminism, several sophisticated record&replay mechanisms have been developed. However, the substantial problem of the waiting time during re-execution was not sufficiently investigated in the past. This paper shows that the waiting time is in some cases unlimited with currently available methods, which prohibits efficient interactive debugging tools. In contrast, the new *shortcut replay* method combines checkpointing and debugging techniques. It controls the replayed execution based on the trace data in order to minimize the waiting time during debugging long-running parallel programs.

1 Introduction

High Performance Computing (HPC) technologies have been substantially improved in terms of usability and programmability over the last decade. The latest approaches to low-cost HPC computing on clusters of workstations on the one hand, and high-performance, high-throughput computing on computational grids on the other hand [8], have further pushed the HPC technology into the mainstream market. This fact is underlined by many scientific applications that either have been or are being developed to run on PC clusters or the Grid [1-6]. However, there are still some problems, which are not sufficiently solved. One of them is debugging of long-running parallel programs. This is especially important in the context of HPC platforms, because many applications of computational science and engineering suffer from a long execution time of days, weeks, or even months.

Nowadays the typical program development cycle of programmers is "edit, compile, run, debug". The same cycle applies to parallel programming, but the process is more complex [7]. A parallel program consists of a number of processes that are executed in parallel by different communicating processors. These programs may produce non-deterministic behavior, i.e. consecutive runs may result in different executions, even if the same input data is provided, which prohibits using cyclic debugging for parallel programs. This is a popular debugging technique, where a

A. Jean-Marie (Ed.): ASIAN 2002, LNCS 2550, pp. 34-46, 2002.

program is executed repeatedly in order to examine occurring program states by using breakpoints, watch-points, etc. and finally to detect the origins of erroneous behavior.

To overcome this problem, so-called deterministic replay techniques [24] or record&replay mechanisms [17] have been developed. These methods are based on two steps: (1) during an initial record phase, a trace of the program's nondeterministic choices is recorded, and (2) the trace data may afterwards be used to ensure that the re-execution is equivalent to the initially observed execution.

Despite these efforts in combining cyclic debugging and deterministic replay, debugging long-running parallel programs is still a challenge, since long execution times are quite common. Every time, the programmer wants to inspect the value of a variable at an intermediate point, the program must be re-executed from the beginning to that point. Since cyclic debugging usually requires several iterations, the debugging task may become very time-consuming.

A solution is provided by checkpointing [23], which can be used to pass "uninteresting parts" during re-executions in order to minimize the waiting time. The same idea was introduced in incremental replay methods [21][29][30], but it only supports to re-execute a part of one process at a time. In order to stop at an arbitrary distributed breakpoint as fast as possible and to replay all processes later, methods used to establish recovery lines in fault tolerance computing can be applied. However, they do not satisfy the strict requirements of interactive debugging tools because the waiting time may still be rather long in some cases.

As an advanced approach, a new replay technique called *shortcut replay* is described in this paper. This method applies a checkpointing technique to reduce the waiting time. It is flexible enough to choose a recovery line so that the rollback/replay distance [25] is shorter than in other methods. The rollback/replay distance is the gap between the recovery line and the corresponding distributed breakpoint. Consequently, the replay time is small due to the short replay distance. In addition, a new method to find a suitable recovery line for the new replay method is presented. This replay technique can be applied for both message-passing and shared memory programs. However, due to space limitations, details are only described for message-passing programs.

This paper is divided into 8 sections. Definitions of checkpointing and rollback recovery are introduced in Section 2. A short survey of deterministic replay methods and possibility of combining checkpointing and debugging are shown in Section 3. In Section 4, the shortcut replay technique is described and two methods to detect orphan messages for message-passing programs are shown in Section 5. The new graph model, which is used to find a suitable recovery line for the shortcut replay method, is presented in Section 6. The results of successful application of the shortcut replay are placed in Section 7. Finally, conclusions are given in Section 8.

2   Definitions Used in Checkpointing and Rollback Recovery

Before starting with details about our debugging approach, some basic definitions are needed. The *global state* of a message-passing program is the collection of the individual states of all participating processes and the states of the communication channels [12]. A *consistent global state* is one in which every message that has been received is also shown to have been sent in the state of the sender [9].

A *global checkpoint* is a set of local checkpoints, one from each process. When considering a global checkpoint G, two categories of messages are particularly important:

- *Orphan messages*, which are messages that have been delivered in G, although the corresponding send events occur only after the local checkpoints comprising G.
- *In-transit messages*, which are messages that have been sent but not delivered in G.

A global checkpoint is *consistent* if there is no orphan message with respect to it [15]. This condition can be described in the following way in order to check the consistency of a global checkpoint: if $(C_0, C_1,..., C_n)(n \geq 1)$ is a consistent global checkpoint, then $(\forall i,j)(i \neq j, 0 \leq i,j \leq n) \neg (C_i \rightarrow C_j)$, where "$\rightarrow$" is "happened-before" relation [18]. On contrary, an *inconsistent global checkpoint* is a global checkpoint that is not consistent.

In Figure 1, message m_1 is an in-transit message of $(C_{0,0}, C_{1,1}, C_{2,0})$ and $(C_{0,0}, C_{1,2}, C_{2,0})$. Message m_2 is an orphan message of $(C_{0,0}, C_{1,2}, C_{2,0})$ and $(C_{0,1}, C_{1,2}, C_{2,0})$. $(C_{0,0}, C_{1,1}, C_{2,0})$ is a consistent global checkpoint but $(C_{0,0}, C_{1,2}, C_{2,0})$, and $(C_{0,1}, C_{1,2}, C_{2,0})$ are inconsistent global checkpoints due to $C_{2,0} \rightarrow C_{1,2}$ or orphan message m_2.

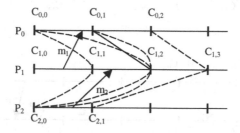

Fig. 1. Global checkpoints

Assume that $G = (C_{0,2}, C_{1,3}, C_{2,1})$ is the global state that a user wants to reach. The rollback/replay distance between recovery line $(C_{0,0}, C_{1,1}, C_{2,0})$ and G is two intervals and between $(C_{0,1}, C_{1,2}, C_{2,0})$ and G is one interval, where interval is the maximum distance between two consecutive checkpoints on the same process.

3   Related Work

A prerequisite of a parallel debugging tool is to ensure reproducibility, which is resolved by deterministic replay or record&replay methods. These methods can be classified into two kinds: content-based and ordering-based methods [24]. In content-based replay, the choices of nondeterministic events are recorded and later on used in re-execution [22]. This method is based on the fact that each process will produce the same behavior each time if it is supplied the same input value (corresponding to the contents of messages received or the values of shared memory locations references) [19]. In particular, each process will produce the same output values in the same order. Each of these output values may then serve as an input value for some other process. On contrary, ordering-based replay methods try to guarantee that the order of interprocess dependencies during the replay phase matches the order of the dependencies that were observed during the record phase. In message passing programs, the critical dependencies are the pair-wise orders of corresponding send and receive operations [20]. In message passing systems prohibiting message overtaking, it is even sufficient to trace the actual sender of messages received by promiscuous receive operations [11][16]. (For a more complete survey of deterministic replay methods see [24].)

A problem occurs when replay methods and interactive setting of breakpoints are combined in cyclic debugging. Setting breakpoints is a technique, which helps to halt and examine a program at interesting points during its execution [14]. The waiting time may be rather long in each debugging cycle if a program is replayed from the beginning state to the breakpoint state. Developing a technique to minimize this waiting time seems necessary.

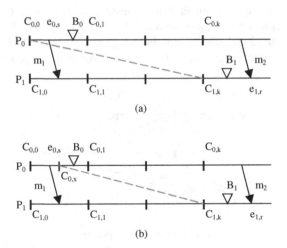

Fig. 2. Consistent and inconsistent recovery lines

A solution is offered by checkpointing techniques. Checkpointing is applied in fault tolerance computing to minimize the waste time, i.e. whenever a program's execution fails, the execution of the program may proceed from the last available checkpoint to avoid to restarting at the beginning state. The construction of recovery lines is extensively examined in fault-tolerant computing [9][12][15][27], where recovery lines can only be established at consistent global checkpoints, because inconsistent global states prohibit failure-free execution.

A variety of solutions have been proposed to restart the program from intermediate code positions in order to minimize the waiting time [21][22][30]. These incremental replay techniques allow us to replay only one part of one process at a time.

Despite the existence of several methods for taking checkpoints and establishing recovery lines, the rollback/replay distance may be rather long in some cases. In Figure 2a, the best recovery line for the consistent global state (B_0, B_1) is $(C_{0,0}, C_{1,k})$. However, due to orphan message m_1, this recovery line is inconsistent and cannot be used by the available approaches. Instead, the most recent consistent recovery line is

$(C_{0,0}, C_{1,0})$. The replay distance between $(C_{0,0}, C_{1,0})$ and (B_0, B_1) is nearly $k+1$ intervals. If the value of k is rather large, the replay distance is obviously long.

The above problem can be solved by using CASBR (Checkpoint-After-Send-Before-Receive) method [28], i.e. an additional checkpoint $C_{0,x}$ is taken immediately after send event $e_{0,s}$ as shown in Figure 2b. In this case, the recovery line $(C_{0,x}, C_{1,k})$ can be used for (B_0, B_1) with a short replay distance.

During debugging, the problem is that process P_0 does not have enough information at send event $e_{0,s}$, e.g., where a breakpoint will be established, or which send and receive events will happen on processes P_0, P_1. Thus it cannot decide whether to take an additional checkpoint or not. The traditional solution to limit the replay distance is to take checkpoints immediately after every send event. Unfortunately, the overhead of this technique is rather high because many checkpoints are required.

This problem cannot be solved by current checkpointing and rollback recovery techniques, when recovery lines are only chosen at consistent global checkpoints. Unfortunately, all previous replay techniques prohibit inconsistent global checkpoints as recovery lines, although the short waiting time is an important requirement of interactive debugging tools.

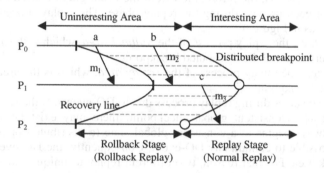

Fig. 3. Two stages in replay process

4 Shortcut Replay

The shortcut replay technique applies checkpointing to minimize the waiting time under the constraints presented above. In this case, the waiting time is the replay time of the uninteresting area as shown in Figure 3, where users want to replay (re-execute) only the area after the distributed breakpoint. This method allows us to construct recovery lines more flexible than other methods by supporting recovery lines at both consistent and inconsistent global checkpoints; the waiting time is thus reduced. The main idea is based on the following observations:

-   The necessity of using only consistent global checkpoints for establishing recovery lines is to avoid processing a special kind of events called *O-event* (Output Event). O-events are events that create only affection on other processes such as send events in message-passing programs. If a program is recovered in an inconsistent global state, it leads to a situation that a process P_p processes an O-event and this will affect another process P_q, while process P_q is a state that the affection has happened. The final result is thus influenced by the repeated affection. This kind of O-event is called *DO-event* (Dangerous O-event).

-   With record&replay mechanisms, the re-execution can enforce the same event ordering as observed during the record phase by skipping O-events (or rather DO-events) when needed.

For message-passing programs, unexpected effects may be observed through orphan messages. Given recovery line $(C_{0,0}, C_{1,k})$ in Figure 2a, message m_1 will be an orphan message. By using this recovery line, receive event $e_{1,r}$ may accept message m_1 instead of m_2, leading to incorrect results. The send events, which create orphan messages, are DO-events. For example, in Figure 3, a is a DO-event while b, c are not.

The above observations allow us to develop the shortcut replay technique, where the recovery line can be chosen at both consistent and inconsistent global checkpoints. This replay technique is based on the event graph model, which represents events and their relations as observed during a program's execution [17], and includes two phases: record phase and replay phase. In record phase, the relations between events are recorded. Afterwards, the information from the event graph is used to control the re-execution of each process during the replay phase. The replay process is divided into two stages as in Figure 3:

1.   *Rollback stage*: the replay process of the *rollback area*, which is the area between the recovery line and the distributed breakpoint.
2.   *Replay stage*: the replay process of the *replay area*, which is the area behind the distributed breakpoint.

There are two stages during replay process due to DO-events. If the recovery line is established at an inconsistent global checkpoint, there may exist DO-events. The replay area always begins at a consistent global state (a distributed breakpoint) and thus it is impossible to contain any DO-event. Consequently, the DO-events are only in the rollback area. For that reason, two different replay techniques are used for the two areas.

On the one hand, the *normal replay method* is used in the replay stage. This normal replay method is the same as record&replay mechanisms in [17], where all deterministic events are ensured to receive messages from the same senders as in the initial execution based on the trace data. On the other hand, the *rollback replay method* is used in the rollback stage, where all DO-events can be distinguished based on the trace data and they are thus skipped in the replay process. Consequently, the affections of DO-events are disappeared by this replay method. The rollback replay method executes other events in the same way with the normal replay method.

The efficiency of this replay method can be evaluated through the rollback distance length. Because recovery lines can be chosen at any global checkpoint, the rollback distance is often shorter than other methods.

The shortcut replay technique can be applied for message-passing programs, where the O-events are send events. During the record phase, information of communication events is traced. During re-execution in the replay phase, all send events are examined based on the trace data. If they create orphan messages, they are skipped. For example, in Figure 2a all orphan messages of the recovery line $(C_{0,0}, C_{1,k})$ are determined, such as message m_1. During re-execution, the send events of the orphan messages can be skipped, e.g. message m_1 is not created, and the re-execution path of each process is equivalent to the initial execution. This replay method is called *bypassing orphan messages* [25].

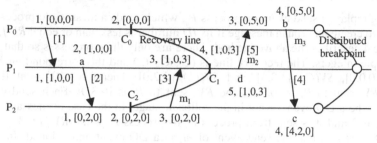

Fig. 4. The method to detect orphan messages

5 Detecting Orphan Messages

In message-passing programs, DO-events are orphan messages. Thus a problem is to know when a send event is responsible for an orphan message in re-executions. Two solutions are suggested here.

Firstly, all orphan messages of a recovery line and all correlative send events (DO-events) are identified based on the event graph. A list of these DO-events is sent to each process and they are skipped during re-execution. A disadvantage of this method is the requirement of searching the event graph and the extra communication overhead. It is thus not an optimal solution if the event graph data is large and there are many processes.

Secondly, identification of orphan messages is processed based on a small comparison at each send event during replay phase. Each event has a sequential number, called *ID* number, and this number is the same in the initial execution and the re-execution. *IDs* of send events are piggybacked on the messages. Each process P_p manages a vector SV_p, which includes n elements, where n is the number of processes. Element $SV_p[q]$ ($q \neq p$) is used to keep the *ID* of the send event of the last message coming from process P_q. All elements are initially set to 0. Whenever process P_p receives a message from process P_q, $SV_p[q]$ is assigned to the *ID* value attached on the coming message. *SV* vector is similar to vector timestamp [13] but their meanings are different. Vector timestamps are used to track down the happened-before relation between events, while *SV* vectors show the send events of the last coming messages from other processes. For example, in Figure 4, the *SV* vector of event c on process P_2 is [4,2,0], which shows that the last coming messages from processes P_0 and P_1, which are received, are created by event b (ID = 4) and a (ID = 2). If a vector timestamp is used, the vector timestamp of c shows that the last events on processes P_0 and P_1, which are happened-before c, are b and d. Consequently, the vector timestamp of c must be [4,5,x].

The *SV* vector is stored in the trace data of each checkpoint event. During the recovery process, all *SV* vectors of checkpoint events in the recovery line are used to compute the useful vector *RVs* sent to other processes as following:

*Vector RV_q is sent to process P_q where $RV_q[q]=0$ and $RV_q[i]= SV_i[q]$
($\forall i \neq q$ in [0,n), where n is the number of processes) with SV_i is the SV
vector of checkpoint event on process P_i at the recovery line.*

During replay, a send event on process P_q, which sends a message to process P_p, is detected to create an orphan message if its *ID* number is less than or equal $RV_q[p]$.

Figure 4 describes the above method. There are only three processes so that *SV* is a set of triple integers. The recovery line is (C_0, C_1, C_2) and the corresponding *SV*s are $SV(C_0)=[0,0,0]$, $SV(C_1)=[1,0,3]$, and $SV(C_2)=[0,2,0]$. Therefore, RV_0 sent to P_0 is [0,1,0], RV_1 sent to P_1 is [0,0,2], and RV_2 sent to P_2 is [0,3,0]. Each send event is checked to be a DO-event or not in the rollback stage. In the case of message m_1, the ID of m_1 is 3 and it is sent from process P_2 to process P_1 while $RV_2[1]=3$ (which is equal ID of m_1) so that the send event of m_1 is a DO-event and skipped. In case of message m_2 and m_3, ID(m_2)(=5) is greater than $RV_1[0]$(=0) and ID(m_3)(=4) is greater than $RV_0[2]$(=0) so that they are not DO-events and executed.

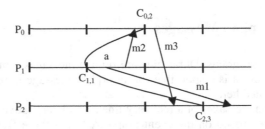

Fig. 5. Identifying orphan messages in FIFO-Computation

Please notes, that vector timestamps [13] cannot be applied to solve this problem in FIFO-computation [10]. The idea that a send event creates an orphan message if it is happened-before the corresponding checkpoint is critical. Figure 5 gives an example. The recovery line is ($C_{0,2}$, $C_{1,1}$, $C_{2,3}$). Message m_1 is not an orphan message although $a \rightarrow C_{2,3}$. Although vector timestamp cannot be used to identify the orphan message, it can be used to create the vector *SV*, i.e. if vector timestamp is piggybacked on message, the time value of the sending process in vector timestamp is used instead of the *ID* number.

6 Rollback Reduced Message Graph: R2-Graph

In practice, a problem of the shortcut replay method is to find a suitable global checkpoint so that the *R2-graph* can be developed. This graph is constructed based on checkpoints and in-transit messages, which are not logged. Such a graph is developed in order to find global checkpoints, which are enough in-transit messages, used as recovery lines in shortcut replay method. It is different from other checkpoint graphs such as rollback-dependency graph, and checkpoint graph [12], where relation among checkpoints is the key characteristic for constructing the graph. They are only used to find consistent global checkpoints. Otherwise, any global checkpoint can be a recovery line in the shortcut replay method, and other graph models do not often provide the best recovery line due to long replay distance described in section 3. R2-graph is thus necessary for shortcut replay.

Figure 6b displays an image of the R2-graph for the event graph of Figure 6a. Each node represents a checkpoint and a directed edge m is drawn from $C_{p,i}$ to $C_{q,j}$ if (1) $p \neq q$, and a message from $I_{q,j-1}$ to $I_{p,i}$ is not logged or (2) $p=q$ and $j=i+1$. The checkpoints $C_{p,i}$ and $C_{q,j}$ are called head(m) and tail(m).

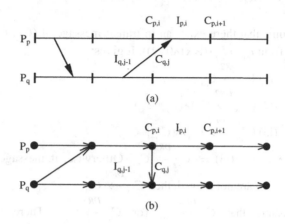

(a)

(b)

Fig. 6. (a) Checkpoints and not required messages; (b) R2-graph

Definition 1:   *R2-Graph*

An *R2-graph* is a directed graph $G=(C, \overset{d}{\rightarrow})$, where C is a non-empty set of local checkpoints on all processes, while $\overset{d}{\rightarrow}$ is a relation connecting checkpoints, such that $C_{p,i} \overset{d}{\rightarrow} C_{q,j}$ means that there is an edge from $C_{p,i}$ to $C_{q,j}$ in G with "head" at $C_{p,i}$ and "tail" at $C_{q,j}$.

The relation $C_{p,i} \overset{d}{\rightarrow} C_{q,j}$ only shows that in-transit messages of $(C_{p,p}, C_{q,j})$ from $I_{q,j-1}$ to $I_{p,i}$ are not logged. This relation can be opened to *direct relation* through the definition of *Direct R2-path (DR2-path)* below:

Definition 2:   *DR2-path*

There is a DR2-path from checkpoint Cp,x on process Pp to checkpoint Cq,y on process Pq in R2-graph, denoted Cp,x $\overset{DR2}{\rightarrow}$ Cq,y, iff a path [m1...mn], n≥1, exists such that

1. $C_{p,x}$ is head(m_1), and
2. for each m_i, $1 \le i < n$, tail(m_i) and head(m_{i+1}) are on P_p or P_q and tail(m_i) is head(m_{i+1}), and
3. $C_{q,y}$ is tail(m_n).

This is called a direct relation because DR2-path is only constructed based on relation among checkpoints on a couple of processes. Direct relation is a extension of the relation in R2-graph by applying transitive characteristic on couple of processes.

This means, that if C_1, C_2, C_3 are checkpoints on processes P_p and P_q and $(C_1 \overset{DR2}{\rightarrow} C_2) \wedge (C_2 \overset{DR2}{\rightarrow} C_3)$, then $C_1 \overset{DR2}{\rightarrow} C_3$.

Lemma 1: There exists an in-transit message of $(C_{p,x}, C_{q,y})$, which is not logged, if and only if $C_{p,x} \overset{DR2}{\rightarrow} C_{q,y}$ or $C_{q,y} \overset{DR2}{\rightarrow} C_{p,x}$.

Proof:

a) ⟹. Assume that there exists an in-transit message of $(C_{p,x}, C_{q,y})$, which is not logged, from $I_{p,i}$ to $I_{q,j}$ $((i<x) \wedge (j \geq y))$. It gives:

(i1) $C_{q,j} \overset{DR2}{\rightarrow} C_{p,i+1}$

(i2) $(C_{q,y} \overset{DR2}{\rightarrow} C_{q,j}) \wedge (C_{q,y} \equiv C_{q,j})$

(i3) $(C_{p,i+1} \overset{DR2}{\rightarrow} C_{p,x}) \wedge (C_{p,i+1} \equiv C_{p,x})$

(i1) ∧ (i2) ∧ (i3) $\Rightarrow C_{q,y} \overset{DR2}{\rightarrow} C_{p,x}$. Otherwise, if messages from $I_{q,j}$ to $I_{p,i}$ $((j<y) \wedge (i \geq x))$ are not logged, then $C_{p,x} \overset{DR2}{\rightarrow} C_{q,y}$.

b) ⟸. Assume that $C_{p,x} \overset{DR2}{\rightarrow} C_{q,y}$ (or $C_{q,y} \overset{DR2}{\rightarrow} C_{p,x}$). There exists $C_{p,i} \overset{d}{\rightarrow} C_{q,j}$ $((i \geq x) \wedge (j < y))$ (or $C_{q,j} \overset{d}{\rightarrow} C_{p,i}$ $((j \geq y) \wedge (i < x))$). It means, that messages from $I_{q,j-1}$ to $I_{p,i}$ (or from $I_{p,i-1}$ to $I_{q,j}$) are not logged. This also shows that there exists an in-transit message of $(C_{p,x}, C_{q,y})$, which is not logged. □

Based on the R2-graph, an available recovery line can be computed by determining the DR2-path following description in theorem 1:

Theorem 1 A global checkpoint $G=(C_0, C_1,..., C_n)(n \geq 1)$ is a recovery line, if and only if there is no DR2-path between any two local checkpoints in G $((\forall i,j$ in $[0,n], i \neq j)$ $\neg (C_i \overset{DR2}{\rightarrow} C_j))$.

Proof:

a) ⟹. Assume that there is an in-transit message of G, which is not logged, and it is thus in-transit message of $(C_i, C_j)(i,j \in [0,n])$. Therefore, we have $C_i \overset{DR2}{\rightarrow} C_j$ or $C_j \overset{DR2}{\rightarrow} C_i$ (lemma 1).

b) ⟸. Assume that $C_i \overset{DR2}{\rightarrow} C_j$ $(i,j \in [0,n])$. There exists thus an in-transit message of (C_i, C_j) which is not logged (lemma 1). This means that G has an in-transit message, which is not logged. □

Theorem 1 can be applied to find the nearest recovery line for a consistent global state with the following 3 steps approach:

1. The initial checkpoint set contains local checkpoints, where each checkpoint is *the nearest checkpoint before* the consistent global state on each process.

2. If there is a DR2-path between any two checkpoints $C_{p,i}$, $C_{q,j}$ $(C_{p,i} \xrightarrow{DR2} C_{q,j})$, then $C_{q,j}$
    is replaced by a checkpoint $C_{q,j-1}$ in the checkpoint set.
3. Continue Step 2 until there is no DR2-path between any two checkpoints in the
    set. The final checkpoint set is the recovery line.

7   Application of Shortcut Replay

The shortcut replay is introduced as a new replay method that allows users to reduce
the waiting time during debugging parallel programs. It has been used in two
methods: Rollback-One-Step (ROS) [25] and MRT [26]. They are checkpointing and
rollback-recovery methods used in debugging. The goals of the methods are to give a
small replay time and a low overhead of message logging for long-running parallel
programs.

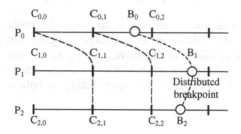

Fig. 7. Recovery lines in ROS and MRT

The same checkpointing method used in both ROS and MRT is index-based
communication-induced checkpointing [12]. It allows any global checkpoint with the
same index, e.g. $(C_{0,k}, C_{1,k}..., C_{n,k})$, to be consistent. However, as mentioned in Section
3, if recovery lines are only placed at consistent global checkpoints, the rollback
distance may be rather long in some cases. Therefore, the shortcut replay is used to
allow users to establish the recovery lines more flexible. Obviously, the most recent
checkpoints can be chosen as the recovery line, e.g. $(C_{0,1}, C_{1,2}, C_{2,2})$ in Figure 7, but the
number of transferred messages, which must be logged, may be great because any
message could become a transferred message. Consequently, ROS and MRT allow
the recovery line to contain either the most recent checkpoint or the last one before it
on each process, i.e. if the most recent checkpoint is $C_{p,k}$ (k≥1), then the recovery line
contains either $C_{p,k}$ or $C_{p,k-1}$. For example, in Figure 7 the recovery line of (B_0, B_1, B_2)
are only established between $(C_{0,0}, C_{1,1}, C_{2,1})$ and $(C_{0,1}, C_{1,2}, C_{2,2})$. Such the way to
establish a recovery line proves that the rollback distance is either less than or equal to
two checkpoint intervals. In other words, the rollback distance in both ROS and MRT
has an upper bound two checkpoint intervals. Furthermore, MRT ensures that the
replay time is also limited in two checkpoint intervals [26].

The overhead of message logging in both ROS and MRT is small, e.g. the ratio
between the number of logged messages per the number of the total messages is less
than 5% [25] [26]. The detail methods to store transferred messages can be seen in
[25] [26].

The above results prove that the shortcut replay is an efficient replay method, which can be used to reduce the waiting time during debugging parallel programs.

8 Conclusions

A short waiting time is an important characteristic of interactive debugging tools. This paper shows the limits of current techniques to minimize this waiting time during debugging long-running parallel programs. The shortcut replay technique gives a new method to control re-executions of parallel programs and thus allows us to flexibly choose recovery lines. Consequently, the rollback/replay distance and the replay time are minimized. In addition, a method to construct a suitable recovery line based on R2-graph and DR2-path is introduced. These techniques are successfully applied in Rollback-One-Step method [25] and MRT method [26] in order to limit the rollback distance or the replay time about two checkpoint intervals. All of these techniques can be used to develop interactive debugging tools in order to build long-running parallel programs.

The shortcut replay technique allows us to limit the replay time but the ratio between replay time and overhead of message logging always depend on the checkpointing method. In addition, the event graph gives us more information of the running program and the intercommunication of its processes. Our future work in this project intends to use the event graph for determining an optimal replay method with a low overhead and a short replay time.

References

1. GiPhyN Particle Physics Grid Project Site, http://www.griphyn.org/
2. International Virtual Data Grid Laboratory, http://www.ivdgl.org/
3. NEES Earthquake Engineering Grid, http://www.neesgrid.org/
4. SCEC Earthquake Science Grid, http://www.scec.org/
5. The European CrossGrid Project, http://www.eu-crossgrid.org/
6. The European DataGrid Project, http://www.eu-datagid.org/
7. Appelbe B., and Bergmark, D. "Software Tools for High Performance Computing: Survey and Recommendations", Scientific Programming (Fall 1996), Vol. 5, No. 4.
8. Baker, M., Buyya, R., and Laforenza, D. "Grids and Grid Technologies for Wide-Area Distributed Computing", Software: Practice and Experience (SPE) Journal, Wiley Press, USA (2002).
9. Chandy, K. M., and Lamport, L. "Distributed Snapshots: Determining Global States of Distributed Systems", ACM Transactions on Computer Systems 3 (1985), pp. 63-75.
10. Charron-Bost, B., Mattern, F., and Tel, G. "Synchronous, Asynchronous, and Causally Ordered Communication", Distributed Computing (1996), Vol. 9, No. 4, pp. 173-191.
11. Chassin de Kergommeaux, J., Ronsse, M., and De Bosschere, K. "MPL*: Efficient Record/Replay of Nondeterminism Features of Message Passing Libraries", In J. Recent Advances in Parallel Virtual Machine and Message Passing Interface (EuroPVMMPI99) (September 1999), Vol. 1697 of Lecture Notes in Computer Science, pp. 234-239.

12. Elnozahy, E. N., Alvisi, L., Wang, Y. M., and Johnson, D. B. "A Survey of Rollback-Recovery Protocols in Message-Passing Systems", Technical Report CMU-CS-99-148, School of Computer Science, Carnegie Mellon University (June 1999).
13. Fidge, C. "Fundamentals of Distributed System Observation", IEEE Software (November 1996), Vol. 13, No. 6, pp. 77-84.
14. Haban, D., and Weigel, W. "Global Events and Global Breakpoints in Distributed Systems", Proc. of the 21st Annual Hawaii International Conference on System Sciences, Software Track, IEEE Computer Society (January 1988), Vol. 2, pp. 166-175.
15. Hélary, J. M., Mostefaoui, A., and Raynal, M. "Communication-Induced Determination of Consistent Snapshot", IEEE Transaction on Parallel and Distributed Systems (September 1999), Vol. 10, No. 9.
16. Kranzlmüller, D., Volkert, J. "NOPE: Nondeterministic Program Evaluator", Proc. of ACPC99 (February 1999), pp. 490-499.
17. Kranzlmüller, D. "Event Graph Analysis for Debugging Massively Parallel Programs", PhD Thesis, GUP Linz, Johannes Kepler University Linz, Austria (September 2000), http://www.gup.uni-linz.ac.at/~dk/thesis.
18. Lamport, L. "Time, Clocks, and The Ordering of Events in a Distributed System", Communications of the ACM (July 1978), Vol. 21, No. 7, pp. 558-565.
19. LeBlanc, T. J., and Mellor-Crummey, J. M. "Debugging Parallel Programs with Instant Replay", IEEE Transactions on Computers (April 1987), Vol. 36, No. 4, pp. 471-481.
20. Netzer, R. H. B., and Miller, B. "Optimal Tracing and Replay for Debugging Message-Passing Parallel Programs ", Proc. of Supercomputing'92, Minneapolis, MN (November 1992), pp. 502-511.
21. Netzer, R. H. B., and Xu, J. "Adaptive Message Logging for Incremental Program Replay", IEEE Parallel & Distributed Technology (November 1993), Vol. 1, No. 4, pp. 32-40.
22. Pan, D.Z., and Linton, M.A. "Supporting Reverse Execution of Parallel Programs", Proc. of the ACM SIGPLAN and SIGOPS Workshop on Parallel and Distributed Debugging (May 1988), University of Wisconsin, Madison, Wisconsin, USA, SIGPLAN Notices (January 1989), Vol. 24, No. 1, pp. 124-129.
23. Plank, J. S. "An Overview of Checkpointing in Uniprocessor and Distributed Systems, Focusing on Implementation and Performance", Technical Report of University of Tennessee, UT-CS-97-372 (July 1997).
24. Ronsse, M., De Bosschere, K., Chassin de Kergommeaux, J. "Exection Replay and Debugging", Proc. of the 4th International Workshop on Automated Debugging (AADEBUG2000) (August 2000), pp. 5-18.
25. Thoai, N., Kranzlmüller, D., and Volkert, J. "Rollback-One-Step Checkpointing and Reduced Message Logging for Debugging Message-Passing Programs", Proc. of the International Meeting on Vector and Parallel Processing (VECPAR'2002), Porto, Portugal (June 2002).
26. Thoai, N., and Volkert, J. "MRT - An Approach to Minimize the Replay Time During Debugging Message-Passing Programs", Proc. of the 4th Austrian-Hungarian Workshop on Distributed and Parallel Systems, Linz, Austria (September-October 2002), pp. 117-124.
27. Wang, Y. M. "The Maximum and Minimum Consistent Global Checkpoints and Their Applications", Proc. IEEE Symp. Reliable Distributed Systems (September 1995), pp. 86-95.
28. Wang, Y. M. "Consistent Global Checkpoints That Contains a Set of Local Checkpoints", IEEE Transactions on Computers (1997), Vol. 46, No. 4, pp. 456-468.
29. Zambonelli, F., and Netzer, R. H. B. "An Efficient Logging Algorithm for Incremental Replay of Message-Passing Applications", Proc. of the 13th International Parallel Processing Symposium and 10th Symposium on Parallel and Distributed Processing (1999).
30. Zambonelli, F., and Netzer, R. H. B. "Deadlock-Free Incremental Replay of Message-Passing Programs", Journal of Parallel and Distributed Computing 61 (2001), pp. 667-678.

On the List Colouring Problem

Olivier Cogis, Jean-Claude König, and Jérôme Palaysi

LIRMM, 161 rue Ada, 34392 Montpellier Cedex 5, France
{cogis, konig, palaysi}@lirmm.fr

Abstract. To colour a graph G from lists $(L_v)_{v \in V(G)}$ is to assign to each vertex v of G one of the colours from its list L_v so that no two adjacent vertices in G are assigned the same colour. The problem, which arises in contexts where all-optical networks are involved, is known to be $\mathcal{NP}$-complete. We are interested in cases where lists of colours are of the same length and show the $\mathcal{NP}$-completeness of the problem when restricted to bipartite graphs (except for lists of length 2, a well known polynomial problem in general). We then show that given any instance of the list colouring problem restricted to lists having the same length ℓ, a solution exists and can be polynomially computed from any k-colouring of the graph, provided that the overall number of available colours does not exceed $k\frac{\ell-1}{k-1}$.

1 Introduction

Because of their low cost, low error rates and high capacity, optical fibers are becoming the standard transmission medium for networks used to convey signals on long distances and serve as the backbone of a complex network hierarchy that organizes lower bandwidth connections.

Using the Wavelength Division Multiplexing (WDM) technology, an optical fibre can convey several messages at the same time, provided that not two of them make use of the same wavelength [Tan97].

In some all-optical networks [BBG+97], mainly for cost reasons, routers are not intended to act as wavelengths converters. Thus, the problem consists in assigning to a request both a path in the network and a wavelength to be uniquely used all along this path by the request.

As the number of available wavelengths in WDM optical networks is limited, scarcity is likely to be a crucial problem as there is no anticipation for dramatic progress in the near future as opposed to the increasing demand for communication resources. Therefore it is of importance that path and wavelength allocation should be performed at best.

We are interested in path and wavelength allocation where packages of requests are treated one after the other, requests from the last package being to be satisfied while some of the requests from preceding packages are still under connection. This means to say that the allocation problem is to be solved while not every wavelength is available along some edges.

One way to solve the problem is to first allocate the paths, then assign wavelengths to the paths, according to the rule that no two paths should be

A. Jean-Marie (Ed.): ASIAN 2002, LNCS 2550, pp. 47–56, 2002.

assigned the same wavelength whenever they use a common line of the network, bearing in mind that wavelengths available to a path are those which are not in use in any of the lines it has to go through.

Assigning the wavelengths is usually modelled through the **paths conflicts graph**. To each communication request in the network corresponds a vertex of the graph, two vertices of the graph being adjacent whenever their corresponding requests have been assigned paths that share at least a common line in the network. Moreover, to each vertex of the graph is attached the set of wavelengths that are available all along its corresponding path in the network. Which leads to the so-called **list colouring problem**.

Recall that, given a graph G, to colour G is, given some set called the set of colours, assign one colour to each vertex v of G in such a way that no two adjacent vertices in G are assigned the same colour. The least number of colours needed to colour a graph G is called the **chromatic number** $\chi(G)$ of G.

Given a graph $G = (V, E)$ together with a family $(L_v)_{v \in V(G)}$ of sets, we call L_v the list of colours assigned to vertex v. **To colour G from lists** $(L_v)_{v \in V(G)}$ is to assign to each vertex v of G one of the colours from its list L_v in such a way that no two adjacent vertices in G are assigned the same colour.

In other words, a list colouring of G is a colouring of G, except that the colour assigned to each vertex must be picked up from its own list of colours.

More formally, the **list colouring problem** can be defined as

INSTANCE : A graph $G = (V, E)$ together with a family $(L_v)_{v \in V(G)}$ of sets called the lists of colours assigned to the vertices of G.

QUESTION : Can G be coloured from lists $(L_v)_{v \in V(G)}$? That is, does there exist a mapping $c : V(G) \to \bigcup_{v \in V(G)} L_v$ such that :

1. $\forall v \in V(G) \quad c(v) \in L_v$
2. $\forall v, v' \in V(G) \quad \{v, v'\} \in E(G) \Rightarrow c(v) \neq c(v')$

When there is no ambiguity about $(L_v)_{v \in V(G)}$, we simply refer to G as an instance of the list colouring problem, and still speak of list colourings of G.

Given some integer $k \geq 1$, the graph G is called k-**choosable** if, for every family $(L_v)_{v \in V(G)}$ such that $|L_v| = k$ for all $v \in V(G)$, it is list colourable from $(L_v)_{v \in V(G)}$. The least integer k such that G is k-choosable is called the **choice number** $ch(G)$ of G.

If a graph G is k-choosable for some k, then assigning the list $\{1, 2, ..., k\}$ to every vertex of G ensures that a list colouring of G exists. Thus $ch(G) \geq \chi(G)$ for every graph G.

Similarities between $ch(G)$ and $\chi(G)$ have been investigated. For instance, any planar graph is 5-choosable [Tho94], but there exist planar graphs which are not 4-choosable [Voi93].

On the one hand, one has $ch(G) = \chi(G)$ for chordal graphs[Tuz97], but on the other hand, there exist bipartite graphs G (that is such that $\chi(G) = 2$) with arbitrarily large choice number $ch(G)$ [ERT79]. As a matter of facts, the class of

2-choosable graphs has been shown [ERT79] to be the class of graphs of which no subgraph is isomorphic to an even subdivision (one can insert any even number of new vertices along any edge of the graph) of any of the bipartite graphs of figure 1, ensuring that the 2-choosability problem is polynomial.

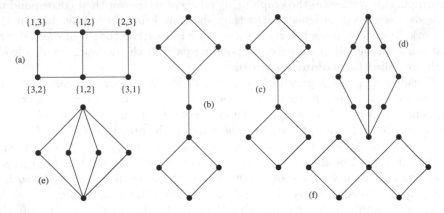

Fig. 1. The six minimum not 2-choosable bipartite graphs. For one of these graphs, a list of colours is provided for which there exists no list colouring of the graph.

But choosability is too strong a condition when faced with solving instances of the list colouring problem. Indeed, K_n, the complete graph with n vertices, satisfies $ch(K_n) = n$, but if each vertex is assigned a different colour in a list of length 1, the instance is trivially list colourable.

Therefore, besides choosability, the list colouring problem itself deserves both theoretical and practical attention (see [Tuz97] for a survey).

For instance, the list colouring problem is known to be polynomial when graphs are complete graphs [Tuz97], and $\mathcal{NP}$-complete when graphs are interval graphs, while the chromatic number can be polynomially computed for both families of graphs.

As a matter of fact, the list colouring problem is easily shown to be polynomial when lists are of length 2, but it is $\mathcal{NP}$-complete when restricted to instances where each lists contains at most 3 colours, each colour occurs in at most 3 lists, and G is a planar bipartite graph of maximum degree 3 [KT96], while bipartite planar graphs are 3-choosable [AT92], which shows the importance of restricting the length of the lists to be equal to 3 rather than less or equal to 3.

Based on this $\mathcal{NP}$-completeness, we are interested whether the knowledge of some colouring of a graph, not necessarily optimum, might be of any significance to its list colourability.

In this paper, we present results on the list colouring problem, involving colourings of the graph, from different points of view.

In section 2, we extend to the special case of lists of equal length (called the k-LC problem in [Tuz97]) the $\mathcal{NP}$-completeness of the list colouring problem restricted to instances where the graph is bipartite and the lists are of length at most ℓ, for some given $\ell \geq 3$ ([Gra97], a weaker form of the result cited above from [KT96]). Therefore, contrary to planar graphs, $\ell \leq 3$ or $\ell = 3$ are indifferent with regards to complexity.

In section 3, we give a polynomial construction to solve an instance of the list colouring problem from a known colouring of the graph, under some sufficient condition involving the number of colours of the colouring, and the length of the lists and the total number of available colours of the instance. Follows, involving the chromatic number, the length of the lists and the total number of available colours, a sufficient condition, best possible in general, to ensure lists colourability.

In sections 2 and 3, we define a **sub-instance** of an instance $I = \big(G, (L_v)_{v \in V(G)}\big)$ of the lists colouring problem as an instance $I' = \big(G', (L'_v)_{v \in V(G')}\big)$ such that:

1. G' is a subgraph of G, that is G' is a graph such that $V(G') \subseteq V(G)$ and $E(G') \subseteq E(G)$
2. $L'_v \subseteq L_v$ for all $v \in V(G')$

If an instance $I' = \big(G', (L'_v)_{v \in V(G')}\big)$ is a sub-instance of an instance $I = \big(G, (L_v)_{v \in V(G)}\big)$ of the list colouring problem, we call a list colouring c of G from $(L_v)_{v \in V(G)}$ an **extension** of a list colouring c' of G' from $(L'_v)_{v \in V(G')}$ when $c(v) = c'(v)$ for all $v \in V(G')$. Colouring c' is then called a **restriction** to I' of colouring c.

A sub-instance $I' = \big(G', (L'_v)_{v \in V(G')}\big)$ of an instance $I = \big(G, (L_v)_{v \in V(G)}\big)$ of the list colouring problem is said to be a **strong sub-instance** of I if any list colouring of G from $(L_v)_{v \in V(G)}$ restricted to I' induces a list colouring of G' from $(L'_v)_{v \in V(G')}$, while conversely, any list colouring of G' from $(L'_v)_{v \in V(G')}$ is the restriction to I' of some list colouring of G from $(L_v)_{v \in V(G)}$.

2   Bipartite Graphs

The list colouring problem being $\mathcal{NP}$-complete in general, one may investigate instances of the same problem when restricted to specific families of graphs. It turns out [Gra97, pages 28-31] that, given any integer $\ell \geq 3$, the problem remains $\mathcal{NP}$-complete when restricted to bipartite graphs with lists of colours of length at most ℓ.

We will focus on the special case where all the lists are of the same length.

Let $B_{\ell,c}$ be the complete bipartite graph defined, up to isomorphism (that is, one can change the names of vertices and/or colours at will) as $B_{\ell,c} = (V_1, V_2, V_1 \times V_2)$ for $\ell \geq 2$ and $c \geq \ell(\ell - 1)$, where :

$$V_1 = \big\{ v_i | v_i = \{i\ell, i\ell + 1, ..., i\ell + \ell - 1\}, 0 \leq i \leq \ell - 2 \big\}$$

$$V_2 = v_0 \times v_1 \times v_2 \times ... v_{\ell-2} \times \{c\}$$

and let each vertex stand for its own list of colours, that is let $L_v = v$ for each $v \in V_1 \cup V_2$. As stated before, for the sake of simplicity, we still call $B_{\ell,c}$ the bipartite graph together with this particular list assignment.

Given some graph G and some vertex v of G, **to stick** $B_{\ell,c}$ **to** v **in** G means to build the graph G' from G by adding a disjoint copy of $B_{\ell,c}$ (using colours of its own) and linking vertex v by an edge to every vertex of V_2. A sticking of $B_{3,c}$ is shown in figure 2.

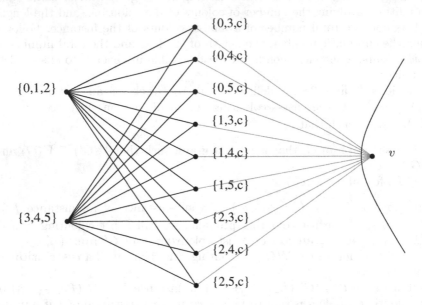

Fig. 2. A sticking of $B_{3,c}$ to v in G.

Lemma 1. $B_{\ell,c}$ $B_{\ell,c}$
c V_2

1. Choose colour c for each vertex in V_2 and pick any colour in its list for each vertex in V_1. This choice is a list colouring of $B_{\ell,c}$.
2. Given any list colouring of $B_{\ell,c}$, assume n_i is the colour chosen for vertex v_i of V_1, $0 \leq i \leq \ell - 2$. Then $w = (n_0, n_1, ..., n_{\ell-2}, c)$ is a vertex of V_2 adjacent to every vertex v_i of V_1. As vertex w stands for its own list of colours, c has to be the chosen colour for w.   □

Lemma 1 implies that, if G' is a graph built from some graph G by sticking $B_{\ell,c}$ to some vertex v in G, then colour c cannot be chosen for v in any list colouring of G'.

Moreover, if $\chi(G) \geq 2$, G' has the same chromatic number as G. Note that sticking $B_{\ell,c}$ to v in G adds $\ell^{\ell-1} + \ell - 1$ vertices and ℓ^{ℓ} edges to G.

Proposition 1. $\qquad\qquad\qquad\qquad \ell \qquad\qquad\qquad\qquad\qquad\qquad\qquad I =$
$\big(G, (L_v)_{v\in V(G)}\big)$ $\qquad\qquad\qquad\qquad\qquad\qquad \ell \qquad\qquad\qquad \chi(G) \geq 2$
$\qquad\qquad\qquad\qquad\qquad\qquad\qquad\qquad\qquad\qquad I^* = \big(G^*, (L_v^*)_{v\in V(G^*)}\big)$

$G \qquad\qquad\qquad\qquad\qquad\qquad G^*$
$\chi(G^*) = \chi(G)$
$\forall v \in V(G^*) \quad |L_v^*| = \max\limits_{v\in V(G)} \{|L_v|\}$
$I^* \qquad\qquad\qquad\qquad\qquad\qquad\qquad I$

Let $p \leq \ell$ be the largest size of the lists of colours in I, that is $|L_v| \leq p$ for all $v \in V(G)$. Let w be any vertex of G with $L_w = \{c_1, c_2, ...c_q\}$. If $q = p$, let $L_w' = L_w$. If $q < p$, let $L_w' = L_w \cup \{c_1', c_2', ...c_{p-q}'\}$ where $\{c_1', c_2', ...c_{p-q}'\}$ is a set of colours disjoint from L_w. Now, G' being the graph built from G by sticking to w every $B_{p,c'}$ for $c' \in \{c_1', c_2', ...c_{p-q}'\}$, one can see from lemma 1 that I is a strong sub-instance of the new instance $I' = \big(G', (L_v')_{v\in V(G')}\big)$, where w and the added vertices are assigned lists of colours of length equal to ℓ, while $\chi(G') = \chi(G)$. Repeating the construction for every other vertex of G in G' yields the instance I^*, of which I is still a strong sub-instance, with $\chi(G^*) = \chi(G)$. As ℓ is a constant to the problem, I^* is constructible in polynomial time. $\qquad\square$

Theorem 1. $\qquad\qquad\qquad\qquad \ell \geq 3$
$\qquad\qquad\qquad\qquad\qquad\qquad\qquad \ell \quad \mathcal{NP}$

The result stems from applying proposition 1 to the Gravier's result referred to at the beginning of this section. $\qquad\square$

3   List Colouring Using a Given Colouring

With $N \geq 1$ and $0 \leq \ell \leq N$, let S_N^ℓ denote the graph defined, up to isomorphism, by $V(S_N^\ell) = \{v|v \subseteq \{1, 2, ..., N\}, |v| = \ell\}$, $E(S_N^\ell) = \emptyset$, together with the lists of colours assignment where $L_v = v$ for all $v \in V(S_N^\ell)$.

A sample of S_4^2 is shown in figure 3.

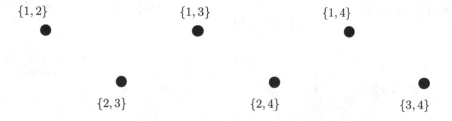

$\{1,2\}$ $\qquad\qquad\qquad\qquad\qquad \{1,3\} \qquad\qquad\qquad\qquad\qquad \{1,4\}$

$\qquad\qquad \{2,3\} \qquad\qquad\qquad\qquad\qquad \{2,4\} \qquad\qquad\qquad\qquad\qquad \{3,4\}$

Fig. 3. Each vertex stands for its own list of colours.

Lemma 2.
$\ell + 1$ $N - \ell + 1$ S_N^ℓ $N -$ $\{1, 2, ...N\}$ ffi
S_N^ℓ

1. Assume that S_N^ℓ is coloured using $N - \ell$ colours at most, and let A be a set of cardinality ℓ made of unused colours. Then A is a vertex of S_N^ℓ which has not been coloured.
2. Let A be a set of colours of cardinality at least $N - \ell + 1$. Then at least one colour of A is choosable in the list of colours of any vertex in S_N^ℓ.   □

With $k, N \geq 1$ and $0 \leq \ell \leq N$, let $H_k^{N,\ell}$ denote the graph defined, up to isomorphism, as the complete k-partite graph built on k disjoint copies of S_N^ℓ (S_N^ℓ is defined up to isomorphism too, but the k copies must be copies of the same S_N^ℓ, not just isomorphic images). Then two vertices are adjacent in $H_k^{N,\ell}$ if and only if they belong to two different copies of S_N^ℓ, yielding $\chi(H_k^{N,\ell}) = k$. As with S_N^ℓ, each vertex of $H_k^{N,\ell}$ stands for its own list of colours.

Lemma 3. $H_k^{N,\ell}$ $N \leq k\frac{\ell - 1}{k - 1}$

The overall number of available colours is N. From lemma 2, at least $N - \ell + 1$ colours are used in order to colour each sample of S_N^ℓ, not two samples being allowed to use any colour in common. Therefore $k(N - \ell + 1) \leq N$, that is $N \leq k\frac{\ell - 1}{k - 1}$.

Conversely, this inequality ensures that $H_k^{N,\ell}$ is list colourable. Indeed, one can partition the set of the N available colours into k classes, each of cardinality at least $N - \ell + 1$, and assign one different class to each copy of S_N^ℓ in $H_k^{N,\ell}$. Following lemma 2, one can list colour each S_N^ℓ using the class it has been assigned, producing a list colouring of $H_k^{N,\ell}$.   □

The above results entitle us to state a sufficient condition for list colourability of a graph based on a given colouring of the graph.

Proposition 2. $\ell \geq 1$ $I =$
$(G, (L_v)_{v \in V(G)})$ $|L_v| = \ell$ $v \in V(G)$
            $c \rightarrow \{1, 2, ..., k\}$ · k N

$$N = \left| \bigcup_{v \in V(G)} L_v \right|$$

$N \leq k\frac{\ell - 1}{k - 1}$ I
c

Let $\{V_1, V_2, ..., V_k\}$ be the partitioning of $V(G)$ into k independent subsets induced by colouring c of G. Now modify G into graph G' by identifying any two vertices of a same V_i, $1 \leq i \leq k$, whenever they are assigned the same list of colours in G, the resulting vertex being adjacent to the vertices that where adjacent to any of the two collapsed vertices, and bearing their common list of colours. Clearly, any list colouring of G', yields a list colouring of G. It suffices to note that $(G', (L_v)_{v \in V(G')})$ is a strong sub-instance of some $H_k^{N,\ell}$ while lemma 3 ensures its list colourability.

All transformations involved in the proof are polynomial, as well as the list colourability of $H_k^{N,\ell}$, from lemma 3.   □

The above results entitle us to link together the chromatic number of a graph, the length of lists of colours, assuming vertices are assigned lists of equal length, and the overall number of available colours into a (best) sufficient condition for list colourability.

Theorem 2. $\ell \geq 1$ $(G, (L_v)_{v \in V(G)})$
$$|L_v| = \ell \qquad v \in V(G) \qquad (*)$$
ffi G $(L_v)_{v \in V(G)}$
$(*)$ fi

$$\left| \bigcup_{v \in V(G)} L_v \right| \leq \chi(G) \frac{\ell - 1}{\chi(G) - 1} \quad (*)$$

ffi

Proposition 2 is valid for any colouring of G. Thus the first part of the claim.

Now, considering $H_k^{N,\ell}$, whose lists of colours are of length ℓ, while $\left| \bigcup_{v \in V(G)} L_v \right| = N$, and $\chi(G) = k$. Because of lemma 3 (necessary condition), condition $(*)$ is best possible in general.   □

Again assume that $(G, (L_v)_{v \in V(G)})$ is an instance satisfying condition $(*)$ with $|L_v| = \ell$ for every $v \in V(G)$, and put $N = \left| \bigcup_{v \in V(G)} L_v \right|$ and $k = \chi(G)$.

By definition, the list colouring problem implies that $\ell \leq N$, and it is clear that no list colouring is possible unless $k \leq N$. Moreover, one cannot ensure a list colouring for every distribution of the N colours into lists of length ℓ unless $k \leq \ell$ (otherwise, just set every list to $\{1, 2, ..., \ell\}$).

Therefore, seeking for any sufficient condition for list colourability in general doesn't make sense unless $k \leq \ell \leq N$. Under such conditions one has $\ell \leq k \frac{\ell - 1}{k - 1}$, and condition $(*)$ of theorem 2 can be rephrased as :

$$N \in \left[\ell, k \frac{\ell - 1}{k - 1} \right], \text{ with } k \leq \ell \quad (**)$$

Values of N for low values of ℓ and k are shown in figure 4.

It might be worthwhile to view the valid interval assigned to N as :

- $[\ell, \ell + \frac{\delta}{k-1}]$ if one puts $\ell = k + \delta$;
- $[\ell, \ell + \alpha - 1 + \frac{\alpha - 1}{k-1}]$ if one puts $\ell = \alpha k$.

Table 1. On the one hand, a bipartite graph making use of 2 (respectively 18 or 38) colours distributed into lists of length 2 (respectively 10 or 20) is sure to be list colourable, no matter how many vertices. On the other hand, distributing the colours into lists of length 20, no matter how many vertices, it appears that for $\chi(G) = 11$ up to 15, a list colouring cannot be ensured unless lists are made of the same 20 colours.

k	max N	2	3	4	5	6	7	8	9	10	11	12	13	14	15	16	17	18	19	20
2		2	4	6	8	10	12	14	16	18	20	22	24	26	28	30	32	34	36	38
3			3	4	6	7	9	10	12	13	15	16	18	19	21	22	24	25	27	28
4				4	5	6	8	9	10	12	13	14	16	17	18	20	21	22	24	25
5					5	6	7	8	10	11	12	13	15	16	17	18	20	21	22	23
6						6	7	8	9	10	12	13	14	15	16	18	19	20	21	22
7							7	8	9	10	11	12	14	15	16	17	18	19	21	22
8								8	9	10	11	12	13	14	16	17	18	19	20	21
9									9	10	11	12	13	14	15	16	18	19	20	21
10										10	11	12	13	14	15	16	17	18	20	21
11											11	12	13	14	15	16	17	18	19	20
12												12	13	14	15	16	17	18	19	20
13													13	14	15	16	17	18	19	20
14														14	15	16	17	18	19	20
15															15	16	17	18	19	20

4   Conclusion

The list colouring problem being $\mathcal{NP}$-complete in general, a great deal of work has been devoted to restrictions of the problem.

In this paper, we focused on special cases where lists are all of equal length, and where the chromatic number of the graph is known, or simply a colouring, not necessarily optimal.

On the one hand, we proved the $\mathcal{NP}$-completeness when lists are of equal length for bipartite graphs in general (the least non trivial chromatic number). Recall that when restricted planar graphs, asking for $\ell = 3$ in place of $\ell \leq 3$ moves the list colouring problem from $\mathcal{NP}$-complete to $\mathcal{P}$.

On the other hand, we proved a sufficient condition involving the chromatic number to ensure a solution to an instance of the list colouring problem where lists are all of equal length (a best condition in general). More generally, we gave a condition ensuring a solution to an instance of the list colouring problem where lists are of equal length, the solution being polynomially computable from any available colouring of the graph (under some bounding of the overall number of available colours, in terms of parameters from the instance and from the given colouring).

References

[AT92]   N. Alon and M. Tarsi. Colorings and orientations of graphs. *Combinatorica*, 12:125–134, 1992.

[BBG+97] B. Beauquier, J-C. Bermond, L. Gargano, P. Hell, S. Pérennes, and U. Vac-
          caro. Graph problems arising from wavelength-routing in all-optical net-
          works. In *2nd Workshop on Optics and Computer Science*, April 1997.
[ERT79]   P. Erdös, A.L. Rubin, and H. Taylor. Choosability in graphs. In *West
          Coast Conference on Combinatorics, Graph Theory, and Computing*, pages
          125–157. Congressus Numerantium XXVI, 1979.
[Gra97]   Sylvain Gravier. *Coloration et Produits de graphes*. PhD thesis, Université
          Joseph Fourier, Grenoble, 1997.
[KT96]   J. Kratochvil and Zs. Tuz. Algorithmic complexity of list colorings. *Dis-
          crete Applied Mathematics*, 50:297–302, 1996.
[Tan97]   Andrew Tanenbaum. *Réseaux*. Dunod, troisième edition, 1997.
[Tho94]   C. Thomassen. Every planar graph is 5-choosable. *J. Combin. Theory*,
          pages 180–181, 1994.
[Tuz97]   Zs. Tuza. Graph colorings with local constraints - a survey. *Discussionnes
          Mathematicae Graph Theory*, pages 261–228, 1997.
[Voi93]   M. Voigt. List colourings of planar graphs. *Discrete Mathematics*, pages
          215–219, 1993.

On Determining the Minimum Length, Tree-Like Resolution Refutation of 2SAT, and Extended 2SAT Formulas *

K. Subramani

LDCSEE
West Virginia University,
Morgantown, WV
ksmani@csee.wvu.edu

Abstract. This paper is concerned with the design of polynomial time algorithms to determine the shortest length, tree-like resolution refutation proofs for 2SAT and Q2SAT (Quantified 2SAT) clausal systems. Determining the shortest length resolution refutation has been shown to be `NP-complete`, even for HornSAT systems (for both tree-like and dag-like proofs); in fact obtaining even a linear approximation for such systems is `NP-Hard`. In this paper we demonstrate the existence of simple and efficient algorithms for the problem of determining the *exact* number of steps in the minimum length tree-like resolution refutation proof of a 2SAT or Q2SAT clausal system. To the best of our knowledge, our results are the first of their kind.

1 Introduction

Research in Propositional Proof Complexity is directed towards answering the following question: $($ $)$

From an algorithmic perspective, we are interested in two related but orthogonal questions: (a) $\mathbf{P_1}$: Is there a polynomial time algorithm to produce the shortest length proof of a tautology, (b) $\mathbf{P_2}$: Is there a polynomial time algorithm that outputs the size of the shortest length proof of a tautology? Problems $\mathbf{P_1}$ and $\mathbf{P_2}$ are related in the sense that they are both interested in shortest length proofs of tautologies; further a polynomial time algorithm for $\mathbf{P_1}$ immediately implies a polynomial time algorithm for $\mathbf{P_2}$. However, it is possible for a formula to have a minimum proof length that is of exponential size (with respect to the input clause set) in the given proof system (see [Hak85], for instance). Consequently, there may not exist a polynomial time algorithm for $\mathbf{P_1}$, but there could still exist a polynomial time algorithm for $\mathbf{P_2}$ [ABMP98]. It is at least reasonable to compute the running time of an algorithm for problem $\mathbf{P_1}$ with respect to the length of the shortest proof for that clause set; in this case, the lower bound on

---

* This research was supported in part by the Air Force Office of Scientific Research under Grant F49620-02-1-0043

A. Jean-Marie (Ed.): ASIAN 2002, LNCS 2550, pp. 57–65, 2002.

the shortest proof does not preclude the existence of a polynomial time algorithm [BP98]. Implicit in the discussion of shortest length proofs is the type of proof system under discussion; in this paper, we are concerned with ˙ proof systems only.

Progress in propositional complexity research has been along two directions, viz. establishing lower bounds on methodologies or proof systems (such as resolution refutation, [Hak85]) and showing that for certain clause sets, determination of the exact proof complexity is computationally "hard", irrespective of the proof system under consideration [ABMP98]. In this paper, we focus our efforts on determining the proof complexity of a collection of 2SAT and Q2SAT clauses. We show that for these classes of Boolean formulas, both problems $\mathbf{P_1}$ and $\mathbf{P_2}$ can be decided in polynomial time (when the proof system is tree-like resolution). When we talk of deriving the shortest length proof of a tautology, it is understood that the clausal set is specified in DNF form. An alternative and equivalent problem is that of deriving the shortest length refutation of an unsatisfiable set of clauses; it is to the latter problem that we shall devote our attention.

The rest of this paper is organized as follows: Section §2 provides a formal description of the problem(s) under consideration. The motivation for our work as well as work in related problems are discussed in Section §3. In Section §4, we provide algorithms for the problems detailed in Section §2 and analyze their complexity. We conclude in Section §5 by summarizing our contributions and outlining problems for future research.

2   Statement of Problem(s)

Definition 1.

$$(D,E) \quad \frac{D\cup\{x\} \qquad E\cup\{\bar{x}\}}{(D,E)} \qquad\qquad \frac{E\cup D \qquad (D,x)\wedge(E,\bar{x}) \to}{D\cup\{x\} \qquad E\cup\{\bar{x}\}}$$

A detailed discussion on the soundness and completeness of resolution is available in [Pap94].

Definition 2.

$$(\square) \qquad\qquad \frac{C \qquad\qquad \text{fi}}{C}$$

Note that $\square$ can be derived from C if and only if the unit clauses (x_i) and $(\bar{x}_i)$ can be derived from C, for some variable x_i.

Definition 3.   fi C

Note that if a given clause C' is required more than once in the refutation, then it has to be derived each time, to make the refutation tree-like. ˙   ; if the refutation is a tree, then it is called a Read-Once Resolution refutation [Iwa97,IM95]. A non-tree-like resolution refutation is also called a dag-like refutation.

Definition 4.   ( )

$$fi$$

Let $C = C_1 \wedge C_2 \wedge \ldots C_m$ be a clausal system defined on the variable set $X = \{x_1, x_2, \ldots, x_n\}$. Each clause C_i is constituted of exactly 2 literals corresponding to the variables in X [1]. We assume that C is unsatisfiable and we wish to provide the shortest length resolution refutation of C.

Let $C' = Q_1 x_1 Q_2 x_2 \ldots Q_n x_n \; C$ be an instance of a Q2SAT formula, where every Q_i is either $\exists$ or $\forall$ and C is a 2SAT formula as defined above. We assume that C' is unsatisfiable and we wish to provide the shortest length resolution refutation of C'.

We assume that there are m clauses in each unsatisfiable formula, defined over n variables.

Definition 5.   Extended 2SAT fi
           one

Note that the non-2SAT clause in Definition (5) is completely arbitrary (i.e., Horn, 3SAT or even a clause having $\Omega(n)$ literals).

Definition 6.   Extended Q2SAT fi

                                                          fi

           fi

We will show that the techniques developed for determining the propositional proof complexity of 2SAT and Q2SAT formulas (under tree-like resolution refutation) can be carried over to the case of Extended 2SAT and Extended Q2SAT formulas.

3   Motivation and Related Work

Our work is motivated from both the theoretical and the practical aspects of proof complexity. From the theoretical perspective, the study of proof complexity has fundamental implications for complexity theory; it was shown in [CR73] that there exists a propositional proof system giving rise to short (polynomial-sized) proofs for all tautologies if and only if NP=coNP. Our results are interesting for the following reasons: (a) They represent one of the few "positive" results for a naturally occurring subset of Boolean formulas, (b) They seem to be the first to consider the proof complexity of QBFs (Quantified Boolean Formulas). One of the more common application areas of Satisfiability is Real-Time Databases [BFW97]. Queries to the database are converted into equivalent tautologies which in turn are converted to refutation problems; the search for efficient procedures to find the shortest length resolution refutation of an unsatisfiable formula is thus directly connected to practical concerns.

---

[1] A literal corresponding to variable x_i is either x_i or $\bar{x}_i$.

[Hak85] was one of the earliest results showing an exponential lower bound for any proof system; they proved that any proof of the pigeonhole principle using resolution would generate exponentially many clauses. A similar lower bound using Bounded Arithmetic proof systems was proved in [Raz96]. Stronger and simpler resolution lower bounds for the pigeonhole principle are derived in [BP96]. In [ABM01], an example of a sharp threshold is given; they show that randomly generated "dense" 3SAT formulas satisfying certain properties almost certainly require resolution proofs of exponential size. Exponential lower bounds for propositional formulas using cutting plane proof systems were first shown in [Pud97]; applications of cutting plane theory to propositional proof systems are also discussed in [BE]. Exhaustive surveys of Propositional proof complexity can be found in [BP98] and [Urq95].

From an optimization perspective, [ABMP98] argues NP-Hardness and in-approximability results for a number of proof systems; the weakest proof system that they consider is Horn resolution, i.e. resolution as applied to a set of Horn-SAT clauses. Their hardness result holds for both tree-like and dag-like resolution refutations. In this paper, we show that the exact length of the shortest tree-like resolution refutation of an unsatisfiable 2SAT (or Q2SAT) formula can be determined in polynomial time. To the best of our knowledge, our results are the first of their kind [Bus].

4   Algorithms and Complexity

Our algorithms for the problems discussed in Section §2 exploit the graphical nature of 2SAT and Q2SAT problems [Pap94,APT79]. We shall first use the directed graph representation of 2SAT formulas as described in [Pap94] to develop an algorithm for deciding problems $\mathbf{P_1}$ and $\mathbf{P_2}$ (Section §4.1); the extension of this method to Q2SAT formulas, as discussed in [APT79] will follow in Section §4.2. The applicability of these techniques to Extended 2SAT and Extended Q2SAT is discussed in Section §4.3.

4.1   Minimum Length Resolution Refutation for 2Sat

Given a collection of m 2SAT clauses $C_i, i = 1, \ldots, m$, over the n boolean variables $x_1, x_2, \ldots, x_n$, construct graph $\mathbf{G}$ with vertex set $x_1, x_2, \ldots, x_n, \bar{x}_1, \bar{x}_2, \ldots, \bar{x}_n$. Corresponding to each clause C_i of the form (x_i, x_j), add edges $(\bar{x}_i \rightsquigarrow x_j)$ and $(\bar{x}_j \rightsquigarrow x_i)$. Thus $\mathbf{G}$ has $2 \cdot n$ vertices and $2 \cdot m$ edges. Without loss of generality, we assume that every clause has exactly 2 literals.

For instance, the formula

$$F = (\bar{x}_1, x_2)$$
$$(\bar{x}_1, x_3)$$
$$(\bar{x}_2, \bar{x}_3)$$

is represented by the graph in Figure (1).

Each edge of the graph represents an implication; the clause (x_i, x_j) represents the conjunction of the two implications $(\bar{x}_i \to x_j)$ and $(\bar{x}_j \to x_i)$. Thus following the path $x_i \rightsquigarrow x_j \rightsquigarrow x_k$ (say) is equivalent to taking the conjunctions of $(\bar{x}_i \to x_j)$ and $(\bar{x}_j \to x_k)$, which is equivalent to resolving on the variable x_j. The graph $\mathbf{G}$ is called the implication graph corresponding to the formula F.

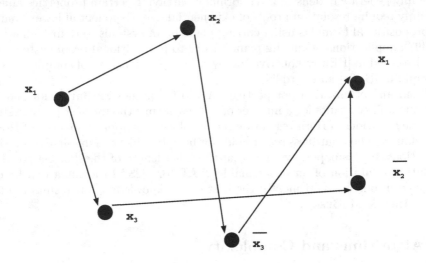

Fig. 1. Graph representation of a 2SAT formula

Theorem 1. $\qquad F \qquad fi$
$$x_i$$
$$\bar{x}_i \qquad\qquad\qquad\qquad \bar{x}_i \qquad x_i$$

Proof:
Suppose that the given formula C is unsatisfiable. Then as per Theorem (1), there must exist one or more variables x_i, such that there is a directed closed trail containing x_i and $\bar{x}_i$. Each of these directed closed trails provides evidence that C is unsatisfiable; in that it provides a resolution refutation in the following sense. A path from vertex x_i to vertex $\bar{x}_i$ corresponds to a resolution derivation of $(\bar{x}_i)$, while a path from vertex $\bar{x}_i$ to vertex x_i corresponds to a resolution derivation of (x_i), from the input clause set. In fact, every candidate for a shortest resolution derivation of $(\bar{x}_i)$ corresponds to tracing out a path from vertex x_i to vertex $\bar{x}_i$; likewise for derivations of (x_i) (recall that there are no input unit clauses). It is possible to derive (x_i) using the derivation of $(\bar{x}_i)$; (or vice versa) however, such a derivation can always be made shorter!

Lemma 1. $\qquad R$
$$C \qquad\quad \square \qquad\qquad\qquad\qquad\qquad\qquad (x_i) \qquad (\bar{x}_i) \qquad R \qquad\qquad R$$
$$(x_i)$$

$$(\bar{x}_i)$$

Proof: (x_i)

$(\bar{x}_i)$

R

$(\bar{x}_i)$

It follows that finding the shortest tree-like resolution refutation for C, corresponds to finding the shortest resolution derivations for (x_i) and $(\bar{x}_i)$ over all variables x_i.

From the above discussion, it is clear that Algorithm (4.1) can be used to determine the shortest length resolution refutation of a 2SAT formula.

Function MIN-LENGTH-RESOLUTION (C)

1: Construct the implication graph corresponding to C
2: **for** ($i = 1$ **to** n) **do**
3:    Perform a breadth-first search using x_i as the root vertex; let $s_i =$ distance of $\bar{x}_i$ from x_i in the BFS tree, if $\bar{x}_i$ is reachable from x_i; otherwise set $s_i = \infty$. Note that the shortest derivation of $(\bar{x}_i)$ is $s_i - 1$, in terms of new clauses generated.
4:    Perform a breadth-first search using $\bar{x}_i$ as the root vertex; let $s_i' =$ distance of x_i from $\bar{x}_i$ in the BFS tree, if x_i is reachable from $\bar{x}_i$; otherwise set $s_i' = \infty$. Note that the shortest derivation of (x_i) is $s_i' - 1$, in terms of new clauses generated.
5: **end for**
6: Sort the sums $(s_i + s_i')$; output the smallest sum (say $(s_j + s_j' - 2)$ as the length of the shortest refutation of C
7: Convert the derivations of (x_j) and $(\bar{x}_j)$ into a resolution refutation of C.

Algorithm 4.1: Shortest Length Tree-Like Resolution for 2SAT formulas

---

The running time of the Algorithm (4.1) is clearly dominated by the time required to find the BFS tree of each literal, which is clearly $O(2 \cdot n(m + n)) = O(m \cdot n + n^2)$. We need to emphasize the following point:

(x_i) $(\bar{x}_i)$

$(\ )$

4.2   Minimum Length Refutation for Q2SAT

[APT79] describes the implication graph construction of Q2SAT formulas. The clause set C is converted into a graph, exactly as for the 2SAT case. Note that some of the vertices (literals and their complements) are existential vertices while the others are universal vertices; accordingly, each vertex contains a bit which represents its quantifying type, i.e. universal or existential.

Theorem 2. $C' = Q(x_1, x_2, \ldots, x_n)$ C

$Q(x_1, x_2, \ldots, x_n)$ fi C

C' fi

x_i $\bar{x}_i$

$$j < i \quad x_j \qquad \frac{x_i}{x_i} \qquad fi \qquad Q_i \qquad \frac{x_j}{x_j}$$

Since, we are concerned with determining the shortest resolution refutation of an unsatisfiable Q2SAT formula, at least one of the conditions described in Theorem (2) must hold. Note that we cannot use simple resolution as we did for 2SAT formulas; rather we need to use a form of resolution called **Q**-resolution, which applies to Quantified Boolean formulas. **Q**-resolution has been proven to be both sound and complete for Quantified Boolean Formulas in [BKA95]. The mechanics of **Q**-resolution are as follows: Assume that the existentially quantified variables are represented by y_i and that the universally quantified variables are represented by x_i. We also assume that there is no clause that contains only universally quantified variables, since then we have a resolution refutation of size 1 (the clause itself!). Let C_1 be a clause with the $\exists$-literal y_l and C_2 be a clause with the $\exists$-literal $\bar{y}_l$. Then the **Q**-resolvent of C_1 and C_2 is obtained by:

1. Removing all the occurrences of y_l and $\bar{y}_l$ in $C_1 \vee C_2$;
2. Removing all the occurrences of $\forall$-literals that do not precede any $\exists$-literal in the resulting clause.

For details of the proof, see [BKA95]. Note that resolution is carried out only on the existentially quantified variables.

Thus as in the simple 2SAT case, we construct one BFS tree for each quantified vertex in the implication graph (with the source being that vertex). Note that as **Q**-resolution is being performed, on the clause set, we may derive a clause with only $\forall$-literals. This is considered to be the empty clause $\square$ and thus we can count the number of edges in the graph on this resolution path to obtain its length. From the BFS trees, it is easy to check for all three conditions and output the minimum length resolution refutation tree as in the 2SAT case. Once again the complexity of the algorithm is $O(m \cdot n + n^2)$.

4.3 Minimum Length Resolution Refutation for Extended 2SAT and Extended Q2SAT Formulas

As defined in Section §2, an Extended 2SAT formula is a 2SAT formula, augmented with a single non-2SAT clause. Let us denote the non-2SAT clause as C_l, i.e., the input formula is $C = \wedge_{i=1}^{m-1} C_i \wedge C_l$. We first decompose C_l into a collection of 2SAT clauses as: $(x_{l_1}, x_{l_2}) \vee (x_{l_3}, x_{l_4}) \ldots (x_{l_{p-1}}, x_{l_p})$, where p represents the total number of literals in C_l. (We are assuming without loss of generality that p is even.) We now find the minimum resolution refutation of each 2SAT formula $\wedge_{i=1}^{m-1} C_i \wedge (x_{l_{2j-1}}, x_{l_{2j}})$, $j = 1, 2, \ldots, \frac{p}{2}$ and take the smallest one!

It is easily seen that the above technique can be used in conjunction with the discussion in Section §4.2 to derive the shortest length resolution refutation for Extended Q2SAT formulas.

5   Conclusions

In this paper, we provided polynomial time algorithms to determine the size of the shortest tree-like resolution refutation of 2SAT formulas. Our algorithms are straightforward and can be easily implemented in practical AI systems and databases.

Our work has the effect of classifying natural classes of Boolean formulae in the following resolution refutation complexity hierarchy:

1. 3SAT formulas - A short resolution refutation exists only if NP = coNP [CR73];
2. HornSAT formulas - A short resolution refutation exists, but even obtaining a linear approximation to its length is NP-Hard [ABMP98] (for both dag-like and tree-like proof systems);
3. 2SAT formulas - A short resolution tree-like refutation exists and its exact length can be determined in polynomial time (this paper).

An extremely interesting an open area of research is concerned with analyzing the resolution complexity of 2SAT forumulas under dag-like proof systems.

Acknowledgements. We are indebted to Sam Buss for his pointers on Extended 2SAT formulas.

References

[ABM01]   Achlioptas, Beame, and Molloy. A sharp threshold in proof complexity. In *STOC: ACM Symposium on Theory of Computing (STOC)*, 2001.

[ABMP98]   M. Alekhnovich, S. Buss, S. Moran, and T. Pitassi. Minimum propositional proof length is np-hard to linearly approximate. In *Mathematical Foundations of Computer Science (MFCS)*. Springer-Verlag, 1998. Lecture Notes in Computer Science.

[APT79]   Bengt Aspvall, Michael F. Plass, and Robert Tarjan. A linear-time algorithm for testing the truth of certain quantified boolean formulas. *Information Processing Letters*, (3), 1979.

[BE]   Alexander Bockmayr and Friedrich Eisnbrand. Combining logic and optimization in cutting plane theory. In *Proceedings of Frontiers of Combining Systems (FROCOS) 2000*, pages 1–17. Springer-Verlag. Lecure Notes in Artificial Intelligence.

[BFW97]   Azer Bestavros and Victor Fay-Wolfe, editors. *Real-Time Database and Information Systems, Research Advances*. Kluwer Academic Publishers, 1997.

[BKA95]   H. Kleine Buning, M. Karpinski, and A.Flogel. Resolution for quantified boolean formulas. *Information and Computation*, 117:12–18, 1995.

[BP96]   Paul Beame and Toniann Pitassi. Simplified and improved resolution lower bounds. In *37th Annual Symposium on Foundations of Computer Science*, pages 274–282, Burlington, Vermont, 14–16 October 1996. IEEE.

[BP98]   Paul Beame and Toniann Pitassi. Propositional proof complexity: Past, present, future. *Bulletin of the EATCS*, 65:66–89, June 1998.

[Bus]   Samuel Buss. personal communication.

[CR73]   Stephen A. Cook and Robert A. Reckhow. Time bounded random access machines. *Journal of Computer and System Sciences*, 7(4):354–375, August 1973.

[Hak85]   A. Haken. The intractability of resolution. *Theoretical Computer Science*, 39(2-3):297–308, August 1985.

[IM95]   K. Iwama and E. Miyano. Intractability of read-once resolution. In *Proceedings of the 10th Annual Conference on Structure in Complexity Theory (SCTC '95)*, pages 29–36, Los Alamitos, CA, USA, June 1995. IEEE Computer Society Press.

[Iwa97]   K. Iwama. Complexity of finding short resolution proofs. *Lecture Notes in Computer Science*, 1295:309–319, 1997.

[Pap94]   Christos H. Papadimitriou. *Computational Complexity*. Addison-Wesley, New York, 1994.

[Pud97]   Pavel Pudlák. Lower bounds for resolution and cutting plane proofs and monotone computations. *The Journal of Symbolic Logic*, 62(3):981–998, September 1997.

[Raz96]   Alexander A. Razborov. Lower bounds for propositional proofs and independence results in bounded arithmetic. In Friedhelm Meyer auf der Heide and Burkhard Monien, editors, *Automata, Languages and Programming, 23rd International Colloquium*, volume 1099 of *Lecture Notes in Computer Science*, pages 48–62, Paderborn, Germany, 8–12 July 1996. Springer-Verlag.

[Urq95]   Alasdair Urquhart. The complexity of propositional proofs. *The Bulletin of Symbolic Logic*, 1(4):425–467, December 1995.

Data Storage and Stream Caching for Video on Demand Servers

Putra Sumari[1] and Hailiza Kamarulhaili[2]

[1] Multimedia Computing Research Group, School of Computer Science,
University Science of Malaysia, Minden, Penang, Malaysia 11800
[2] School of Computer Science, University Science of Malaysia,
Minden, Penang, Malaysia 11800
{putras, hailiza}@cs.usm.my

Abstract. Video on demand (VOD) is an electronic video-rental services over a computer network. VOD provides a service to users to browse and to watch any videos at any time. One of the most challenging aspects in designing VOD system is to design a data storage for VOD server with a capability of retrieving and transmitting different blocks of videos simultaneously to support simultaneous streams. Real time and latency characteristics are the major hurdles in devising server's data storage for producing maximum number of simultaneous streams as well as reducing the average service waiting time. In this paper we present a new data storage scheme for VOD server that eliminates latency and hence producing maximum number of simultaneous streams. The scheme introduces a disk-region layout technique on an array of disks. The disk-region layout uses a residue class theory concept for overall mechanism of disk partition and data distribution within disks. We also present our approach of stream caching in minimizing the average service waiting time of the system.

1 Introduction

A video on demand (VOD) is an electronic video rental service over the network [2, 4, 6, 9, 10, 13, 14]. It has three main components, they are VOD server, transport network and user display equipment. The VOD server stores a large number of videos and the role is to distribute videos to users when requested. Transport network is a medium for video delivery between the server and the users. The user display equipment is a television type device for viewing purpose. VOD application eliminates a specific time schedule characteristic as in traditional television programmes [4] and introduces a scenario in which viewing any videos at any time. The VOD server is one of an important component in this application as its responsible to retrieve blocks of videos and send them to users in simultaneous fashion. In other words, different blocks of videos are retrieved in order to support a maximum number of streams that can be simultaneously supported. This is not an easy task due to the real time and large volume characteristics posses by the video. Real time characteristic requires a continuous presentation in time [6]. Video blocks have to be retrieved from the disk

A. Jean-Marie (Ed.): ASIAN 2002, LNCS 2550, pp. 66-75, 2002.

subsystem of the server and have to be sent continuously to different users within deadline. Failure to meet the deadline will result in jerkiness during viewing. A large volume characteristic at the other hand is simple due to the nature of digitized processing. For example, a frame with color depth of 24-bit-colour with 640 pixels x 480 pixels resolution produces 900 Kbytes of data. At 30-frames-per-second presentation speed, the amount is 27 Mbytes [5]. Even in the format of MPEG 1 and 2 standard with 1.5 Mbps and 4 Mbps playback rates respectively are also still considered large in this area.

In building a VOD server to bring a video presentation service to users from the disks, the major factor that constraint the maximum number of streams is the data storage method for reading the streams out of the disks. Due to the real time requirements, the VOD server must be able to deliver the blocks on time, while still supporting a large number of simultaneously users retrieving the blocks from it. A part from this, it is also important to consider that the average service waiting time performance is within acceptable period during the design of data storage for VOD server. The effort to produce a maximum number of simultaneous streams that the server can support should not result in a long average service waiting time.

In order to support a maximum number of simultaneously streams and to provide a low average service waiting time, we present a new storage method for video in VOD server. We introduce a disk-region concept for disk partitioning and data distribution on an array of disks. In this scheme latency is eliminated and hence maximum number of simultaneous streams is achieved. In our method we also provide a stream caching technique to further reduce the average service waiting time. RAM as a caching component is used to cache the ongoing streams and used to serve the new requests. In overall our scheme, when applied to multiple disks environment yield a simple retrieval mechanism while supporting maximum number of simultaneous streams and has a good load balancing.

This paper is organized as follows. Background and related works are described in section 2. The VOD server and our data storage architecture are presented in section 3. Stream caching technique is presented in section 4. Case study and simulation results are presented in section 5. Finally, the conclusion is presented in section 6.

2 Background and Related Studies

VOD server is an important component in video on demand application. It stores large number of videos and acts as an engine to distribute data from the disks to users. A more specific responsibility is to retrieve different blocks of videos either belongs to the same or different videos and then to send them simultaneous to support simultaneous streams (stream is referred to the transmission channel of video from the server to users) to the network. This is a challenging task since video holds real time characteristic. Video blocks are scattered on the disk surface and yet they should be retrieved and sent to the network within the deadline. This has caused much latency and decreased the number of simultaneous streams that the system can support. One technique to handle this is to devise an intelligent block placement scheme on the disk with aim to optimize the retrieval mechanism to support simultaneous streams and also to reduce latency without affected the real time constraint of each stream.

Numerous researchers have done great contributions to the data storage design. In [7, 8], storage issues in supporting real time data are investigated. The work focused on traditional random and contiguous data allocation. These approaches however are facing to much latency and not suitable for the read only category like VOD services. In [2], a circular skip cluster scheme is proposed to enhance data retrievals technique in the VOD server. Small latency in this scheme has decreased the number of simultaneous stream that the system can support. In [7, 1], disks are partitioned into regions. Data are distributed within regions with aim to reduce latency and hence increase the number of simultaneous streams. The number of simultaneous streams however still not achieved maximum level. In [16], the disks are divided into zones and latency is reduced. This scheme however provides a small number of zones and due to the real time constraint the number of blocks sits in each region is small. Hence it limits the number of simultaneous stream that the system can support. In [3, 10, 12], proposed Phase based storage scheme. The video is organized into a column-row representation. In physical disk data are stored in column order and concentric fashion. Latency is eliminated and number of concurrent streams is maximized. This works however the performance of the average service waiting time (the duration period between the moment of users press the button (selecting particular video title) and the moment playback starts) is not been discussed. We focus our work on devising storage architecture with the following objectives namely, (i) to maximize the number of simultaneous streams and at the same time, (ii) to minimize the average service waiting time of the system. These two objectives are related to each other. A good storage layout with latency-free characteristic (for maximum number of simultaneous streams) has to face with an increment of average service waiting time. This happen because of when a new request arrives, it has to wait until R/W heads finishes to serve all ongoing streams.

3   Overall Video Server Architecture

The assume architecture of VOD server in our study is shown in figure 1. The video server consists of an array of disks and a buffer. Disks are used to store videos and are fetched (blocks form) and placed temporarily in the buffer before being sent to the network. The buffer then delivers the blocks to the network as simultaneous streams as an example shown in figure 1 of five simultaneous streams label by $s1$, $s2$, ... , and $s5$. The number of blocks read into the buffer is determined by the data storage policy being implemented in the disks. The scheme/policy normally has the characteristics of small latency (or zero latency), higher number of simultaneous streams and small average service waiting time.

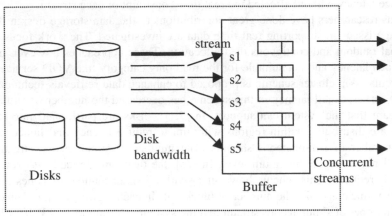

Fig. 1. Video-on-demand servers architecture

3.1 Disk-Region Layout and Data Placement

In this scheme the disk surface is divided into regions of equal size as shown in figure 2. The figure shows *n* regions labels by *R1* to *Rn*. The first region is labeled by *R1* and the last region is labeled by *Rn*. We now derive the number of regions (*n*) as follows:

$$n = (disk\_size/disk\_rate)/s \qquad (1)$$

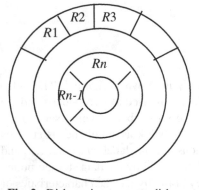

Fig. 2. Disk_region concept: disk is divided into *n* regions

Table 1. Parameter used in the study

Ri	Region *i*th
disk_size	Disk capcity
disk_rate	Disk bandwidth
video_rate	Playback rate
p	Number of blocks/ streams
d	Block size
a_i	*i*th block of stream *a*
a_{i+1}	(*i*+1)th block of stream *a*
m	Matrix row

We then derive the number of blocks (*p*) sit in a single region as follows:

$$p = disk\_rate/video\_rate. \qquad (2)$$

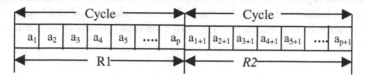

Fig. 3. The bounded of gap between block a_i and a_{i+1} for real time characteristic.

Equation (1) tells that the size of each region is *disk_rate* (equal to the size of disk bandwidth) and equation (2) tells that each region can occupy the maximum of p blocks of size *video_rate* each. Therefore, with equation (1), equation (2) and the size of p is *video_rate* we can conclude that p are actually the maximum number of blocks sit in single region. We now look at how p blocks are arranged in a region. We explain using figure 3. Figure 3 shows the allocation of p blocks at every region. Region R1 consists of p block labeled by a_1, a_2, a_3, ..., and a_p (parameter definition is referring to table 1). Region R2 consists of next subsequent p blocks labeled by a_{1+1}, a_{2+1}, a_{3+1}, ..., and a_{p+1}. It is important to note here is that block a_{1+1} is the next to be retrieved after block a_1, block a_{2+1} is the next to be retrieved after block a_2 and so on with the others. We conclude that equation (1) and (2) guarantee the gap between two subsequent blocks is at the right distance to preserve the playback continuity. E.g. two subsequent blocks of a_i and a_{i+1} (see figure 3) are at the right distance for preserving the real time playback. There is no gap between blocks and hence latency is eliminated. It is worth to note here that if all p blocks in single region are read by the R/W head and kept in the buffer then the buffer can send them simultaneously to the network to form maximum P simultaneous streams.

3.2 Buffering and Simultaneous Streams

As in previous section the R/W head read the region in sequential manner that is the reading is begin from the first region then followed by the next region until to the last region. In this scheme we use double buffering approach for buffering mechanism[3, 11]. In this scheme buffers of size $2pd$ is required. To visualize the buffering operation, lets buffer is divided into two rooms (two regions) of size pd each. While the first buffer is filled with data of size pd, the second buffer sent out data of size pd. Then the role switch that is the second buffer now is filled with data of size pd and at the same time the first buffer sent out data of size pd. This buffering policy preserved the real time constraint of video data. When the R/W head reaches the last region, it returns back to the first region and repeat the operation.

3.3 Data Placement on Multiple Disks

The previous section 3.1 and section 3.2 elaborated the disk region layout and video blocks distribution within regions. In multiple disks, we assume all disk are identical in capacity and therefore the number of regions of each disk is same to each other.

With m disks and n regions, we can represent as $(m \times n)$ matrix as shown in figure 4. The row indicates number of disks and the column indicates number of regions. The (m,n) is the indicator of block location. E.g. position (m,n) means block i sits on disk m and at region n.

region0 region1 region2 region3..region n-1

Disk 0 — (0,0) (0,1) (0,2) (0,3) ... (0,n-1)

Disk 1 — (1,0) (1,1) (1,2) (1,3) ... (1,n-1)

Disk m-1 — (m,0)(m,1)(m,2) (m,3)..(m-1,n-1)

Fig. 4. Matrix representation for
region concept

region0   region1   region2   region3   region4

Disk 0 — (b1,b16,..) (b7,...) (b13,..) (b4,..) (b10,..)

Disk 1 — (b11,0) (b2,b17,..) (b8,2) (b14,..) (b5,..)

Disk 2 — (b6,..) (b12,..) (b3,b18,..) (b9,..) (b15,)

Fig. 5. Block b1, b2, ..., bk are striped across
disks and regions

Our data placement based on mathematical number theory known as residual classes. We denote that the set of all integers such that $m \equiv i \ mod \ (y)$, we call residual classes i modulo y. For instance if $y = 3$, then we have 3 residual classes which are 0, 1 and 2. The class of 0 contains all integers that when divided by 3 leave no residue. The class of 1 contains is all the integers when divided by 3 leaves 1 as residue and so on. For our case, we have two integers m and y with $(m, y) =1$. Another word, the greatest common factor of m and y is equal to 1, with an additional condition that $y = [n]_m$, where $[n]_m$ means the greatest relative less or equal to n which is relatively integer to prime m. From the following formula, the i-th block of video is then stripped and scattered across m disk and n regions. That is, the i-th block is place in

$$(\text{region number} \equiv i \ (mod) \ m \ , \text{disk number} \equiv i \ (\ mod) \ n \ ) \qquad (3)$$

with condition: maximum number of blocks in each region is equal or less than p blocks

Example, let the number of disk (m) is 3 and the number of region (n) is 5. The video is composed of blocks b1, b2, b3,.., bk. The data placement of block is shown in figure 5. With equation (3), block b1, b16 are stored at location (0,0), subsequent block b2, b17 are stored at location (1,1) and so on until end of block. In our scheme the R/W heads of all disks should be synchronized and should be simultaneously read the same block at the same region. By the above placement, blocks of video are striped across disks and spread over all disks. It is a good property of load balancing during reading.

4 Average Waiting Time

The waiting time is the time taken by the R/W head to travel from the current position to the first region. Returning to the first region is simply because of the first block of the video is resided here where users can start the playback. In our scheme the worst-case waiting time is the total length of the regions. To further explain let assume that first block of video i is located in region 1 and the current location of R/W head is at region 2 (the R/W head just passed region 1). In this assumption, when a new request arrives and to be served, it will have to wait until the R/W head arrives at the first region. To arrive at the first region the R/W head have to finish the reading of all remaining regions, namely region 3 then region 4 until the last region. When arrive at the last region then the R/W head will read next the first region. Therefore in the worst case the service waiting time is the total length of regions. We can conclude that for the average service waiting time is half of the total length of the regions. Let look an example, if we look at scenario with 200 regions. The worst-case service waiting time is 200 seconds (3.3 minutes), that is the total length of all regions. The average service waiting time is 100(200/2) seconds (1.6 minutes).

To minimize the average service waiting time we use a stream caching technique. One characteristic of video is popularity. The most popular videos will be viewed by most of the users at any certain of time. Therefore by granting popular videos to be cached in the RAM and allow users to view the video from the cache the average service waiting time will be reduced. We referred to the new stream as a replicated stream. This mechanism let the new request do not have to wait until R/W head get back at the first region instead it is served by cache (replicated stream).

To further detail of the technique, we use figure 6 with explanation. Figure 6a shows m disks with n regions. Blocks of video i are distributed within regions of m disks using equation (3). A pool of RAM acts as a cache. A pool of RAM consists of replicated buffers as in figure 6b. Caching operation works as follow, when the R/W head reads the first block of video i and place it in the buffer, at the same time the block is copied into replicated buffer as shown by solid arrow in figure 6. When second block is read and place in the buffer, at the same time the block is copied into the second room of replicated buffer. This operation goes on until all rooms in replicated buffer are occupied (as in the example where the fourth block is copied into the last room of replicated buffer). At this moment the new requests are served using replicated stream. To sustain the continuity of replicated stream, the current block (the fifth block) read by R/W head is copied into the first room at replicated buffer as shown by dotted line in figure 6, to replace the first block just sent to network. This fashion will go on until end of video. If we set the size of replicated buffer is $n/2$, waiting time is reduced up to 50%. The replicated buffer will be used until nothing left and at this moment the operation will back to original scheme as without a cache.

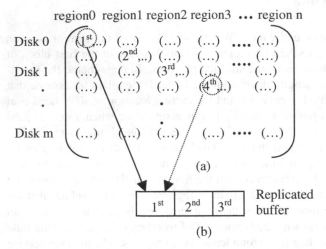

Fig. 6. (a) Data placement of video i using residual classes theory, (b) Replicated buffer use to cached blocks of video i

5 Simulation Study

In this section we conduct a simulation for measuring waiting time performance of the system. We consider four disks with the following characteristics: Seagate Baracuda with 2.25 GB capacity and 75 Mbps bandwidth rate. We use five MPEG 1 standard videos with 60 minutes in length. With four disks we derive 240 regions to form (4 x 240) matrix. The size pool of RAM is 500 MB. The placement of blocks satisfy equation (1), (2) and (3). The simulation was developed using the CSIM/C++ discrete event simulation language [15]. The popularity of each video is determined based on Zifpian (z) [3, 17] distribution and the characteristic of users arrival rates is based on Poisson (p) distribution [3]. The popularity of each video and the characteristic of users arrival rate can be varied by changing the distribution factor z and p respectively. We adopt the default value of both Zipfian and Poisson parameter by $z = 0.2$ and $p = 8$ respectively [3].

Figure 7 shows the effect of different video popularity against the average waiting time. The value of p is fixed at 8 as default value. In overall figure 7 shows that the scheme without cache gives two minutes average waiting time. With 0.5 GB replicated buffer, the average waiting time is decreased 20%. The decrement is because of most popular videos are cached in the replicated buffers and new requests are served from it instead of to wait until the R/W head arrives at first region. In the case of $z = 0.1$ the lowest waiting time is obtained. This is because as z become smaller, the access pattern more localized to individual video that is identified as the most popular. The case of $z = 0.3$, a slight increase of waiting time due to fair popularity among

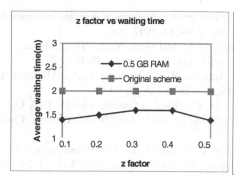
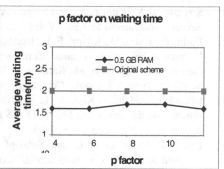

Fig. 7. Popularity vs. Avg. waiting time   **Fig. 8.** Arrival rate vs. Avg. waiting time

video and therefore the access pattern is distributed fairly to all videos. Figure 8 shows the effect of different users arrival rate against the average service waiting time. The z is fixed at 0.2 as default value. The figure shows that the different access pattern due to p variability does not affect the average waiting time of the system.

6 Conclusion

This paper presents a new data storage scheme for video on demand server. The scheme eliminates latency and hence produces maximum number of simultaneous streams. The scheme introduces a disk-region technique. Disks are divided into small regions and data are distributed within regions using a mathematical number theory known as residue class concept. The data placement within regions is design that subsequent blocks of same video are placed at different region bounded by real time characteristic. Our scheme achieved a good load balancing when applied to an array of disks. We also provide the RAM known as a cache for stream caching purpose. The ongoing blocks are copied into cache so that new requests can be served. The simulation work shows that with a caching stream the average service waiting time of the system is reduced while the number simultaneous streams is maximized.

References

[1]   Chang, E., and Garcia-Molina, H., "Reducing Initial Latency in Media Servers," *IEEE Multimedia*, Vol. pp. 50-61, 1997.
[2]   Chang, C. K., and Shih, C.-C., "A circular skip-cluster scheme to support video-on-demand services.," *Multimedia System*, Vol. 7, No. 2, pp. 107-118, 1999.
[3]   Chua, T. S., Li, J., Ooi, B. C., and Tan, K. L., "Disk Stripping Strategies for Large Video-on-Demand Servers," in *The 4th ACM International Multimedia Conference*, Boston, MA, pp. 297-306, 1996.

[4]   Srivastava, A., Kumar, A., and Singru, A., "Design and Analysis of a Video-on-demand Server," *Multimedia Systems* , Vol. 5, No. 4, pp. 238-254, 1997.

[5]   Furht, B., Kalra, D., Kitson, F. L., Rodriguez, A. A., and Wall, W. E., "Design Issues for Interactive Television Systems," Computer, 1995, Vol. 28, No. 5, pp. 25-39.

[6]   Gemmell, D. J., Vin, H. M., Kandlur, D. D., Rangan, P. V., and Rowe, L. A., "Multimedia Storage Server: A Tutorial," Computer, 1995, Vol. 28, No. 5, pp. 40-49.

[7]   Ghandeharizadeh, S., Kim, S. H., and Shahabi, C., "On Configuring a Single Disk Continuous Media Server," in *SIGMETRICS Performance Evaluation, Ottawa Ontario Canada*, Vol. 23, No. 1, pp 37-46, 1995.

[8]   Liu, J. C. l., Du, D. H. C., and Schnepf, J. A., "Supporting random access on real-time retrieval of digital continuous media," Computer Communications, 1995, Vol. 18, No. 3, pp. 145-159.

[9]   Li, V. O. K., and Liao, W., "Distributed multimedia system," *Proceeding of the IEEE* , Vol. 85, No. 7, pp. 1063-1108, 1997.

[10]   Ozden, B., Rastogi, R., and Silberschatz, A., "On the design of a low-cost video-on-demand storage system," *Multimedia system*, Vol. 4, No. 1, pp. 40-54, 1996.

[11]   Rotem, D. and Zhao, J. L., "Buffer Management for Video Database Systems," *Proceeding of The 11th Int. Conf. On Data Engineering* , pp. 439-448, 1995.

[12]   Subrahmanium, V. S., and Jajoda, S., *Multimedia Database Systems: Issues and Research Directions*: Springer, New York, 1996, pp. 237-261.

[13]   Sumari, P., Merabti, M., and Pereira, R., "Video On Demand Server: Storage Architecture with Disk Arrays," in *Proceeding of the Eurograpics workshop (Multimedia '99)*, Milan, Italy, pp. 73-81, 1999.

[14]   Sumari, P., Merabti, M., and Pereira, R., "Video-on-demand Server: Strategies for improving performance.," *IEE Proceedings Software*, Vol. 146, No. 1, pp. 33-37, 1999.

[15]   Schwetman, H., "CSIM18 - The simulation Engine in Mesquite Software, Inc, Austin, TX.," , 1996.

[16]   Wu, C.-S., Ma, G.-K., and Liu, M.-C., "A scalable storage supporting multistream real-time data retrieval," *Multimedia System*, Vol. 7, pp. 458-466, 1999.

[17]   Zipf, G. K., *Human Behaviour and the Principle of Least Effort* . Reading, MA: Addision-Wesley, 1949.

Analysis of Caching Mechanisms
from Sporting Event Web Sites

Zhen Liu, Mark Squillante, Cathy Xia, S. Yu, Li Zhang,
Naceur Malouch, and Paul Dantzig

IBM Research Division
Thomas J. Watson Research Center
Yorktown Heights, NY 10598
{zhen, mss, hhcx, shuzheng, zhangl, nmmalouc, pauldant}@watson.ibm.com

Abstract. Caching mechanisms are commonly implemented to improve the user experience as well as the server scalability at popular web sites. With multi-tier, geographically distributed caches, it is often difficult to quantify the benefit provided by each tier of caches. In this paper we present and analyze the design of a web serving architecture that has been successfully used to host a number of recent, popular sporting event web sites with two tiers of caches. Special mechanisms are incorporated in this design that allow us to infer the cache performance at the middle-tier of reverse-proxy caches. Our results demonstrate a very high hit ratio (i.e., around 90%) for the reverse-proxy caches employed in this web serving architecture, which is sustained throughout the day and across all geographical regions being served. This is primarily due to system design mechanisms that allow almost all of the dynamic content to be cached, as well as to a significantly larger locality of reference among the users of sporting event web sites than that found in other web environments. These mechanisms also make it possible for us to separate the true user request patterns at the page level from any additional requests induced by the server architecture and implementation.

1 Introduction

With the growing popularity of the World Wide Web, a dominant amount of information and services are delivered to many people around the world from web sites of various companies and organizations. The techniques used to handle user requests for information and services at such web sites must provide levels of performance and scalability that can accommodate the growth and evolution of these environments.

A particularly challenging and interesting class of web sites are those that support sporting events that are of interest to people all over the world. These web sites tend to have some of the highest certified peak and sustained hit rates, with each event setting new records over previous events; e.g., see [5,1]. Moreover, such web sites must provide the latest information about various aspects of the sporting event that are constantly changing, and thus much of the content being served by these sites is dynamic. This in particular makes the problem of effectively caching the web content, in order to handle the high-volume request rates, especially difficult.

To address this problem, we present the design of a web serving architecture with features that make it possible to serve dynamic content at the performance level of serving

A. Jean-Marie (Ed.): ASIAN 2002, LNCS 2550, pp. 76–86, 2002.

static content. This architecture has been successfully used to host the web sites for a large number of recent, popular sporting events, including the 2000 Olympic Games held in Sydney, Australia, the 2000 – 2002 Australian Open, the 2000 and 2001 US Open, the 2000 and 2001 French Open, and the 2000 and 2001 Championships at Wimbledon. We then use various sources of measurement data from a representative instance of these high-volume sporting event web sites to analyze the benefits and limitations of our web serving architecture and design. This web serving architecture embeds tiny uc.gif files in all cacheable pages, which makes it possible for us in our analysis to separate the true user request patterns at the page level from any additional requests induced by the web server architecture and implementation. Since each uc.gif file contains the number of images embedded within the particular page, we can infer the performance characteristics at the middle-tier reverse-proxy caches of the web architecture.

The results of our analysis demonstrate a very high hit ratio, consistently around 90%, for the reverse-proxy caches employed in our web serving architecture, which is sustained throughout the day and across all geographical regions being served. This is in stark contrast to the significantly lower hit ratios reported in the research literature. Once again, such high hit ratios are primarily made possible by the high-volume web server design presented in this paper, which allows almost all of the dynamic content to be cached. Another reason for such high cache hit ratios is the significantly larger locality of reference among the users of sporting event web sites than that found in other web site environments.

The remainder of this paper is organized as follows. We first present an overview of the design of our web serving architecture and the corresponding measurement data used in our study. A representative sample of some general statistical results from our analysis are then presented in Section 3, followed by an analysis of the request-level patterns observed at different tiers of the system architecture. Our concluding remarks are provided in Section 4.

2   Web Site Design and Architecture

We consider the web site for the 2000 Olympic Games held in Sydney, Australia, which also has been exploited at other sporting event web sites such as recent Australian Opens, French Opens and Championships at Wimbledon. The system architecture of this web site consists of cache and/or server complexes at six different geographic locations. Specifically, as illustrated in Figure 1, cache and server complexes were located in: Bethesda, MD; San Francisco, CA; and Schaumburg, IL; a cache complex was located in: Los Angeles, CA; and New York, NY; and a server complex was located in Sydney, Australia. All user requests are routed to one of the cache complexes based in part on the geographical origin of the user, with the exception of Sydney where all user requests are routed to the corresponding server complex.

The web site consists of the four-tier web serving architecture shown in Figure 2, where the first tier represents a cache complex and the second and third tiers represent a server complex. Each cache complex, which consists of a set of eNetDispatcher routers (eND) and a set of cache boxes, is located at an Internet Hub and functions as a set of reverse-proxy servers (in the sense that it provides a proxy for the server to the clients).

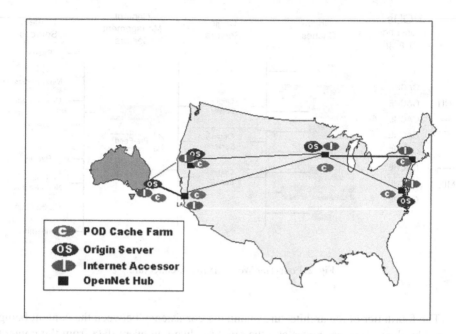

Fig. 1. Sporting and Event Web Site Technology Infrastructure.

Having this set of caches close to the end users can reduce the delivery time of a page by 3 to 5 times if the page is in the cache. A server complex consists of a set of eNDs together with a set of cache boxes (second tier) in front of a set of SP2 machine frames (third tier, origin servers). All requests are routed to one of the eNDs of a cache complex (with the exception of Sydney, where requests are routed to one of the eNDs of the server complex), which employs a weighted round-robin policy to route the user requests to a specific cache box in the cache complex [3,4], where the weight for a cache is a function of its current estimated load. Having the second tier caches in front of the origin servers allows enough capacity at these servers to handle the updates for the pages from the caches and to serve the uncached dynamic content, such as search requests, etc.

If the content requested at a cache complex is resident in the cache, it is returned directly to the client. Upon a miss in this cache, the request is sent to one of the server complex eNDs which employs a weighted round-robin policy to route the user request to a specific cache box in the server complex according to the description above for the cache complex. If the requested content is resident in the second-tier cache, then it is returned directly to the cache complex acting (in this scenario) as a client proxy. Otherwise, one of the second-tier eNDs employs a weighted round-robin policy to route the user request to a specific node of a particular SP2 machine frame, where (again) the weight for a node is a function of its current load. Each SP2 frame is composed of 10 uniprocessor nodes, and the size of all cache boxes is 512MB. An LRU replacement policy is used in each of the caches together with a time-to-live (TTL) specification for every object.

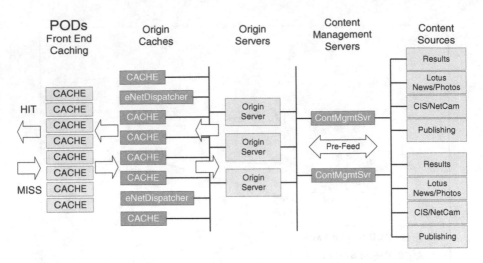

Fig. 2. Four-Tier Web Serving Architecture.

The fourth tier of the architecture maintains consistency between the content being served by the web server nodes and the quickly changing event data from the content sources at the sporting event site. When event data from a content source is updated, the content management servers employ a Data Update Propagation (DUP) algorithm to rebuild the (dynamic) pages that are effected by this modification of the event data, and then they push these rebuilt pages to each of the server nodes [2]. The DUP algorithm is used to maintain up-to-date (static) copies of the dynamic pages cached at each server, and thus the web server nodes can serve dynamic content at the performance level of serving static content. A specific TTL time is chosen for each page based on its characteristics, with a frequently changing page staying active (via a specific TTL time) for up to a few seconds. In this way, all of the cache complexes, origin caches and origin servers are kept consistent with each other. This approach makes it possible for almost all of the content being served by the web site architecture to be cacheable, which is a key feature of the architecture design and implementation. The only exceptions to this are search requests, requests for a uc.gif embedded in almost all pages, and a very small number of special dynamic pages that are not cacheable.

A small uc.gif image is embedded in each page, it is marked non-cacheable, and it contains the number of embedded objects that comprise the page. Whenever a request is made to any page, the origin web servers may not be aware of the requests to some of the embedded objects within the page because they may be served by the various caches at different levels, including the browser cache, proxy caches, etc. By embedding a uc.gif image in every page, all requests to the uc.gif in a given page will reach the origin servers and this makes it possible for us to record all user request information at the page level. This also makes it possible for us to infer the total number of requests that the web site would experience if there were no caches anywhere.

The measurement data used as the basis for our analysis consist of the standard access logs maintained at each server node and the cache reference logs maintained at

Table 1. Sydney 2000: General Statistics for Request Patterns at Different Server Complexes

	Sydney	Bethesda	San Francisco	Schaumburg	Overall
Request (one day)	8.6M	15.5M	9,9M	6,5M	40.6M
Req / Sec (ave)	99	179	114	75	
Req / Sec (std)	66	70	36	27	
Byte (one day)	46.7B	109.8B	66.2B	47.6B	270.3B
Byte / Sec (ave)	540.3K	1,270.6K	766.4K	550.9K	
Byte / Sec (std)	440.9K	839.3K	502.1K	390.9K	
Dyn_Page (one day)	4.2M	8.3M	5.7M	3.2M	21.4M
Dyn_Page / Sec (ave)	48	95	66	37	
Dyn_Page / Sec (std)	37	43	21	18	
Object (one day)	211.2M	385.4M	258.4M	139.8M	995.0M
Obj / Sec (ave)	2,444	4,461	2,991	1,618	
Obj / Sec (std)	1,808	2,368	894	875	

each cache box in every cache complex. We also have the cache reference logs maintained at each cache box in the server complex at Sydney, which has no cache complex. The cache reference logs contain the number of cache hits, the number of cache misses, and the number of bytes transmitted every minute. These logs also contain the per-minute memory utilization at the cache boxes.

3   General Statistical Behavior of Web Site

In this section we consider the general statistical behavior of the foregoing web serving architecture, with a particular interest in caching effects. While a tremendous amount of web data and analysis results are available to us, we shall focus on the data and results from a particular day (actually the peak day) at the 2000 Olympic Games held in Sydney. Due to space limitations, we omit the corresponding data and results from other days at the Sydney site, as well as the corresponding day and results from other sporting event web sites exploiting the same architecture. We note, however, that the data and results presented herein are also representative of these other instances of the web serving architecture.

To provide an overall picture, we first present some general statistics for the web environment under consideration. We consider the cache-reference and server-access logs from each of the cache and server complexes for the peak day of the Sydney Games, namely September 25, 2000. Starting with the server logs, we provide in Table 1 some general overall statistics on the request patterns found at each of the 4 server complexes. Note that the total number of requests at each of the geographical server locations ranges from 6 million requests in the day to 15 million requests in the day. The average number of requests per minute ranges from 4,000 to 10,000.

A breakdown of the types of pages that were requested at the 4 server complexes is provided in Table 2. We note that the percentages of requests and bytes shown in Table 2 are reasonably consistent across the different server complexes, and thus the per-complex statistics are not provided. Almost all of the pages at the web site are generated dynamically. These pages contain static objects (such as gif and jpeg images) as well as dynamic objects (such as those generated upon queries). The majority of requested uncacheable objects are composed of uc.gif objects (45% of requests seen at server) and search results (10% of Bytes seen at server). The cacheable objects transfered from the servers represent 47% of the requests and 85% of the bytes.

Table 2. Sydney 2000: Page Request Information at Server Complexes.

Type	cache	Req(#)	Req(%)	Byte(#)	Byte(%)
uc.gif	no	18.3M	45.03	0.8B	1.55
?	no	3.1M	8.00	7.0B	13.43
*.html	yes	5.0M	12.36	26.0B	50.10
img_etc	yes	14.1M	34.61	18.1B	34.92

We now turn to the cache reference logs. Some of the statistical behavior of the cache boxes at the 5 cache complexes together with those from the Sydney server complex are provided in Table 3. We observe the very high hit ratios in these caches, which are consistently around 90%. This is significantly higher than the hit ratios found in proxy caches reported in the research literature. One of the primary reasons for such a high proxy cache hit ratio is the design features of the web serving architecture presented in Section 2 which makes almost all of the content being served by the web site cacheable. Another important reason concerns the larger fraction of content being shared among the users and the greater reference locality, which tends to be found at sporting event web sites. This clearly demonstrates and quantifies the benefits of the design of our web server architecture for such environments.

Table 3. Request Information at First-Tier Cache Complexes.

Cache	Hit	Miss	HitRate	Byte	Byte/Hit
Syd	55.8M	6.3M	89.90	114.5B	2.0K
Beth	86.8M	9.2M	90.46	200.9B	2.3K
LA	49.7M	7.2M	87.41	103.7B	2.1K
NY	93.5M	9.2M	91.08	226.6B	2.4K
Sch	61.8M	7.0M	89.81	135.3B	2.2K
SF	65.0M	8.4M	88.61	125.6B	1.9K
Total	412.6M	47.1M	89.75	906.7B	2.2K

We respectively plot in Figures 3 through 5 the hit ratios, the bytes per request, and the memory usage statistics from a representative cache box at the 5 cache complexes and at the Sydney server complex. In each case, the cache statistics are plotted as a function of the time of day together with the corresponding request patterns encountered at each of the cache boxes. We first observe that the cache hit ratios are consistently high throughout the day (see Figure 3). The only exceptions are some (usually small) drops in the hit ratio when the request rates are very low, which result from a combination of object TTL expiration together with the low request rates. From Figure 4, we observe a fairly close tracking between the number of bytes transferred and the number of user requests. The same trends basically hold between the memory usage in the cache boxes and the user request patterns, although with some delays (see Figure 5).

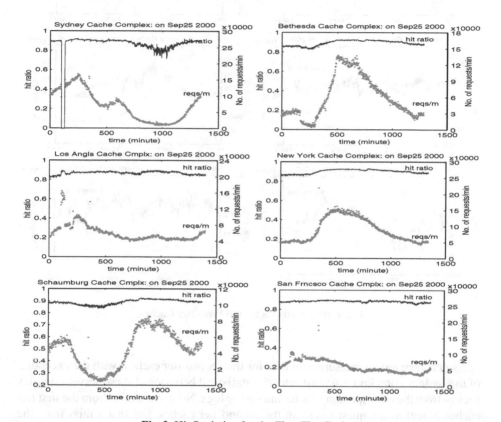

Fig. 3. Hit Statistics for the First-Tier Caches.

Table 4. Requests from First-Tier Caches at Different Server Complexes.

Server Complex	Req	Byte	Byte / Req
Sydney	5.5M	44.5GB	8.1K
Bethesda	7.3M	101.0GB	13.9K
San Francisco	4.6M	62.9GB	13.7K
Schaumburg	3.5M	44.4GB	12.7K
Total	**20.9M**	**252.9GB**	

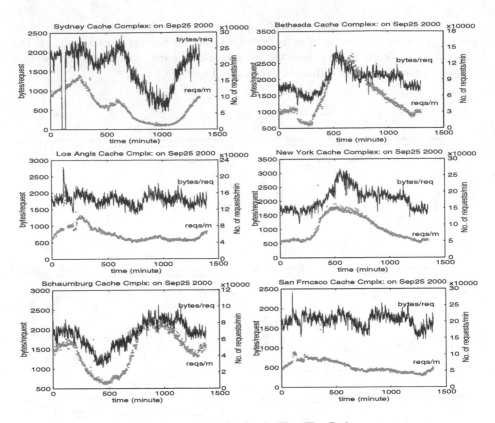

Fig. 4. Byte Statistics for the First-Tier Caches.

Since there are no measurement data for the second-tier caches (with the exception of the Sydney complex), we must infer the statistical behavior of these server-complex caches from the corresponding cache and server logs. Note that a miss from the first tier caches is sent as a request to one of the second tier caches, and that a miss from the second-tier caches are sent to the web servers. This information makes it possible for us to infer the number of hits and misses at the second-tier cache.

Table 3 provides the hit and miss information for the first-tier cache complexes, and Table 4 provides the corresponding statistics for the requests from the first-tier caches that eventually get routed to one of the server complexes. The miss ratio for all of the tier-two caches can then be obtained by taking the ratio of the number of requests from caches in Table 4 to the number of misses from the cache complexes in Table 3, which yields (not including Sydney) $(20.9M - 5.5M)/(47.1M - 6.3M) = 37.7\%$. The tier-two cache hit ratio (not including Sydney) is then 62.3%. More detailed information for the number of hits and hit ratios at the second-tier caches, as a function of time, is provided in Figure 6.

The uc.gif mechanism allows us to obtain the *offered hits*, which is the number of object requests that would be experienced by the web site if there were no caches

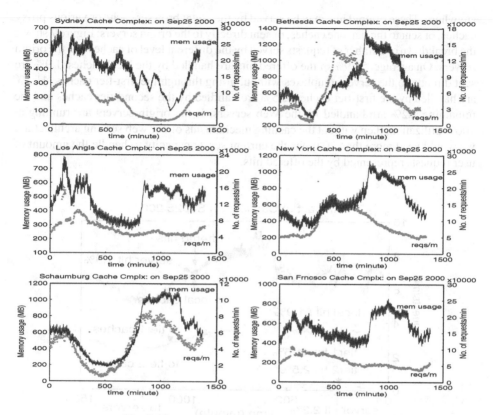

Fig. 5. Memory Statistics for the First-Tier Caches.

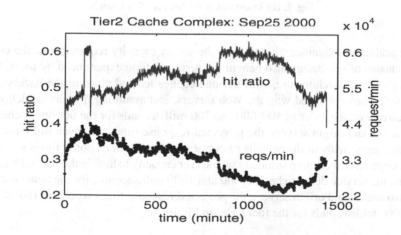

Fig. 6. Hit Statistics for Second Tier Caches

anywhere. These offered hits may be served by the client browser cache or various proxy caches, or sent to the tier-one caches, or sent directly to the origin servers. Figure 7 shows the breakdown or number of requests served by the different level of caches and the origin servers. On average, 51.9% of the offered hits are handled by the local caches, 1.9% are sent directly to the server complexes without going through the first-tier caches, 41.5% are handled by the first-tier caches, 2.5% are handled by the second-tier caches and the remaining 2.2% are handled by the Web servers. If the origin servers are running at 100% utilization, then without the caching mechanisms of our web serving architecture, we would need more than 20 times the current server capacity to handle the amount of user requests represented by the offered hits.

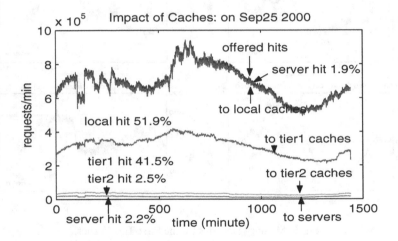

Fig. 7. Hit Information for Second Tier Caches.

In addition to significantly reducing the server capacity requirements, the caching mechanisms of our design also benefit the response time experienced by users. Under our web serving architecture, with tier-one caches located close to the backbone and tier-two caches colocated with the Web servers, and assuming the service delay to be respectively on the order of $100, 500$ and 750 milliseconds for the tier-one caches, tier-two caches and origin servers, the projected response times are given in Figure 8. On the other hand, without the benefits of our design, the client response times would be 9 times larger even assuming sufficient web server capacity to handle the offered hits. If we assume the service delay to be $300, 800$ and 1000 milliseconds, for the tier-one caches, tier-two caches and origin servers, the projected response times would be $185, 190, 480$ and 1000 milliseconds for the four cases in Figure 8.

4   Conclusions

In this paper we have presented the design of a web serving architecture with multiple tiers of caches and a special mechanism to record the embedded images within each

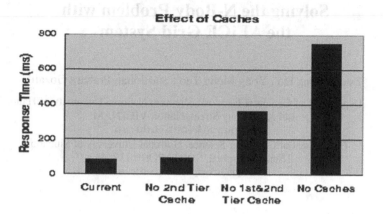

Fig. 8. Effect of Caches on Response Times

page. This architecture has been used to successfully host a large number of recent, popular sporting event web sites. These web sites are designed with a large portion of dynamic content, which are cached at two tiers of the architecture that function as reverse-proxy servers. Using the server and cache data from a specific sporting event web site, we find that these servers exhibit various important characteristics that have not been demonstrated in the web literature to date. In particular, the reverse-proxy cache hit ratios are extremely high, consistently around 90%, and this is achieved by exploiting various design features of our web serving architecture.

References

1. M. Arlitt and T. Jin. Workload Characterization of the 1998 World Cup Web Site. Technical Report HPL-1999-35(R.1), HP Laboratories, Palo Alto, CA, September 1999.
2. J. Challenger, A. Iyengar, and P. Dantzig. A Scalable System for Consistently Caching Dynamic Web Data. In *Proceedings of IEEE INFOCOM'99*, March 1999.
3. D. Dias, W. Kish, R. Mukherjee, and R. Tewari. A Scalable and Highly Available Web Server. In *Proceedings of the 1996 IEEE Computer Conference (COMPCON)*, February 1996.
4. G. Hunt, G. Goldszmidt, R. King, and R. Mukherjee. Network Dispatcher: A Connection Router for Scalable Internet Services. In *Proceedings of the 7th International World Wide Web Conference*, April 1998.
5. A. K. Iyengar, M. S. Squillante, and L. Zhang. Analysis and characterization of large-scale web server access patterns and performance. *World Wide Web*, 2, June 1999.

Solving the N-Body Problem with the ALiCE Grid System

Dac Phuong Ho[1], Yong Meng Teo[2], and Johan Prawira Gozali[2]

[1]Department of Computer Network, Vietnam National University of Hanoi
144 Xuan Thuy Street, Hanoi, VIETNAM
hdphuong@vnuh.edu.vn
[2]Department of Computer Science, National University of Singapore
3 Science Drive 2, SINGAPORE 117543
teoym@comp.nus.edu.sg

Abstract. The grid enables large-scale aggregation and sharing of computational resources. In this paper, we introduce a method for solving the N-body problem on a cluster-grid using our grid system, ALiCE (Adaptive and scaLable internet-based Computing Engine). The modified Barnes-Hut algorithm allows the N-body problem to be solved adaptively using compute resources on-demand. The N-body program is written using ALiCE object programming template. Our experiments varying the number of bodies per task and the number of computation nodes demonstrate the feasibility of exploiting parallelism on a grid system.

1 Introduction

The grid [4, 5] promises to change the way we tackle complex problems. It enables large-scale aggregation and sharing of computational, and data resources across institutional boundaries. As technologies, networks, and business models mature, it is expected to become commonplace for small and large communities of scientists to create "Science Grids" linking their various resources to support human communication, data access and computation.

The N-body problem is the study of how n number of particles will move under one of the physical forces. Modern physics has found that there are only four fundamental physical forces, namely: gravity, electro-magnetic, strong nuclear, and weak nuclear. These forces have a few things in common: they can be expressed by using simple formulas, they are all proportional to some properties of a particle (mass, electrical charge, etc.), and they get weaker the further apart the particles are from each other [3]. However, very small differences in initial conditions of an N-body problem can lead to unpredictably differing results.

The simplest and most straightforward manner of modeling the N-body problem is the direct method. Here, each pair of particles is visited in turn to calculate and accumulate the appropriate forces. Conceptually, this solution is implemented as two nested loops, each running over all particles. This algorithm scales as N-squared, and cannot be considered sufficiently efficient to enable the solution of interesting (large N) problems. A galaxy might have, to say 10^{11} stars. This suggests repeating 10^{22}

A. Jean-Marie (Ed.): ASIAN 2002, LNCS 2550, pp. 87-97, 2002.

calculations. Even using an efficient approximate algorithm, which requires $Nlog_2N$ calculations, the number of calculations is still enormous $(10^{11}log_210^{11})$. It would require significant time on a single processor system. Even if each calculation takes one microsecond, it would take 10^9 years for N^2 algorithm and almost a year for $Nlog_2N$ algorithm. Therefore, there is a need for a better and faster way to solve the N-body problem.

This paper presents a distributed object-oriented method for solving the N-body problem using our grid system ALiCE (the Adaptive and scaLable internet-based Computing Engine). ALiCE also makes it possible to solve the N-body problem adaptively, using resources on-demand. Our experiments showed a reduction in parallel execution times as we increase the number of available compute resources.

This paper is organized as follows. Section 2 presents the Barnes-Hut algorithm - an algorithm that uses a divide-and-conquer strategy to recursively sub-divide the N-body problem space to facilitate calculation of inter-particle distances. Section 3 presents ALiCE – our Java-based grid computing system [6]. The mapping of the N-body problem onto the ALiCE framework is presented in Section 4. We present our experimental results in Section 5, and the summary of our work in Section 6.

2   Barnes-Hut Algorithm

Suppose we compute the gravitational force on the earth from the known stars and planets. A glance skyward on a clear night reveals a dauntingly large number of stars that must be included in the calculation, each one contributing a term to the force sum.

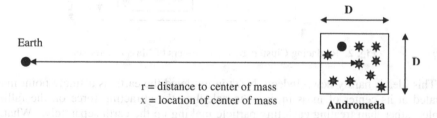

Fig. 1. Viewing the Andromeda Galaxy from Earth

One of those dots of light we might want to include in our sum is, however, not a single star (particle) at all, but rather the Andromeda galaxy, which itself consists of billions of stars. These stars appear so close that they appear as a single dot to the naked eye. We model the Andromeda galaxy as a single point, located at the center of mass of the Andromeda galaxy and with a mass equal to the total mass of the Andromeda galaxy. This is indicated in Fig. 1, with an "x" marking the center of mass.

Since the ratio $\dfrac{D}{r}$, is so small, we can accurately replace the sum over all stars in Andromeda with one term at their center of mass. D denotes the width and height of the box containing Andromeda, and r is the distance between Andromeda and Earth centre of masses. We explain this in more detail below.

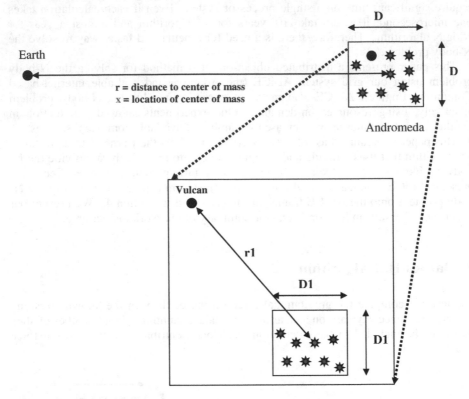

Fig. 2. Replacing Clusters by their Centers of Mass Recursively

This idea is hardly new. Indeed, Newton modeled the earth as a single point mass located at its center of mass in order to calculate the attracting force on the falling apple, rather than treating each tiny particle making up the earth separately. What is new is applying this idea recursively. First, it is clear that from the point of view of an observer in the Andromeda galaxy that our Milky Way galaxy can also be approximated by a point mass at its center of mass. But more importantly, within the Andromeda (or Milky Way) galaxy itself, this geometric picture repeats itself as shown below: As long as the ratio D1/r1 is also small, the stars inside the smaller box can be replaced by their center of mass in order to compute the gravitational force on, say, the planet Vulcan. This nesting of boxes within boxes can be repeated recursively (see Figure 2).

Details of Barnes-Hut algorithm can be found at [2]. This algorithm consists of two main phases:

a. Creating a data structure to represent the space. For example, in 3D this can be modeled as the *OctTree*, and in 2D using the *QuadTree*.

b. Traversing the tree to carry out the force calculations. This is accomplished by a simple post-order traversal of the tree, i.e., the child nodes are processed before their parent node. Since the primary objective is to maximize efficiency in calculating inter-particle distances, a group of particles "far away enough" is treated as a single particle with a composite mass, located at the center of mass of the array. Thus, for each particle in turn, the tree is traversed starting from the topmost "universe" node. The spatial extent of the node is divided by the distance from the center of mass of the node to the particle. If this quotient is less than a specified quantity called the theta parameter, the particles in the node are "far away enough" to be considered as a single particle. If the quotient is greater than theta, the tree is recursively descended.

2.1 Task Partitioning

With the Barnes-Hut algorithm mentioned above, the first phase of creating tree and calculating the center of mass and total mass must be done serially. But, with the QuadTree created, new positions for each body can be calculated independently. Thus, second phase of the algorithm can be done in parallel.

Another important aspect of the algorithm is that execution time for the first phase is much lower than that of the second phase. In Table 1 below, we can see the greater the number of bodies, the lower the ratio of time between the first stage and the total of time. Therefore, we can reduce total execution time by calculating positions for each body in parallel.

Table 1. Sequential Execution Time Varying the Number of Bodies

Number of bodies	First Phase Execution Time (s)	Total Sequential Execution Time (s)
1000	1	23
2000	4	193
4000	5	403
8000	9	1537
10000	11	2401
15000	17	5349
20000	23	9428

3 The ALiCE Grid System

ALiCE (Adaptive and scaLable internet-based Computing Engine) is a portable software technology for developing and deploying general-purpose grid applications and systems [5]. It virtualizes computer resources on the Internet/intranet into one computing environment through a platform-independent consumer-producer resource-sharing model, and harnesses idle resources for computation to increase the usable power of existing systems on the network.

3.1 ALiCE Consumer-Producer Model

Fig. 3 shows our ALiCE consumer-producer model. Applications are submitted by the consumer for execution on idle computers (referred to as producers) through a resource broker residing on another computer. The resource broker regulates consumer's resource demand and producer idle cycles, and dispatches tasks from its task pool for execution at the producers. A novel application-driven task-scheduling algorithm allows a consumer to select the performance level for each application.

ALiCE supports *sequential* or parametric computer applications to maximize computer throughput. For *parallel* computer applications, ALiCE breaks down large computations into smaller tasks and distribute for execution among producers tied to a network to exploit parallelism and speedup.

Parallel programming models are supported through a programming template library. Task and result objects are exchanged between consumers and producers through the resource broker.

ALiCE is scalable and is implemented in Java, Java Jini [1] and JavaSpaces [7] for full cross-platform portability, extensibility and scalability. To the best of our knowledge, ALiCE is the first grid-computing implementation in the world developed using Sun's Java Jini and JavaSpaces.

Efficient task scheduling on a non-dedicated distributed computing environment is a critical issue especially if the performance of task execution is important. The main contributing factors include dynamic changes in computer workload and variations in computing power and network latency. ALiCE's load distribution technology is based on a novel application-driven, adaptive scheduling strategy.

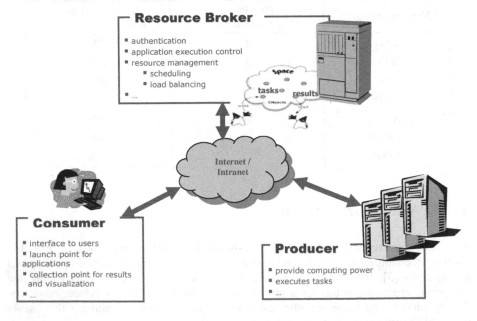

Fig. 3. ALiCE Architecture

3.2 ALiCE Components

ALiCE consists of the following main components:

- A programming model consisting of class libraries and a set of design patterns to support both sequential and parallel computer applications.
- A user interface supports the submission of task by consumers.
- A generic computing engine at each producer supports a number of functions. It notifies the resource broker of its availability, monitors and sends its performance to the resource broker, accepts tasks from the resource broker for execution and estimates its execution performance and returns the result to the resource broker.
- A resource broker that hides the complexities of distributed computing, and consists of three main components:
  o Task Manager – This includes a consumer list containing all registered consumers, a task pool containing computer applications submitted by consumers, a task monitor that monitors the progress of task execution, and for storing the application's data and computed results.
  o Resource Manager – This includes a producer list containing all registered producers, a performance monitor containing workload and performance information received from producers, and a security manager.
  o Task Scheduler – Based on the information supplied by the task manager and resource manager, the scheduler performs task assignments by matching the consumer's computational requirement with the available resources in the network.

3.3 ALiCE Object-Based Programming Model

The ALiCE Programming Template in Figure 4 implements our *TaskGenerator-ResultCollector model*. This model describes the basic components of a parallel ALiCE application.

The TaskGenerator-ResultCollector model defines two entities: TaskGenerator and ResultCollector. The TaskGenerator is executed at the Resource Broker, and is responsible for generating new tasks. The Resource Broker distributes these tasks to the Producers for execution. The Producers upon completion will send back the results to the Resource Broker which in turn will send the results back to the ResultCollector. The ResultCollector is executed at the Consumer, and it is responsible for collecting results from the Resource Broker.

There are four components that make up the ALiCE programming template: TaskGenerator, ResultCollector, Task, and Result. TaskGenerator component allows application to be invoked at the resource broker by invocation of the user's main method.   ResultCollector component allows application to be invoked at the Consumer node, waiting for results to be returned from the Resource Broker. Task component allows the producer nodes to return a Result object to the Resource Broker upon completing the execution. Result component provides an interface for producer to instantiate and returns any evaluated or intermediate data.

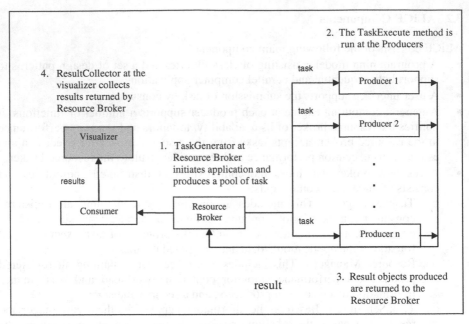

Fig. 4. ALiCE Execution Model

4   Mapping the N-Body Problem onto ALiCE

In our implementation, the Consumer reads data for each body consisting of its position, velocity, and mass, from a file. Data is transferred to the Resource Broker to construct the QuadTree.

The Resource Broker would then send the tree and the body data to the Producers. Each Producer will calculate the new position and velocity of body assigned to it. The result of each calculation is returned to the Consumer.

However, if Producers calculate new positions one body at a time, the volume of data transferred through network is very large, making the network's latency as a possible bottleneck for performance. This is true especially when the number of bodies is large; thus, the ratio between computation time and data transfer time is small.

We can overcome this problem by calculating not only one but many (say m) body at each Producer. As the result, we will save (m-1) network latency delays as the data for the m bodies is sent to each producer in bulk.

Fig. 5 shows the mapping of the application onto the ALiCE architecture.

Our algorithm takes the number of bodies (N) as an argument. The number of tasks that the Task Generator creates is N/M, where M is the number of bodies executed on a producer. Section 2.1 discussed the partitioning algorithm. We cannot implement the distributed Barnes-Hut trees because with the current version of ALiCE, producers cannot communicate with each other. The N-body program is outline in Figure 6.

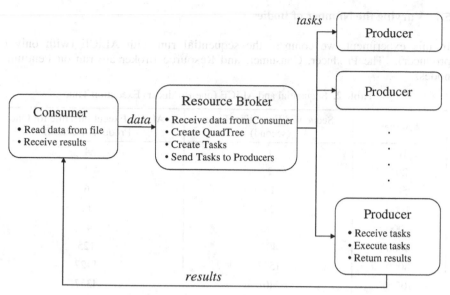

Fig. 5. Mapping N-Body onto ALiCE Architecture

```
TASK_GENERATOR
1: A ← new Tree
2: Initialize (A) //Compute particle mass & center of mass
3: for i in 1 to N/M
4:     T ← new TASK containing (Tree A, NodeID body[M])
5:     send T to Resource Broker
6: endfor

RESULT_COLLECTOR
1: for i in 1 to N
2:     RESULT R ← incoming Result from Resource Broker
3:     Write R to the file
4: endfor

TASK_EXECUTE (Tree A, NodeID i)
1: Calculate the total force of all bodies to node i
2: Calculate the new position of M bodies in array body[M]
3: Result R ← new Result
4: Insert new positions into R
5: Return R
```

Fig. 6. N-Body Problem Algorithm in ALiCE

5   Experiments

Our experiments were conducted on a cluster of 24 nodes consisting of eight Intel Pentium III 866MHz with 256MB of RAM, and sixteen Intel Pentium II 400MHz with 256MB of RAM running Red Hat Linux 7.0. Nodes are inter-connected via a 100Mbps switch.

5.1 Varying the Number of Bodies

In this experiment, we compare the sequential run with ALiCE (with only one producer). The Producer, Consumer, and Resource Broker are run on Pentium III nodes.

Table 2. Sequential and ALiCE (one Producer) Execution Time

#Bodies	Sequential Execution Time (second)	ALiCE Execution Time for One Producer (second)
100	1	4
200	2	4
500	13	6
1000	23	12
2000	193	41
4000	403	125
8000	1537	1427
10000	2401	4357
15000	5349	33457
20000	9428	43721

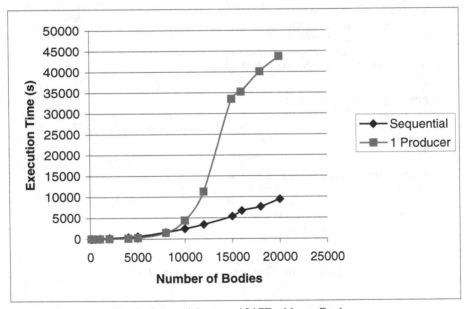

Fig. 7. Sequential versus ALiCE with one Producer

We observe that a single producer runs significantly slower than the sequential version. We attribute this slow-down to the communication overhead between the various components of the ALiCE system, i.e. the Resource Broker, the Producer and the Consumer. Such communication overheads do not exist in the sequential version.

5.2 Varying Task Sizes and the Number of Tasks

We vary the numbers of producers and we partitioned the problem into different number of bodies per ALiCE task yielding different number of tasks. The problem size is 25,000 bodies.

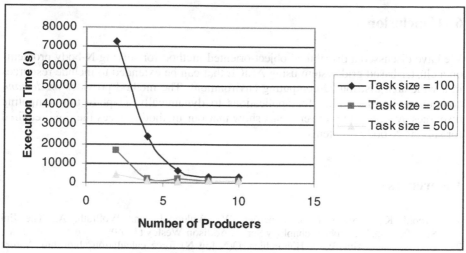

Fig. 8. Grid Computation Time for 25,000 Bodies

Table 3. Varying the Number of Bodies per Task and Task Size

Task size (#Bodies/task)	#Tasks	#Producers	Execution Time (s)
100	250	2	72951
200	125	2	16574
500	50	2	4218
1000	25	2	1582
100	250	4	23673
200	125	4	2044
500	50	4	932
1000	25	4	957
100	250	6	6476
200	125	6	1900
500	50	6	713
1000	25	6	731
100	250	8	3350
200	125	8	1178
500	50	8	1141
1000	25	8	1239
100	250	10	2910
200	125	10	1100
500	50	10	980
1000	25	10	789

As shown in Figure 8, the communication overheads due to data transfer and the overhead of ALiCE can be amortized over task of larger granularity. For example, the sequential execution time of over three hours is reduced to 16 minutes on four producers with 25 tasks (1000 bodies per task).

6 Conclusion

We have discussed a distributed object-oriented method for solving N-body problems on a cluster-based grid system using ALiCE that can be extended to include resources in a wide-area distributed computing environment. The method provides *on-demand* computing, i.e. the ability for applications to dynamically adapt to the computing resources available. Our experiments show that our method reduces the time required for solving N-body problems.

References

1. Arnold, K., O'Sullivan, B., Scheifler, W., Waldo, J., and Wollrath, A.: The Jini Specification. The Java Technology Series. Addison-Wesley (1999)
2. Barnes, J. and Hut, P.: A Hierarchical O(N log N) force calculation algorithm. *Nature* (1986) 324:446—449
3. Feynman, R.: The Character of Physical Law. The MIT Press (1965)
4. Foster I. and Kesselman C., editors.: The Grid: Blueprint for a Future Computing Infrastructure. Morgan Kaufmann Publishers (1999)
5. Foster, I., Kesselman, C., and Tuecke, S.: The Anatomy of the Grid: Enabling Scalable Virtual Organizations. *International J. Supercomputer Applications* (2001) 15
6. Gozali, J.P., ALiCE: Java-based Grid Computing System.: Honours Year Thesis. National University of Singapore (2001)
7. Sun Microsystems: JavaSpaces Specification (1998)

The Experience and Practice of Developing a Brain Functional Analysis System Using ICA on a Grid Environment

Takeshi Kaishima[1], Yuko Mizuno-Matsumoto[12],
Susumu Date[3], and Shinji Shimojo[4]

[1] Department of Information Systems Engineering
Graduate School of Engineering, Osaka University, Osaka, Japan
{takeshi, yuko}@ais.cmc.osaka-u.ac.jp
[2] Department of Child Education and Welfare
Osaka Jonan Women's Collage, Osaka, Japan
[3] Department of Bioinformatic Engineering
Graduate School of Information Science and Technology
Osaka University, Osaka, Japan
sdate@ist.osaka-u.ac.jp
[4] Cybermedia Center, Osaka University, Osaka, Japan
shimojo@cmc.osaka-u.ac.jp

Abstract. For the effective and early diagnosis of brain diseases, we have been developing a brain functional analysis system on a Grid environment. Until recently, neuroscientists have proposed and exploited numerous methods for the analysis of brain function. Although recently proposed analysis methods tend to be computationally-intensive, they are performed, in most cases, on a single-processor basis such as a commodity personal computer. The system developed on the Grid environment allows researchers and medical doctors to integrate a variety of geographically distributed resources and to analyze functional brain data in a realistic time period without detailed knowledge of the Grid. Through this paper, we show that the system built on the Grid has the capability to deliver enough computational power to perform promising brain functional analysis such as Independent Component Analysis (ICA). In addition, we present the experience and practice related to developing a Grid-enabled system for brain functional analysis mainly from the viewpoint of application building.

1 Introduction

Advances in networking technology and computational infrastructure make it possible to construct large-scale high-performance distributed, computing environments, or   that provide dependable, consistent, and pervasive access to high-end computational resources [1]. These environments have the potential to fundamentally change the way we think about computing, as well as the potential for computation to be no longer limited to the resources we currently have on hand.

A. Jean-Marie (Ed.): ASIAN 2002, LNCS 2550, pp. 98–109, 2002.

Recently, and especially in developed countries, brain science has taken on great importance. The number of patients suffering from brain disorders such as cerebrovascular disease and dementia is increasing in the aging society. To solve this problem, medical measurement devices for brain functional analysis and a variety of analysis and diagnosis methods have been exploited. Magneto-encephalography (MEG) [2] is an example of such medical measurement devices. This device will become commonly used because of its features of accuracy and good spatio-temporal resolution, as well as the device's non-invasiveness in measuring brain activities. In other words, MEG has the ability to detect brain disorders at an early stage and to prevent severe brain diseases. However, the cost for purchase and maintenance of MEG is extremely expensive. One way to get the benefits from this MEG without lowering the quality of medical service is to share MEG modality and increase analysis efficiency.

On one hand, a sophisticated analysis method such as Independent Component Analysis (ICA) has appeared with the advent of the MEG. This analysis method is an example of recently developed analysis methods. ICA allows us to extract arbitrary statistically independent components from mixed data [3]. This fact implies that medical doctors and researchers can detect the components of abnormal waves with ICA. Therefore, this analysis method is promising in the area of brain science, especially in the analysis of brain function with MEG data. On the other hand, ICA is computationally-intensive, which obstructs the advance of brain function analysis.

We have been developing a system for brain functional analysis on a Grid environment. Another analysis method, wavelet cross-correlation analysis, has been optimized on a Grid environment [4]. ICA has computational characteristics different from wavelet cross-correlation analysis. In this paper, we describe the experience and practice necessary in developing an ICA method on a Grid environment. In particular, we focus on computational performance for the ICA method. In other words, we describe not only the experience and practice but also the consideration of computing requirements in adopting the ICA method to a Grid environment in the hope that we can show the future potential of the Grid from a practical point of view.

In section 2, we briefly describe the framework of the system we have been developing and the ICA method. In section 3, we describe our Grid testbed and system implementation of how ICA is adapted into the testbed. In section 4, system performance is evaluated to verify that our system has the ability to make use of the computational characteristics of ICA for the best performance on a Grid environment. Section 5 concludes this paper with suggestions for future direction.

2 Modular System Architecture

2.1 ICA

Recently, ICA has been introduced and applied to separate observed MEG signals into each brain signal. The advantage of ICA for the evaluation of brain function is a blind separation technique based on information-maximization, which uses high-order statistical information. The algorithm has also been shown to produce useful decompositions of MEG or EEG (Electroencephalography) datasets into individual source signals. However, the volume of MEG dataset and the calculations required for ICA are tremendous; for example, 1.4 GB an hour in a general MEG data format. To realize early analysis and diagnosis, we introduce a Grid technology.

ICA is a signal processing method with the ability to separate only given mixtures of a set of underlying sources into their original sources without knowing how the signals are mixed nor the distribution of the sources. This principle has many interesting applications: finding hidden factors in financial data, reducing noise in natural images, separating the user's own signal from other signals in telecommunications, and so on.

When using a MEG record, the clinical investigator may face the problem of extracting the essential features of the neuromagnetic signals in the presence of artifacts such as the heart's electrical activity [5]. The amplitude of the disturbance may be higher than that of the brain signals, and the artifacts may resemble pathological signals in shape. The MEG data consists of recordings of magnetic fields in multiple locations on the scalp. These magnetic fields are presumably generated by mixing some of the underlying components of brain activities with artifacts. This situation is quite similar to the ICA model described below, then ICA can separate not only brain signals from artifacts but also brain activities coming from different parts of the brain into different components.

Due to the fact that magnetic fields of different bioelectric current sources superimpose linearly; therefore, the measured values of the sensor array can be modeled as a linear combination of component vectors

$$x(t) = As(t) \tag{1}$$

where $x = [x_1, \ldots, x_m]^T$, $s = [s_1, \ldots, s_n]^T$, $m \leq n$. For independent component analysis we assume that the observed signals $x(t)$ are linear mixtures of n underlying sources $s(t)$, which are mutually statistically independent, i.e. their joint probability density function factorizes. Within these assumptions one can separate data $x(t)$ into independent components $u(t) = Wx(t)$. This recovers the original sources $s(t)$ from the observed mixtures up to scaling and permutation. As both the mixing process A and the sources $s(t)$ are unknown, this technique is called

In the next section, we describe in detail how the workload for ICA is distributed. However, before doing so, we describe the system framework so as to present how the ICA module is built into the entire system.

2.2   System Framework

Figure 1 depicts the framework of the system we have now been under developing for brain function evaluation on a Grid environment. In this paper, we focus on the analysis module for ICA in the figure to show the effectiveness of the system

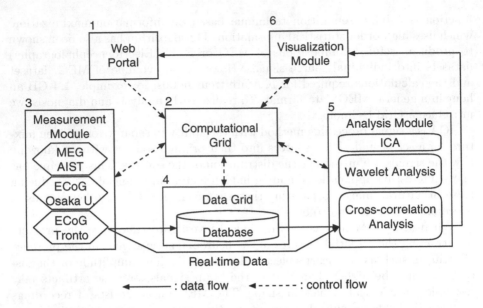

Fig. 1. System framework

performance. Therefore, the experience of developing a Grid-enabled module for the ICA method is mainly presented in the following sections. In this section, we first describe the interaction of the system components in order to clarify our system architecture in detail before we focus on the analysis module. The upper left number of each module box in the figure corresponds to the item number below. This system is composed of six parts:

1. A user requests a job through a web portal with considering user requirements such as deadline time.
2. Computational grid assigns the resources on a Grid environment for the requested job based on the user requirements.
3. Datasets are acquired from a medical modality such as MEG and ECoG (Electrocorticography) at the measurement module according to the control of the computational grid.
4. The datasets are stored and replicated with Data Grid functionality, which is realized by accessing to large amounts of distributed data, or the datasets are passed directly to the analysis module for real-time analysis.
5. The datasets are analyzed on various computational resources assigned by the computational grid.
6. The analyzed datasets are visualized for diagnosis and analysis of brain function in a 2-D or 3-D representation to help the user's understanding of the results.

The Grid refers to an infrastructure that enables the integrated, collaborative use of high-end computers, networks, databases, and scientific instruments owned and managed by multiple organizations dynamically. The Grid is motivated by the need to access resources not located within a single computer system:

1. high-performance computers are too expensive to be replicated,
2. an application may require resources that would not normally be co-located, and
3. certain unique resources such as specialized databases and people cannot be replicated.

In each case, the ability to construct networked virtual supercomputers can provide new qualitative capabilities that enable new approaches to solving problems. Grid applications often involve large amounts of data and/or computing and often require secure resource sharing across organizational boundaries, and are thus not easily handled by current Internet and Web infrastructures.

These prominent functionalities provided by the Grid are the building blocks of our system. In the following section, we detail the computational grid part, the analysis module for ICA and the interaction between these components in Fig. 1. Lastly, we evaluate system performance from several aspects to show the ability of our system built on a Grid environment in the particular use.

3   System Implementation

3.1   Environmental Setup

The Globus Project is one of research and development projects focused on enabling the application of Grid concepts to scientific and engineering computing. The Globus Project provides software tools that make it easier to build computational grids and grid-based applications. These tools are collectively called [6].

The system framework has been developed to map a high-performance parallel application in a portable fashion on a   environment. MPICH–G2 is a grid-enabled implementation of the Message Passing Interface (MPI) that allows the user to run MPI programs across multiple computers at different sites using the same commands that would be used on a parallel computer [7]. This library extends the Argonne MPICH implementation of MPI to use services provided by the Globus grid toolkit.

Figure 2 illustrates our system environment for the evaluation of brain function. The data acquired from the MEG modality are transferred via a 100 Mb/s network to Cybermedia Center, Osaka University, Japan, where the calculations and analysis are performed by the personal computers and/or the cluster system. The computation modules for ICA, Fourier transform, wavelet analysis, and correlation analysis have been developed with MPICH–G2. We have developed the ICA module newly and the last three analysis modules have been developed and are being optimized. The analysis results are loaded into the visualization module. The visualization module provides rendered images interactively to the feedback monitor via the high-speed network and also receives the medical doctor's interaction.

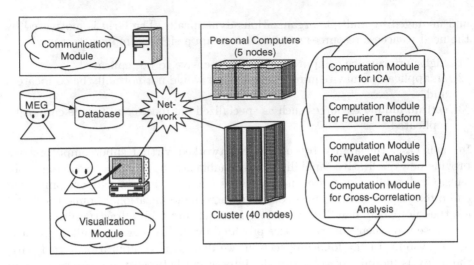

Fig. 2. System environment

Table 1. Machine spec of the testbed

	CPU	Memory	OS
Cluster Nodes	Intel Pentium III 1.4 GHz	1 GB	Linux 2.4.9
Personal Computer Nodes	Intel Pentium 4 1.6 GHz	370 MB	Linux 2.4.9/2.2.19

Table 1 shows the machine spec of the simulated testbed built in Cybermedia Center, Osaka University. We have used a cluster system (Dual Intel Pentium III 1.4 GHz processor, 1 GB memory × 40 nodes) and 6 personal computers (Intel Pentium 4 1.6 GHz processor, 370 MB memory): 1 personal computer for the instruction node (which involves both the communication module and the visualization module), and the other 5 personal computers and all 40 cluster nodes for computational node. These nodes are connected by Fast Ethernet (100Base–TX). To realize the experiment testbed, we have installed Globus toolkit 2.0 and MPICH–G2 on all nodes.

3.2   Implementation of ICA Module

We have adopted the Joint Approximate Diagonalization of Eigenmatrices (JADE) [8] algorithm for the ICA module since its algorithm is simpler than the other ICA algorithms. The JADE algorithm is based on the joint diagonalization of matrices obtained from 'parallel slices' of the fourth-order cumulant tensor. The JADE algorithm parallelizes nicely; each matrix slice in a dataset can be processed independently.

Figure 3 shows part of the data parallelism adopted in the computation module for ICA. The most time-consuming region of ICA is the double loop structure with regard to variable M. Variable M corresponds to the number of

```
while ( more > 0 ) {
  /* One sweep through a stack of K symmetric M*M matrices. */
  more = 0 ;
  for (p=0; p<M; p++)
    for (q=p+1; q<M; q++) {
      theta = GivensStack(A, M, K, p, q) ;
      if (fabs(theta)>threshold) {
        LeftRotStack (A, M, M, K, p, q, theta) ;
        RightRotStack(A, M, M, K, p, q, theta) ;
        LeftRotSimple(R, M, M,    p, q, theta) ;
        more = 1 ; /* any pair rotation triggers a new sweep */
      }
    }
}
```

Original Code

```
while ( more > 0 ) {
  /* One sweep through a stack of K symmetric M*M matrices. */
  more = 0 ;
  for (p=0; p<M; p++)
    for (q=p+1; q<M; q++) {
      theta = GivensStack(A, M, K, p, q, mpiid, mpinum) ;
      if (fabs(theta)>threshold) {
        if (mpiid != 0) {
          LeftRotStack (A, M, M, K, p, q, theta, mpiid, mpinum) ;
          RightRotStack(A, M, M, K, p, q, theta, mpiid, mpinum) ;
        }
        if (mpiid == 0)
          LeftRotSimple(R, M, M,    p, q, theta) ;
        more = 1 ; /* any pair rotation triggers a new sweep */
      }
    }
}
```

Parallelized Code

Fig. 3. Parallelism of JADE

sensors. Parallelized code is modified for use with MPI from the original code of JADE [9], surrounded by the shaded rectangle in the figure. Modified functions calculate over the designated matrix slice with two additional arguments: mpiid (size of MPI communication domain) and mpinum (integer number to specify a process; MPI process rank).

The function called GivensStack finds the angle to rotate the fourth-order cumulant tensor matrix. In this function, $O(M^2)$ time is required and it is needed in all processes to communicate because the rotation angle is retrieved from all elements over the matrix. LeftRotStack and RightRotStack also require

$O(M^2)$ time, but no communications are needed because of calculation independence. Therefore, ICA requests $O(M^4)$ for the number of MEG sensors in a single sweep. In these parallel functions, we have distributed the computational workload equally to the processors using the traditional block mapping manner to calculate equal parts of the matrix.

4   Evaluation

MEG data of a patient with frequent epileptic seizures were recorded from 64 sensors. Each epoch including epileptic discharges of 160 seconds was analyzed. The results of ICA show that the abnormal waves are successfully extracted.

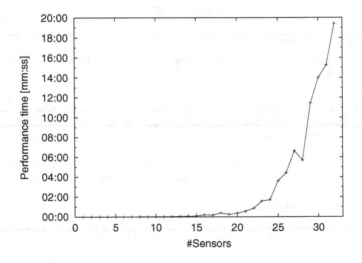

Fig. 4. Computation time with original JADE

To clarify the trend of performance time with ICA when the number of sensors changes, performance time required for non-parallelized code, or original JADE, was measured by changing the number of sensors used, as shown in Fig. 4. This graph shows that performance time is in proportion to $O(M^6)$. When considering the JADE feature, we can see that sweep count, or convergence speed is about $O(M^2)$ because one sweep requires $O(M^4)$ performance time. Based on this consideration, we measured our system performance by changing the number of sensors because the characteristic of performance time changes dramatically. In this paper, we measured performance time in either 64 or 32 sensors; 64 is the number of sensors in the MEG modality and 32 is half the number of sensors.

Experiments were performed to evaluate the computational performance of our system. Each of the two computational systems is located on a different administrative domain. When 1 to 5 processors are assigned, processors only in

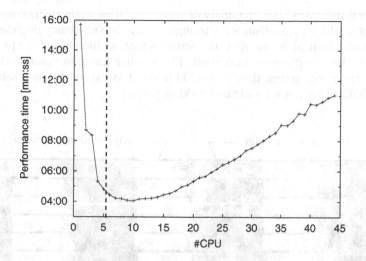

Fig. 5. Performance time (32 sensors)

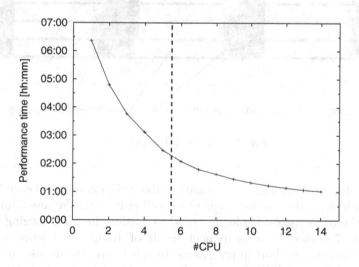

Fig. 6. Performance time (64 sensors)

the personal computers are used. When more than 6 processors are assigned, processors in both the personal computers and the cluster system are used. Performance times were determined using various numbers of processors (1–44) and different data volume (32 and 64 sensors). Figure 5 shows the mean performance time of 32 sensors. The results with processor ID 1 to 5 is on only personal computers and processor ID 6 to 44 on both personal computers and the cluster system. Figure 6 is the measurement results when 64 data are used.

Figure 6 indicates that the analysis time decreases with an increase in the processors used for parallelism, even though parallelism efficiency decreases. Figure 5 indicates that performance time increases with an increase of the processors when more than 10 processors are used. The smaller the data volume, the lower efficiency the performance time shows. This event is caused by increasing both the communication period and the blocking period.

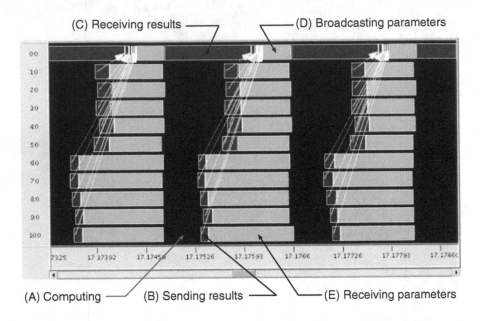

Fig. 7. Results of Jumpshot–3

To investigate either logging information about the execution of each MPI call to a file for later analysis or for tracing each call as it occurs, we used Jumpshot–3 graphical tool for displaying logfiles produced using the MPE logging libraries [10]. Figure 7 shows the measurement result of Jumpshot–3 when 32 sensor datasets were calculated on 10 processors. In this figure, the absussa axis shows time (in seconds), and MPI process ranks are shown from top to bottom.

Time slices indicated in A represent the computational period; time slices in B represent the results-sending period; time slices in C represent the results-receiving period; time slices in D represent the parameters-broadcasting period, and time slices in E represent the parameters-receiving period, respectively. Process ID 0 runs on the communication module. Process ID 0 receives the results from all the other processes, and after collecting all the results, process ID 0 then broadcasts the next parameters to all other processes. Processes ID 1 to 10 wait for broadcasting the next parameters after returning the result.

The length of blocking period E on process ID 1 to 5 is equal to the length of computational period A. The length of E on process ID 6 to 10 is 3 times longer than the length of A. This event is caused by a difference of processor performance. These blocking periods are dynamically extended by the run-time disturbance of the other processes on the distributed multi-user environment.

In addition, Fig. 7 also shows the length of the communication period. Messages from process ID 1to 10 are received one by one, and broadcasted messages from process ID 0 are sent one by one, although this is a specification of MPICH-G2. Therefore, the communication period linearly increases in correspondence to the number of processes. This increase is the main factor for the increase in analysis time in spite of the increasing number of processors when more than 10 processors are used, as shown in Fig. 5.

When the increasing length of the blocking and communication periods is taken into consideration, the increase in performance time is inevitable in ICA with a Grid environment composed of multiple heterogeneous computers. Because of the trade-off between increasing performance effected by load sharing and decreasing performance effected by load imbalance, communication time and blocking time, a minimum performance time is determined by these effects. The number of sensors on a MEG modality tends to increase, for example, to 143 or 275 sensors, and in this situation, parallelism efficiency becomes higher, and performance time becomes shorter with emerging computational resources. Our system, which uses ICA on a Grid environment, is therefore effective for practical use.

5   Conclusion and Future Works

In the hope of showing the future potential of the Grid from a practical point of view, this paper describes not only the experience and practice of computing requirements but also considers the computing requirements for ICA in adopting an ICA method to a Grid environment. The results of our evaluation show that the larger the data volume, the higher the performance efficiency because of the decrease in the ratio of both authentication time before the calculation and data communication period, and because of the blocking time in comparison to the total performance time. Considering the current increase in the number of sensors on a MEG modality, parallelism efficiency becomes higher, and performance time becomes shorter with emerging computational resources.

Furthermore, because of the trade-off between the increasing effect by load sharing and the decreasing effect by load imbalance, communication time and blocking time, performance time does not improve by simply increasing the number of processors. In pursuit of further effective performance on the Grid environment, a scheduling framework that allocates users' tasks to heterogeneous computational resources appropriately is essential. Moreover, this allocation is performed based on dynamic information such as CPU load and network traffic located on heterogeneous environments. When we apply our analysis system to practical clinical use, not only real-time reaction but also a predictable system becomes necessary. Therefore, we intend to focus next on developing a preactive scheduling system, which predicts dynamic resource configuring and realizes effective performance from information during a set time period in the near past.

Acknowledgments. This work was supported in part by a Grant-in-Aid for Scientific Research on the Priority Area, "Informatics Stuies for the Foundation of IT Evolution" (13224059) by the Ministry of Education, Culture, Sports, Science and Technology of Japan. We would like to thank Prof. M. Takeda, Dr. K. Shinosaki and Dr. S. Ukai of the Department of Neuropsychiatry in Osaka University for measuring and offering the MEG data. AIST stands for National Institute of Advanced Industrial Science and Technology.

References

1. Foster, I., Kesselman, C.: The Grid: Blueprint for a New Computing Infrastructure. Morgan Kaufmann, (1998)
2. Sato, S.: Magnetoencephalography. Raven Press (1990)
3. Hyvärinen, A., Oja, E.: Independent Component Analysis: Algorithms and Applications. Neural Networks **13** (2000) 411–430
4. Date, S., Mizuno-Matsumoto, Y., Kadobayashi, Y., Shimojo, S.: An MEG data analysis system using Grid technology. IPSJ Journal **42** (2001) 2952–2962
5. Vigário, R., Jousmäki, V., Hämäläinen, M., Hari, R., Oja, E.: Independent Component Analysis for Identification of Artifacts in Magnetoencephalographic Recordings. in Proc. NIPS'97 **10** (1998) 229–235
6. Foster, I., Kesselman, C.: The Globus Project: A Status Report. in Proc. HCW'98 (1998) 4–18
7. Foster, I., Karonis, N.: A Grid-Enabled MPI: Message Passing in Heterogeneous Distributed Computing Systems. in Proc. SC'98 (1998)
8. Veen, B., Buckley, K.: Beamforming: A Versatile Approach to Spatial Filtering. IEEE ASSP Magazine **25** (1988) 4–24
9. C implementations for JADE, SHIBBS. `http://www.tsi.enst.fr/icacentral/Algos/cardoso/JnS.tar`
10. Zaki, O., Lusk, E., Gropp, W., Swider, D.: Toward Scalable Performance Visualization with Jumpshot. High Performance Computing Applications **13** (1999) 277–288
11. Mizuno-Matsumoto, Y., Date, S., Kaishima, T., Kadobayashi, Y., Shimojo, S.: A Grid Application for an Evaluation of Brain Function using Independent Component Analysis (ICA). in Proc. CCGrid2002 (2002) 111–118
12. Kaishima, T., Mizuno-Matsumoto, Y., Date, S., Kawaguchi, S., Ukai, S., Yamamoto, M., Shinosaki, K., Shimojo, S.: An Application for the Evaluation of Brain Function using Independent Component Analysis (ICA). NeuroImage **16** (2002)

A Scalable Approach to Network Enabled Servers

Philippe Combes[1], Frédéric Lombard[2], Martin Quinson[1], and Frédéric Suter[1]

[1] ReMaP – LIP, École Normale Supérieure de Lyon, 46 Allée d'Italie, F-69364 Lyon Cedex 07
{Philippe.Combes,Martin.Quinson,Frederic.Suter}@ens-lyon.fr
[2] LIFC, Laboratoire d'Informatique de l'Universitéde Franche Comté
16 route de Gray, F-25030 Besançon Cedex
Frederic.Lombard@lifc.univ-fcomte.fr

Abstract. This paper presents the architecture and the algorithms used in DIET (Distributed Interactive Engineering Toolbox), a hierarchical set of components to build Network Enabled Server applications in a Grid environment. This environment is built on top of different tools which are able to locate an appropriate server depending on the client's request, the data location (which can be anywhere on the system, because of previous computations) and the dynamic performance characteristics of the system. Some experiments are reported at the end of this paper, that exhibit the low cost of adding branches in the hierarchical tree of components and the performance increase induced.

Keywords: Metacomputing, Computational servers, Agent hierarchy.

1 Introduction

Huge problems can now be computed over the Internet thanks to Grid Computing Environments [7]. Because most the current applications on the Grid are numerical, the use of specialized libraries like BLAS, LAPACK, ScaLAPACK, PETSc or FFTW is mandatory. But the integration of such libraries in high-level applications using languages such as Fortran or C is far from easy. Moreover the computational power and memory needs of such applications obviously may not be available on every workstation. Thus the RPC paradigm [9,10] seems to be a good candidate to build Problem Solving Environments (PSE) for numerical applications on the Grid [8]. Several tools following this approach exist, such as NetSolve [3], NINF [11], NEOS [6], or RCS [2]. They are most commonly referred to as Network Enabled Server (NES) environments [10]. Such environments usually have five different components: *Clients* that submit problems they have to solve to *Servers*, a *Database* that contains information about software and hardware resources, a *Scheduler* that chooses an appropriate server depending on the problem sent and the information contained in the database, and finally *Monitors* that acquire information about the status of the computational resources.

For instance in the architecture of NetSolve, which is a NES environment developed at the University of Tennessee, Knoxville, we find these components in the form of the client, server, and agent, with the agent containing the database and scheduler. Figure 1(a) shows how these components are organized. A NetSolve session works as follows. First the agent (which has to be unique) is launched. Then servers register to it by sending a list of problems that they are able to solve as well as the speed and the workload of the

A. Jean-Marie (Ed.): ASIAN 2002, LNCS 2550, pp. 110–124, 2002.

machine on which they are running and the network's speed (latency and bandwidth) between them and the agent. Once this initialization step is performed, a client can call the agent to solve a problem. The scheduler selects a set of most suitable servers to this problem and sends back this list to the client. The latter sends input objects to the first of the servers it can reach. The requested tasks are then run on this computational resource and the output objects are returned to the client.

But NetSolve and the other environments previously cited have a centralized scheduler which can become a bottleneck when many clients try to access several servers. Moreover as networks are highly hierarchical, the location of the scheduler has a great impact on the performance of the overall platform. This paper presents the architecture of DIET (Distributed Interactive Engineering Toolbox), a hierarchical set of components to build NES applications and tackle this issue.

This document is organized as follows: Section 2 presents the overall architecture of the DIET platform and its main components and how distributed objects are used to connect these components. In Section 3, we give the algorithms used to discover software and hardware resources that are able to solve a problem submitted by a client. An experimental evaluation of these algorithms is given in Section 4, just before our conclusion and presentation of future work.

2   DIET Architecture and Related Tools

The aim of an NES environment such as DIET is to provide a transparent access to a pool of computational servers. DIET focuses on offering such a service at a very large scale. A client which has a problem to solve should be able to obtain a reference to the server that is best suited for it. DIET is designed to take into account the data location when scheduling jobs. Data are kept as long as possible on (or near to) the computational servers in order to minimize transfer times. This kind of optimization is mandatory when performing job scheduling on a wide-area network.

DIET is built upon *Computational Resource Daemons* and *Server Daemons*. The scheduler is scattered across a hierarchy of *Local Agents* and *Master Agents*. NWS [14] sensors are placed on every node of the hierarchy to collect resource availabilities, which are used by an application-centric performance prediction tool named FAST [13]. Figure 1(b) shows the hierarchical organization of DIET.

2.1   DIET Components

The different components of our software architecture are the following:

Client
A client is an application which uses DIET to solve problems. Many kinds of clients should be able to connect to DIET from a web page, a PSE such as Matlab or Scilab, or from a compiled program.
Master Agent (MA)
An MA receives computation requests from clients. These requests refer to some DIET problems listed on a reference web page. Then the MA collects computation abilities from the servers and chooses the best one. The reference of the chosen

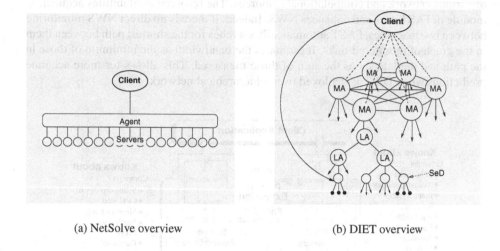

(a) NetSolve overview   (b) DIET overview

Fig. 1. Comparison between two NES environments: NetSolve and DIET.

server is returned to the client. A client can be connected to an MA by a specific name server or a web page which stores the various MA locations.

Local Agent (LA)

An LA aims at transmitting requests and information between MAs and servers. The information stored on an LA is the list of requests and, for each of its subtrees, the number of servers that can solve a given problem and information about the data distributed in this subtree. Depending on the underlying network topology, a hierarchy of LAs may be deployed between an MA and the servers. No scheduling decision is made by an LA.

Server Daemon (SeD)

An SeD encapsulates a computational server. For instance it can be located on the entry point of a parallel computer. The information stored on an SeD is a list of the data available on its server (with their distribution and the way to access them), the list of problems that can be solved on it, and all information concerning its load (memory available, number of resources available, ...). An SeD declares the problems it can solve to its parent LA. An SeD can give performance prediction for a given problem thanks to the FAST module, which is described in next section.

2.2   FAST: Fast Agent's System Timer

FAST [13] is a tool for dynamic performance forecasting in a Grid environment. As shown in Figure 2, FAST is composed of several layers and relies on low-level software. First it uses a network and CPU monitoring software to handle dynamically changing resources, like workload or bandwidth. FAST uses the Network Weather Service (NWS) [14], a tool developed at the University of California, Santa Barbara. This is a distributed system that periodically monitors and dynamically forecasts the performance of various network and computational resources. The resource availabilities acquisition module of FAST uses and enhances NWS. Indeed, if there is no direct NWS monitoring between two machines, FAST automatically searches for the shortest path between them in the graph of monitored links. It estimates the bandwidth as the minimum of those in the path and the latency as the sum of those measured. This allows for more accurate predictions when DIET is deployed over a hierarchical network.

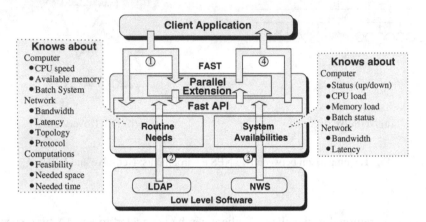

Fig. 2. FAST overview.

In addition to the system availabilities, FAST can also forecast the time and space needs of computational routines, depending on both the parameter set and the machine where the computation would take place. For this, FAST benchmarks the routines at installation time on each machine for a representative set of parameters. After polynomial data fitting, the results are stored in an LDAP tree. The user API of FAST is composed of a small set of functions that combine resource availabilities and routine needs from low-level software to produce ready-to-use values. These results can be combined into analytical models by the parallel extension [4] to forecast execution times of parallel routines.

Thus DIET components, as any FAST client, can access information like the time needed to move a given amount of data between two SeDs, the time to solve a problem with a given set of CRDs managed by an SeD, or the combination of these two quantities.

2.3   Using Corba in DIET

NES environments can be implemented using a classic socket communication layer. NINF and NetSolve are implemented that way. Several problems to this approach have been pointed out such as the lack of portability or the limitation of opened sockets. Our aim is to implement and then deploy a distributed NES environment that works at a wider scale. Distributed object environments, such as *Java*, *DCOM* or Corba have proven to be a good base for building applications that manage access to distributed services. They not only provide transparent communications in heterogeneous networks, but they also offer a framework for the large scale deployment of distributed applications. Being open and language independent, Corba was chosen for the communication layer in DIET.

Corba systems provide a remote method invocation facility with a high level of transparency. This transparency should not dramatically affect the performance, communication layers being well optimized in most Corba implementations [5]. Indeed, the communication time is that of with sockets plus a constant value [1]. Moreover, the time to select a server using Corba should be short compared to the computation time.

Corba is thus well suited to support distributed resources and applications in a large scale Grid environment. New dedicated services can be easily published and existing services can also be used. Thus we can conclude that Corba systems are one of the alternatives of choice for the development of Grid specific services. Our first DIET prototype is based upon *OmniORB* [12], a free Corba implementation which provides good communication performance.

3   DIET Initialization and Operation

In this section we study how to specify the order in which components should be started, giving as an example a DIET platform involving only one MA. This example is actually simpler to discuss and the algorithms presented here are easily extendable to the general case by broadcasting computation requests to the other MAs. Then, we discuss the way a server is chosen to solve a given problem, taking the communication and computation times into account.

3.1   DIET Initialization

Figure 3 shows each step of the initialization of a simple Grid system. The architecture is built in the hierarchical order, each component connecting to its father. The MA is the first entity to be started (1). It waits for connections from LAs or requests from clients.

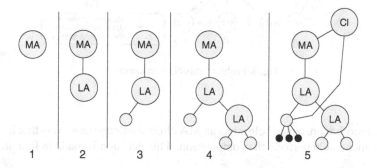

Fig. 3. Initialization of a DIET system.

Then when an LA is launched, it subscribes to the MA (2). At this step of the system initialization, two kinds of components can connect to the LA: an SeD (3), which manages some computational resource, or another LA (4), to add a hierarchical level in this branch. When the SeD registers to an LA, it publishes a list of the services it offers, which is forwarded to the agent father and so on until the MA. Finally, any client can access the registered resource through the platform: it can contact an MA (5) to get a reference to the best server known and then directly connect to it to launch the computation.

The architecture of the hierarchy is described in configuration files and each component transmits the local configuration to its father. Thus, the system administration can also be hierarchical. For instance, an MA can manage a domain like a university, providing priority access to users of this domain. Then each laboratory can run an LA, while each team of the laboratory can run some other LAs to administrate its own servers. This hierarchical administration of the system allows local changes in the configuration without interfering with the whole platform.

3.2   Solving a Problem

Let us assume that the architecture described in section 2 includes several servers able to solve the same problem, and that each operand needed for the computation is available on one single server. The example presented in Figure 4 considers the submission of the problem F() involving data A and B.

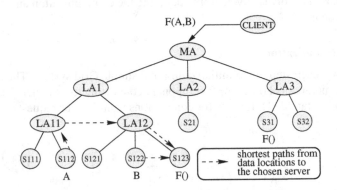

Fig. 4. Problem submission example.

The algorithm presented below lets an MA choose among the servers that it manages the one which could perform the computation. This decision is made in four steps:

 - the MA propagates the client request through its subtrees down to the capable servers ; actually, each agent only knows which among its sons manage the service, and it forwards the client request to them only ;
 - each server that can satisfy the request launches FAST to estimate the computation time necessary to process the request, and it sends this estimation back to their "father" (the LA) ;

- each LA of the tree that receives one or more positive answers from its sons selects a pool of servers among the fastest ones and forwards their answers to the MA, through the hierarchy ;
- once the MA has collected all the answers from its direct sons, it also chooses a pool of fast servers and send their references to the client.

For the problem solving itself, the client connects to one of the servers chosen: it sends its local data and specifies if the results should be kept in-place for further computation or if it should be brought back. The transfer of persistent operand is performed at this time.

3.3   Data Structures and Algorithms

As said in section 3.2 the MA has to locate the capable servers and the persistent data involved in the client request. Thus, this request must be structured in two fields: the problemNickname, and a list of attributes of the data involved, including details about their size and properties in order to evaluate computation and communication times. When the MA receives a request from a client, it builds a request structure and sends it to all its children which either own some of the needed data or are able to solve the problem. The request is transmitted from down to the SeDs across the hierarchy. Each LA labels its children reached by the request and waits for their responses.

Once reached, the SeDs that are able to satisfy the request initiate a response structure and send it back to their father. This structure contains three fields:

myName is the unique id of the component that sends back this response;
data is an array with an entry for each variable involved in the computation, each one containing two fields:
   - location is the name of the component that owns the data,
   - timeToMe is the estimation of the communication time to bring the variable from the component sending the structure, if its location is known;
comp contains an entry for every server (able to satisfy the request) known at this point of the tree. Three pieces of data are kept for each server:
   - name is the id of the server,
   - tComp is the estimated computation time to satisfy the request,
   - tComm is an array containing the estimated time to bring each variable involved to that server;

Transfer times for data are computed dynamically while sending back the answers to the MA. Our idea is that all agents of the hierarchy should be deployed on the underlying network nodes. That is why we just sum the estimated transfer times between the various nodes of the tree. The algorithm is divided in three steps:

1. **SeD answer**
   When an SeD receives a request, it sends a response structure to its father. It fills the data field for the variables it owns, leaving a null value for the others. If the server can also solve the problem, it fills a (tComp) (in a one-element comp array), after FAST has computed the computation time.

2. **Aggregation**

Every LA gathers the responses coming from its children and aggregates them into one single structure. The fields related to communication times are gradually filled as the structures come back up to the MA. FAST computes the transfer time of data to the capable servers, combining information from monitoring and data attributes. The transfer will use the shortest path among those that are monitored, ie among the physical nodes of the hierarchy. Figure 5 gives the complete algorithm used by LAs to aggregate responses coming from their children.

3. **Use**

When the responses come back to the MA, it uses them to make a decision. The evaluated computation and communication times are used to find the servers with the lowest response time to perform the computation.

However, we have to consider the case when a server is chosen twice and the first computation has not already started when the second problem was submitted. It could happen that the penalty of the first computation problem is not considered in the estimation of the computation time for the second one. This is a classical problem in dynamic performance evaluation, and we are presently working on an algorithm, based on contracts between servers and clients, to check that the estimation is still meaningful at the time of client/server connection.

```
for each data D do
    if none of my descendants own D then
        timeToMe = 0
    else if one of my children references D then
        timeToMe = timeToMe for this child + time to send D from this child to me
    else if D is not known by any of my children then
        if a server S of my sub-tree can solve the problem then
            D will be sent through me to S if it's selected.
            ⇒ Increase D's tComm for each server
        else
            D will be sent to a capable server S following a path in which I am not involved.
            ⇒ End tComm's computation for my descendants.
        end if
    end if
end for
```

Fig. 5. Complete result aggregation algorithm for a LA.

4   DIET Architecture Evaluation

In this section we exhibit the first experiments made with the DIET prototype we develop. These experiments only involve one MA and a hierarchy of LAs. Our goal is to validate our architecture and evaluate the performance of the request broadcast algorithm proposed.

The impact of the use of LAs on the request broadcasting on a low bandwidth network is first investigated in section 4.1. This experiment shows that using a hierarchy of LAs can increase notably the speed of the server lookup.

In section 4.2, we examine the cost of adding servers in a DIET architecture with a single agent, then we compare a linear architecture to a binary tree in order to show how parallelism can be introduced in the request processing.

We eventually show in section 4.3 how this parallelism can be used to speed up the request diffusion. Two experiments are lead in this section. The first one consists in adding a new branch to an existing DIET tree. The second one evaluates different ways to add servers to an existing architecture. These experiments show that servers can be added to a DIET tree without additional lookup cost if the tree architecture is chosen wisely.

4.1   Evaluation of the Broadcast Algorithm

We aim here at showing the benefits of the DIET hierarchical approach when a LA is used to optimize communication delays over a slow network link. In such a case, LAs are used to perform an efficient request broadcast from the MA to the SeDs. Figure 6 shows the two configurations used in that experiment. The right part of the figure shows that the introduction of a LA reduces to one the number of messages sent across the slow link. In this section we examine the evolution of the request submission time depending on the number of SeDs with the two configurations shown in Figure 6.

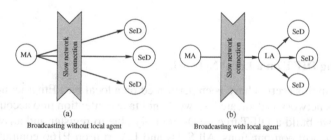

(a)   (b)
Broadcasting without local agent   Broadcasting with local agent

Fig. 6. The DIET broadcasting algorithm validation experiment.

The slow network link has a bandwidth of 2MB/s. This bandwidth is shared with other links. The local network that supports the SeDs (and the LA in configuration shown on Figure 6(b)) is a Fast Ethernet network with several switches. The request processing time being much lower than the communication times on the slow link, up to 25 SeDs have been co-allocated on the same 1GHz Pentium computer. The MA and the client run on the same PIII 500 computer on the other end of the slow link. Figure 7 shows the result of our tests. Experiments have been done with both configurations shown on Figure 6. For each number of SeDs, 50 clients were run sequentially and, as each client only submits a problem to the MA and stops as soon as the reference is answered, the submission time is approximated by the client execution time.

In both cases, results are nearly linear. With the configuration shown on Figure 6(b), the request submission time appears to be 3 (with 42 servers) up to 4 (with 72 servers) times less than without any LA. A linear regression shows that the slope is 4 times greater when no LA is deployed. This corroborates our idea that network bottlenecks are an important issue in NES environments.

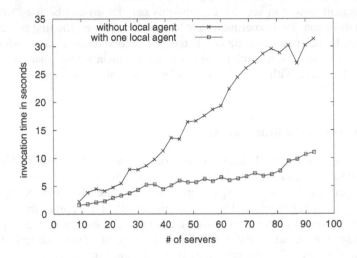

Fig. 7. Time to process a request from submission to answer

4.2   Running DIET on a Local Network

Experiments in this section have been performed on a local Fast Ethernet network with a switch. This network is dedicated, so we do not take contention into account. For each experiment, we build a DIET tree. SeDs are only able to register and answer requests but not to perform computations. All SeDs and LAs run on P166 computers running Linux. The MA and the client run on the cluster entry point, a 1GHz Pentium PC. The problem submitted by the clients is known by every SeD. Thus each request reaches all SeDs. The value measured is the average submission time (i.e., the time elapsed from the submission to the MA to the reception of a server reference).

Adding a server to DIET. Here we aim at evaluating the cost of adding an SeD to an existing DIET architecture by connecting it to the only launched MA. This introduces no parallelism in the broadcast of requests and thus should give the worst performance. Eight experiments have been done with a number of SeDs ranging from one to eight directly connected to the MA. The available number of workstations and the impossibility to co-allocate SeDs on a same machine without changing the results prevented us from running experiments on more servers. When an SeD is added to an existing architecture without adding an LA, the performance loss should be equivalent to the one observed in this experiment. The results of this experiment is given in the following table.

number of SeDs	1	2	3	4	5	6	7	8
request time (ms)	4.4	6.0	6.7	7.4	8.0	9.0	9.8	10.6

In this experiment, the requests are sent by the MA to each SeD sequentially. When a SeD receives a request, it begins to process it immediately. Thus, the requests processing on each SeD is partially parallel and the results above are not linear. By using LAs to increase the amount of parallelism in the request processing, better results may be obtained. Adding four servers to a system with already four other servers adds 3.2 ms to the request processing time. This corresponds to an overhead of 43.24 %. Experiments have been conducted to look for the lowest overhead when adding a server and are compared to this one in the next.

Comparing two architectures of similar depth. Figure 8 shows two DIET architectures that have the same depth and the same number of SeDs. The cost of a communication on a branch of the DIET tree is exactly the cost of the communication through the Ethernet network. Although a linear architecture such as (a) would never be deployed in practice, two LAs are thus used to obtain the same tree depth as for architecture (b). This prevents us from comparing the performance of architectures that have different depths, that is with different costs of a communication between the MA and a SeD.

The average request processing time is 52.2 ms on architecture (a) and only 33.5 ms for (b). The administrators have to carefully build their LA hierarchy to improve the performance. Experiments conducted in section 4.3 aim at providing some simple rules for this task.

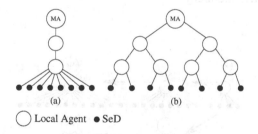

Fig. 8. Comparison between two DIET trees.

4.3   Evaluating the Architecture's Cost

By evaluating the cost of additional servers in the architecture using several strategies, we show here how the request processing can be done in parallel in DIET. The experimental results show that new servers can be added to the system nearly without any overhead to the request processing. The experimental conditions in this section are the same as in section 4.2.

Adding a branch to a DIET tree. Figure 9 shows how it is possible to have twice as many SeDs just by adding one son to the MA. This son heads a hierarchy similar to the existing branch, which consists of a binary tree. The experimental conditions are the same as in section 4.2, in which an overhead of 3 ms has been shown when we increase the number of SeDs in the same proportion. The average submission time is 32.3 ms for the first architecture (a) and 33.5 ms for the second one (b).

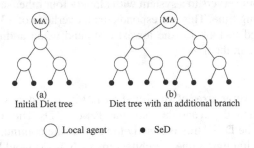

(a)
Initial Diet tree

(b)
Diet tree with an additional branch

○ Local agent   ● SeD

Fig. 9. Adding a branch to a DIET tree.

This results in an increase of 3.71 % (1.2 ms), which is negligible compared to the increased obtained in section 4.2. This simple experiment shows how the requests are processed in parallel when we add servers on an independent branch. Thus, the strategy to add new servers has to be carefully examined. In the next experiment, we test different ways to add new servers on a simple DIET tree and try to figure out some basic rules for establishing a DIET hierarchy.

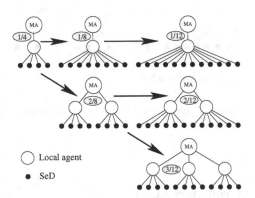

○ Local agent

● SeD

Fig. 10. Tested configurations.

Trying several architectures to add servers. In this experiment, we only consider trees that have a depth of one LA. These configurations can involve more LAs as long as there is one and only one LA between the MA and an SeD. This allows us to make comparisons between them when the number of SeDs is the same. Figure 10 shows the configurations used in this experiment. The name of each configuration depends on its number of LAs and SeDs (e.g., configuration (1/4) involves one LA and four SeDs). Every time we create a new configuration, we add four servers to an existing configuration. Several configurations can be generated this way from one given configuration. We used six of them during this experiment.

The results are as follows:

configuration	1/4	1/8	2/8	1/12	2/12	3/12
request time (ms)	58.8	69.6	60.9	74.4	62.6	62.9

The average submission time is 58.8 ms for the first configuration. When four new servers directly subscribe to the existing LA (configuration 1/8), this leads to an increase of 18.36 %(10.8 ms). If they subscribe to a new LA (configuration 2/8), the overhead cost is only 3.5 % (2.1 ms). This demonstrates the benefits of using two LAs to send requests simultaneously to several servers.

The last column of Figure 10 shows configurations with twelve SeDs. The first one (1/12) is obtained by adding four more SeDs on the only LA of configuration 1/8. This leads to a request process time of 74.4 ms. The two other configurations with twelve SeDs are obtained with two LAs holding six SeDs each and three LAs holding four SeDs each. These two configurations give similar results. This shows that adding a new LA is only necessary for a certain amount of new SeDs. With twelve SeDs, the time difference between the best and the worst architecture is 11.8 ms (which implies an increase of 16 %). This difference may increase with a higher number of SeDs.

This experiment shows the impact of the architecture on the performance of the system. Obviously, architectures that place LAs in parallel perform better than the others. Tuning such an architecture is a matter of knowledge of the underlying network. Some branches may contain more SeDs than others for various reasons (technical or administrative ones) but these results should be kept in mind when building a DIET tree.

5   Conclusion and Future Work

In this paper we have presented our view of a scalable Network Enabled Server system. We believe that hierarchy is mandatory when building such environments for the Grid. When thinking about Grid Computing, scalability should be one of the main concerns of developers. We propose a hierarchical approach to Network Enabled Servers using existing software and standards such as NWS, LDAP or Corba.

Our architecture was also validated experimentally, and it seems that performance of the DIET platform is closely linked to the structure of the tree. Thus, a well suited DIET tree can significantly improve the performance of the system, as long as two main constraints are taken into account:

 – the DIET tree should be mapped onto the physical network architecture for faster request broadcasting and more accurate performance predictions;
 – the use of an LA hierarchy can have an impact on the performance, as soon as a large amount of SeDs is connected, by introducing parallelism in the request processing.

Our future work will first focus on testing this approach on real applications from our project partners. These applications arise from various scientific fields: digital elevation models (tridimensional model computed from two 2D satellite pictures), microwave circuits simulation, molecular dynamics (simulation of atomic trajectories from molecular interactions), as well as an application computing the points of a hypersurface in quantum chemistry. Some other applications (from genetics or sparse solver fields, for instance) aims at using DIET. As one of our target platforms allows 2.5 Gb/s communications between several INRIA research centers in France, connecting several clusters of PCs and parallel machines, such applications written in an RPC mode could benefit from DIET and the whole platform. Thus the powerful computational resources needed for such application can be utilized that could not otherwise be obtained.

After we have implemented a solution to the duplicate choice of a server (see section 3.3), we would like to tackle the issue of fault tolerance. Our work about this domain acts at several levels. Indeed the crash of a server implies to restart computations running on it. For long time computations, checkpoint mechanisms have to be used to reduce the overhead introduced by the crash. When one of the agents is lost, we have to rebuild the hierarchy as soon as possible. Indeed if persistent data are stored in the subtree of that agent, these data are no longer available. The first point to consider is the detection of the crash. A simple solution is to use timeouts on communications between agents. Once a breakdown detected the rebuilding of the hierarchy has to be performed. A possible solution is to stored in each LA the list of LAs connecting it to the MA. Each son of a lost server can then contact its grandfather. When a MA is lost, we only have considered a solution where clients have to contact an other MA and restart their sessions. In such a case the LAs of this branch have to inform servers.

A problem we would also like to address is the optimization of data distribution for parallel library calls using a mixed data and task parallel approach. We also would like to connect our developments to infrastructure toolkits like Globus to benefit from their development as regards security, accounting, and interoperability of services.

Acknowledgements. This work was supported in part by the projects ACI GRID–GRID ASP and RNTL GASP funded by the French department of research.

References

1. J.-L. Anthoine, P. Chatonnay, D. Laiymani, J.-M. Nicod, and L. Philippe. Parallel Numerical Computing Using Corba. In H. R. Arabnia, editor, *Parallel and Distributed Processing Techniques and Applications (PDPTA'98)*, volume III, pages 1221 – 1228. CSREA Press, july 1998.
2. P. Arbenz, W. Gander, and M. Oettli. The Remote Computational System. *Parallel Computing*, 23(10):1421–1428, 1997.
3. D. Arnold, S. Agrawal, S. Blackford, J. Dongarra, M. Miller, K. Sagi, Z. Shi, and S. Vadhiyar. Users' Guide to NetSolve V1.4. Computer Science Dept. Technical Report CS-01-467, University of Tennessee, Knoxville, TN, July 2001. http://www.cs.utk.edu/netsolve/.
4. E. Caron and F. Suter. Parallel Extension of a Dynamic Performance Forecasting Tool. In *Proceedings of the International Symposium on Parallel and Distributed Computing*, Iasi, Romania, July 2002.

5. A. Denis, C. Perez, and T. Priol. Towards high performance CORBA and MPI middlewares for grid computing. In Craig A. Lee, editor, *Proc. of the 2nd International Workshop on Grid Computing*, number 2242 in LNCS, pages 14–25, Denver, Colorado, USA, November 2001. Springer-Verlag.
6. M.C. Ferris, M.P. Mesnier, and J.J. Mori. NEOS and Condor: Solving Optimization Problems Over the Internet. *ACM Transaction on Mathematical Sofware*, 26(1):1–18, 2000. http://www-unix.mcs.anl.gov/metaneos/publications/index.html.
7. I. Foster and C. Kesselman (Eds.). *The Grid: Blueprint for a New Computing Infrastructure*. Morgan-Kaufmann, 1998.
8. E. N. Houstis and J. R. Rice.   On the future of problem solving environments. http://www.cs.purdue.edu/homes/jrr/pubs/kozo.pdf, 2000.
9. S. Matsuoka and H. Casanova. Network-Enabled Server Systems and the Computational Grid.
    http://www.eece.unm.edu/~dbader/grid/WhitePapers/
    GF4-WG3-NES-whitepaper-draft-000705.pdf, July 2000. Grid Forum, Advanced Programming Models Working Group whitepaper (draft).
10. S. Matsuoka, H. Nakada, M. Sato, , and S. Sekiguchi. Design Issues of Network Enabled Server Systems for the Grid.
    http://www.eece.unm.edu/~dbader/grid/WhitePapers/satoshi.pdf,
    2000. Grid Forum, Advanced Programming Models Working Group whitepaper.
11. H. Nakada, M. Sato, and S. Sekiguchi. Design and Implementations of Ninf: towards a Global Computing Infrastructure. *Future Generation Computing Systems, Metacomputing Issue*, 15(5-6):649–658, 1999. http://ninf.apgrid.org/papers/papers.shtml.
12. OMNIORB. http://www.uk.research.att.com/omniORB/.
13. M. Quinson. Dynamic performance forecasting for network-enabled servers in a metacomputing environment. In *International Workshop on Performance Modeling, Evaluation, and Optimization of Parallel and Distributed Systems (PMEO-PDS'02)*, April 15-19 2002.
14. R. Wolski, N. T. Spring, and J. Hayes. The Network Weather Service: A Distributed Resource Performance Forecasting Service for Metacomputing. *Future Generation Computing Systems, Metacomputing Issue*, 15(5–6):757–768, Oct. 1999.

A Server Selection Method Based on Communication Delay and Communication Frequency among Users for Networked Virtual Environments

Kazutoshi Fujikawa[1], Masato Hori[2], Shinji Shimojo[3], and Hideo Miyahara[4]

[1] Information Technology Center, Nara Institute of Science and Technology
8916-5 Takayama, Ikoma, Nara 630-0101, Japan
fujikawa@itc.aist-nara.ac.jp
[2] ORACLE CORPORATION JAPAN
4-1 Kioi-cho, Chiyoda-ku, Tokyo 102-0094, Japan
Masato.Hori@oracle.com
[3] Cybermedia Center, Osaka University
5-1 Mihogaoka, Ibaraki, Osaka 567-0047, Japan
shimojo@cmc.osaka-u.ac.jp
[4] Guraduate School of Information Science and Technology, Osaka University
1-3 Machikaneyama, Toyonaka, Osaka 560-8531, Japan
{m-hori, miyahara}@ics.es.osaka-u.ac.jp

Abstract. In Net-VEs, since a user moves about virtual space and inter-acts with other users, Net-VE system needs to take into consideration the position of the user in virtual space, in addition to the state of a network and a server. In this paper, we propose a new server selection method that can choose the servers from the point of view of both communication delay concerned with the position on a network and the communication frequency concerned with the position on virtual space. Our proposed method collects users with high communication frequency as one group and lets users of the group connect with the same server. In addition, a server where users connect is chosen based on the communication delay from the user in a group to the server. Thus, our Net-VE system can choose servers on which users can exchange updates quickly.

1 Introduction

In recent years, since the Internet spreads rapidly and widely with high-speed backbone networks, Networked Virtual Environments (Net-VEs), where user can share a virtual space and interact with each other, become popular[1,7]. Net-VE offers a virtual space through a network to users and they can share the virtual space. In Net-VE, a user can move about the virtual space freely using the character called "avatar" and have interactions such as conversation and competition by exchanging "updates" of the virtual space.

In the existing Net-VE applications, there are three kinds of architecture, the Peer-to-Peer architecture, the Client-Server architecture, and the Client-Server architecture with Multiple Servers.

A. Jean-Marie (Ed.): ASIAN 2002, LNCS 2550, pp. 125–139, 2002.

On the Peer-to-Peer architecture [4], users exchange "updates" with each other directly. Therefore, the Peer-to-Peer architecture can minimize communication delay. However, the load of each user's computer becomes high rapidly as the number of users increases.

On the Client-Server architecture [8], there is a server which manages the information of virtual space. A server provides a user with virtual space and each user exchanges "updates" through the computer used as a client. On this architecture, virtual space of each client can be kept the same, and the load of a client is mitigated. However, since a server must receive updates of all clients, update the virtual space, and transmit its changes to all clients, if the number of users in virtual space increases, the server will be in a fault load state [3,11].

Client-Server architecture with Multiple Servers can lessen the number of clients that each server manages. In this architecture, it should be considered how to distribute clients to each server. In the existing system using this architecture, virtual space is divided and the method of assigning as space as for which each server carries out management space, and the way each client chooses the server to which communication delay becomes small, and connects based on the position on a network are adopted.

On the other hand, a contents delivery network (CDN) has been developing as technology for distributing data to a user quickly [6]. CDN is a network aiming at distributing contents to a user quickly according to the state of a network and a server. In CDN, multiple distribution servers perform contents distribution other than the server that receives the request of the contents acquisition from a user. The server, which receives the request, connects a user to the optimal distribution server. CDN mainly treats streaming data as contents. Such contents are likely to be distributed to many users, and the contents are seldom changed by users dynamically. Therefore, it is possible to choose a server only based on the state of a network and a server, when a user sends a request. However, in Net-VE system, since a user moves about virtual space and interacts with other users, Net-VE system needs to take into consideration the position of the user in virtual space, in addition to the state of a network and a server.

If all the combination of users and servers is investigated, Net-VE system can ask for the optimal selection of servers. However, since users move about virtual space, if the selection of servers takes much time, it may be meaningless. Then, it is necessary to quickly choose the servers on which users can exchange "updates" of virtual space with short communication delay.

In this paper, we propose a new server selection method that can choose the servers from the point of view of both communication delay concerned with the position on a network and the communication frequency concerned with the position on virtual space. If users that have the high communication frequency with each other connect with the same server, they can exchange updates quickly. Moreover, each user had better connect with the server of short communication delay. Our proposed method collects users with high communication frequency as one group and lets users of the group connect with the same server. A server where users connect is chosen based on the communication delay from the user in a group to the server. Thus, our Net-VE system can choose servers on which users can exchange updates quickly. Moreover, since it is not necessary to investigate all the combination of servers and users, servers can be chosen in short time.

This paper is organized as follows. We discuss the problem of Net-VE system based on multiple servers. Section 3 discusses our proposed method for server selection and section 4 evaluates the proposed method. Finally, section 5 provides our conclusions.

2   Problem of Client-Server Architecture with Multiple Servers

Usually, Net-VE systems of the Client-Server architecture with Multiple Servers, a user connects with a single server, and a user exchanges "updates" of virtual space with other users via servers. Each user transmits updates to a server, and the server which receives updates waits a certain time for updates from any user. Then, the update with the earliest generating time is adopted as an actual update, and virtual space will be updated. The update of the virtual space is transmitted to the user whose visible region of virtual space includes the updated portion.

In the existing Net-VE systems, there are two methods for choosing the server that each user connects: One is the method choosing a server only based on the position on virtual space [5], and the other is the method choosing a server only based on the position on a network [9]. The former method is called "virtual space precedence method" and the latter is called "network precedence method." By the virtual space precedence method, Net-VE system divides virtual space according to the number of the servers. The divided virtual space is assigned to a server. In this method, a user connects with the server which manages the space where he/she exists. Therefore, the communication delay would become large.

By the network precedence method, a user connects with the server corresponding to the position on a network. In this method, since the position relation on virtual space is not taken into consideration at all, the case that users, which interact with each other, have connected to the different servers occurs frequently. Since communication not only between user and server but also between servers occurs, the time for exchanging updates will become large.

In order to solve such problems, Net-VE system should take into consideration both the position on virtual space and the position on a network. If the position on virtual space is taken into consideration, it is better to connect users who interact with each other to the same server, and it is not necessary to connect users who do not exchange data to the same server. Moreover, in case the position on a network is taken into consideration, Net-VE system have to take into consideration not only the communication delay between a user and a server, but also communication delay between users who exchange data. Therefore, by collecting such users as one group and making users in a group connect with the same server, Net-VE system can perform exchange of updates among users efficiently.

3   Server Selection Method

In this section, we propose a new server selection method that can determine which server a user connect with, in consideration of both the position on a virtual space and the position on a network. By using our proposed method, users in virtual space can exchange data with each other in short communication delay.

3.1   User Group Based on Communication Frequency

By collect the users who exchange data frequently as one group, and making the users in a group connect with the same server, users can exchange data via single server. Below, we describe the algorithm for making a user group.

Relation of the Distance between Users and the Communication Frequency. We suppose that a user interacts with users in his/her visible region frequently. Therefore, it is desirable that users whose visible regions are overlapped connect with the same server.

Making User Group. The purpose of making a user group is collecting the users that exchange updates of virtual space. That is, a user belongs to the group that another user in his/her visible region does. Our proposed method uses the size of visible region as a criterion for making a user group. However, when there are few users in virtual space, groups, each of which have only one user, may be created too much. Conversely, when there are many users, the number of users in a group increases too much. Therefore, when there are few users in virtual space, several user groups will be merged into a single group, and when there are many users in virtual space, a user group is divided into several group of small region.

3.2   Server Selection Based on Communication Delay

Now, we explain how to select a server for users in a group. In our proposed method, the two methods, which will be described below, are properly used according to the result of making user group.

- Using a linear programming
- Based on average communication delay between users and servers

Selecting a Server using a Linear Programming. The method of selecting a server using a linear programming is called "linear programming method." When fulfilling the following condition for a set of user groups, the subject of a server selection for each group can be formulized using AMPL [2], and can be solved using linear programming.

- A user exchanges data with only the users in the same group

A server will be selected for a group so that the maximum communication delay between users should not exceed a certain time and the average communication delay may become the smallest.

The formulization using AMPL about selection of a server is explained below. Let a set of users, a set of servers, and a set of groups be $C = \{c_1, c_2, ..., c_i\}$, $S = \{s_1, s_2, ..., s_j\}$, and $G = \{g_1, g_2, ..., g_k\}$, respectively. Any user belongs to one of groups, and all users that belong to the same group connect with the same server. Let the number of users belonging to Group g_l be $|g_l|$. And, let communication delay between the user c_m and the server s_n be $d_{c_m s_n}$. Let $P_{g_p s_q}$ represent whether g_p connects with s_q. $P_{g_p s_q}$ can be defined as follows:

$$P_{g_p s_q} = \begin{cases} 0 & \text{(if } g_p \text{ does not connect with } s_q) \\ 1 & \text{(if } g_p \text{ connect with } s_q) \end{cases} \tag{1}$$

Let N_{max} and D_{max} be the maximum number of users which can be connected to a single server and the maximum permissible communication delay. The constraints for selecting a server are as follows:

- Each group connects with only one server. (Exp. (2))
- The number of users connected to each server does not exceed the maximum permissible number of users. (Exp. (3))
- Communication delay from a user in a group to a server does not exceed the maximum permissible communication delay. (Exp. (4))

$$\sum_{s_u} P_{g_t s_u} = 1 \tag{2}$$

$$\sum_{g_v} |g_v| P_{g_v s_w} = N_{max} \tag{3}$$

$$\max_{c_x \in G_y} (d_{c_x s_z}) \leq D_{max} \tag{4}$$

By defining the objective function of a linear programming under the above constraints and finding the minimum value of the objective function, our proposed method can select the server connected for users of each group.

Selecting a Server based on Average Communication Delay between Users and Servers. The method of selecting a server based on average communication delay between users and servers is called "average communication delay method." If the relation between user groups and servers cannot be adapted as a linear programming, our proposed method will use average communication delay method. In his method, the maximum communication delay as well as average communication delay is considered. A server is selected to each group so that average communication delay may become as small as possible, and in addition, the maximum communication delay should not exceed a certain value. Below, the algorithm of this method will be described.

We suppose that the communication delay to all servers from each user are known. In order that users can exchange data within a certain time, our proposed method defines the maximum permissible communication delay between user and server. When at least one communication delay between a server and users in a group exceeds the maximum permissible one, the server will not be added to a server list for the group. Otherwise, the server will be done. The average communication delay between group and each server in a server list is calculated. The servers in a server list are arranged in order with the small value of average communication delay.

Now, we show an example in Fig. 1. In this figure, there are four user's terminals in a group (Group 1) and three servers. Here suppose that the maximum permissible communication delay is 150 ms. Since the communication delay between User A and Server 3 the maximum permissible one of 180 ms, Server 3 will not be added to the server list of Group 1. The server list of Group 1 is shown in Table 1.

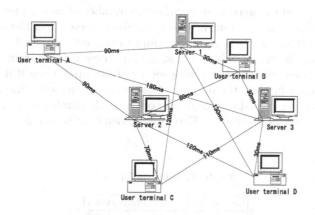

Fig. 1. Communication delay between users and servers

Table 1. Table of server list of Group 1

Group No.	# of users	server IDs
1	4	2,1

Basically, each user selects a server from its own server list. In case of that the maximum permissible number of users in a server exceeds by a group connects with the server, the group cannot select the server. To avoid such a situation, server selection for each group is performed as follows: A group with few servers in its server list can determine a server where users in the group connect, to avoid the situation that all the servers in a server list have been already selected by other groups. When there are several groups with the same number of servers in their own server list, the group with more users can select a server preferentially. Consequently, it makes the average communication delay smaller if the group with more users can select a server preferentially. Thus, our proposed method decides the turn of groups to select a server. Then, each group determine its own server.

As an example of server selection, the case there are four groups and four servers is considered. The server list of each group is shown in Table 2. Here, we suppose that the maximum permissible number of users in a server is 10 users. At first, Server 1 is selected as a server of Group 1 with the fewest number of servers in the server list. The other entire groups have four servers in their server list. Since Group 2 has the most number of users, Group 2 can choose Server 2. Next, Server 2 of a higher rank in the server list of Group 3 has already been chosen as a server of Group 2, and eight users connect with Server 2. If the users of Group 3 connect with Server 2, the number of users of Server 2 will become 13, and will exceed the maximum permissible number of users. Therefore, Server 2 cannot be chosen as a server of Group 3. Since Server 3 in the second of the server list of Group 3 is not chosen by any group yet, Server 3 is chosen as a server of Group 3. Server 3 is the first in the server list of Group 4. Although Server 3 has already been chosen as a server of Group 3, even if it chooses as a server of Group 4 further, the number of users connected with Server 3 becomes eight, and does not exceed the maximum permissible number of users. Therefore, Server 4 is chosen as a server of Group 4. A result of server selection is shown in Table 3.

Table 2. Table of server list

Group No.	# of users	server IDs
1	10	1,2,3
2	8	2,4,3,1
3	5	2,3,1,4
4	3	3,2,4,1

4   Evaluation

4.1   Comparison of Communication Delay

We evaluates whether the exchange of data is efficiently performed by using our proposed method. Let the communication delay between the user c_i and the server s_j and the one between the server s_k and the server s_l be $d_{c_i s_j}$ and $d_{s_k s_l}$, respectively.

Table 3. Selected servers for each group

Group No.	# of users	selected server
1	10	1
2	8	2
3	5	3
4	3	3

We define processing time L_{s_m} of the data in the server s_m as follows:

$$L_{s_m} = \alpha N_{s_m} + \beta R + \gamma \tag{5}$$

where R represents the number of servers in a Net-VE system and N_{s_m} represents the number of users connected with the server s_m. Here, α, β, and γ are constants and we define $\alpha = \frac{1}{10}, \beta = 5$, and $\gamma = 10$.

For the evaluation, the response time between the user c_p and the user c_q is defined as described below. When a user generates an update of virtual space, he/she has to transmit the update to all users in his/her visible region. The formula of response time differs by whether all users in the visible region connect with the same server, or with a different server.

Case 1: All users in the visible region connect with the same server
The user c_p which generates an update transmits the update to a server s_t. The server, which received the update, waits a certain time until it determines whether virtual space reflects the update. The waiting time Wc_{s_t} can be defined by using the largest communication delay between the server and users as in the following expression.

$$Wc_{s_t} = \max_{c_q \in g_i}(d_{c_q s_t}) - d_{c_p s_t} \tag{6}$$

Therefore, the response time $f1_{c_p c_q}$ for an update can be represented by the following expression.

$$f1_{c_p c_q} = d_{c_p s_t} + Wc_{s_t} + L_{s_t} + \max_{c_q \in g_i}(d_{c_q s_{tu}}) \tag{7}$$

Case 2: All users in the visible region do not connect with the same server
The user c_p which generates an update transmits the update to a server s_t. The server, which received the update, waits a certain time until it determines whether virtual space reflects the update. To determine the waiting time, we have to take into consideration the case where an update comes from a user connected with a different server. The waiting time Wd_{s_t} can be defined as in the following expression.

$$Wd_{s_t} = \begin{cases} Wc_{s_t} + d_{s_t s_u} & (Wc_{s_t} + d_{s_t s_u} >= Wc_{s_u}) \\ Wc_{s_u} & (Wc_{s_t} + d_{s_t s_u} < Wc_{s_u}) \end{cases} \tag{8}$$

Therefore, the response time $f2_{c_p c_q}$ for an update can be represented by the following expression.

$$f2_{c_p c_q} = d_{c_p s_t} + L_{s_t} + d_{s_t s_u} + W d_{s_u} + \max_{c_q \in g_i}(d_{c_q s_u}) \tag{9}$$

The average value $Time_R$ of the response time can be expressed as Exp. 10. Here, N_C is the number of users in virtual space.

$$Time_R = \frac{\sum_{c_p \in C} f1_{c_p c_q} + \sum_{c_p \in C} f2_{c_p c_q}}{N_C} \tag{10}$$

4.2   Simulations

We suppose the following two environments for simulations.

- When users spread over the world wide
  - Communication delay between user and server: 50-100 ms
  - Communication delay between servers: 50-250 ms
- When users spread over the nation wide
  - Communication delay between user and server: 50-150 ms
  - Communication delay between servers: 10-50 ms

As a Net-VE system for simulations, there are nine servers, are we suppose that the maximum permissible number of users for a server is ten. In the simulations, we increase the number of users in virtual space from 10 to 90 by five. We will perform 50 simulations to each number of users, to measure the average of response time and the ratio to which data would exchange via several servers. Users are arranged at random on virtual space and a network.

In this paper, we will perform simulation experiments about the following three methods.

1. Average communication delay method that we proposed (Method 1)
2. Virtual space precedence method (Method 2)
3. Network precedence method (Method 3)

We will verify effectiveness of both the way of making user group and the way of server selection.

Making User Group. Here, we verify the effectiveness of making user group discussed in Section 3.1. Servers will be selected by the method mentioned in Section 3.2. Moreover, the simulations for virtual space precedence method and network precedence method will be done using the same servers as selected by average communication delay method. We will measure the response time in each method and the probability of exchange of data will be performed through several servers.

Server Selection. Here, we verify the effectiveness of selecting servers based on the communication delay between users and servers. When the user groups are given, we will compare the response time of using servers selected by the average communication delay method, and the one of using servers selected at random.

Comparison with the Optimal Server Selection. In addition to the above simulations, the following comparison is performed in order to verify the validity of our proposed server selection method. When a set of user groups is given, we will compare the linear programming method, the average communication delay method, and the optimal server selection.

The optimal server selection here can be calculated by investigating all the combination of servers and user groups. To compare these three methods, a set of user groups that fills the following conditions is given so that the linear programming method can be applied.

- A user exchanges data with only the users in the same group.
- The number of users in a group does not exceed the maximum permissible number of users in a server.

The objective function $Time$ for the optimal server selection is defined as follows. The response time $f3_{c_p c_q}$ between user c_p and user c_q is calculated as Exp. (13) by using the communication delay $D_{c_p c_q}$ between c_p and c_q calculated by Exp. (11), and the processing time L_{s_j} in the server s_j calculated by Exp. (12). In the objective function, the response time $f3_{c_p c_q}$ is normalized by the distance between users calculated using the communication frequency between user c_p and user c_q represented by Exp. (15).

$$D_{c_p c_q} = \begin{cases} \sum_{c_p \in g_i} \sum_{c_q \in g_i} \sum_S P_{g_i s_j} d_{c_p s_j} + d_{c_q s_j} & (d_{c_p s_j} >= d_{c_q s_j}) \\ \sum_{c_p \in g_i} \sum_{c_q \in g_i} \sum_S P_{g_i s_j} 2 d_{c_q s_j} & (d_{c_p s_j} < d_{c_q s_j}) \end{cases} \quad (11)$$

$$L_{s_j} = \frac{1}{10} \sum_G |g_i| P_{g_i s_j} + 5 \sum_G \sum_S P_{g_i s_j} + 10 \quad (12)$$

$$f3_{c_p c_q} = D_{c_p c_q} + L_{s_j} \quad (13)$$

$$Time = \frac{\sum_G \sum_{c_p \in g_i} F_{c_p c_q} f3_{c_p c_q}}{N_C} \quad (14)$$

$$F_{c_p c_q} = \frac{\frac{1}{l_{c_p c_q}}}{\frac{1}{l_{c_p c_1}} + \frac{1}{l_{c_p c_2}} + \dots + \frac{1}{l_{c_p c_n}}} \quad (15)$$

Here, let the distance between user c_p and user c_q in a virtual space be $l_{c_p c_q}$.

We assume the network of world wide as simulation environment. In the simulations, there are four servers, and the maximum permissible number of users in a server is defined as 10. Users are arranged at random on virtual space and a network. The simulations are performed for 20 users and 40 users and we measure the average value of response time.

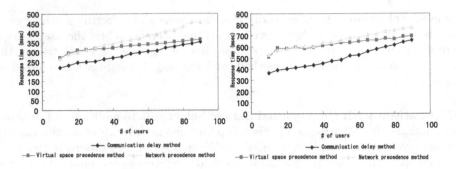

Fig. 2. Average response time of exchanging data in nation wide Internet (left) and in world wide Internet (right)

4.3 Simulation Results

The results of three simulations are shown below and the effectiveness of the proposed method is verified.

Verification of the Effectiveness of Making User Group.

– In the case of the network of nation wide
  Fig. 2 (left) shows the average value of the response time of exchanging data among users on the network of nation wide.
  Table 4 shows the ratio of data exchanging through only one server. Using the virtual space precedence method, the ratio is the highest. When the network precedence method is used, most of the data are exchanged through several servers.

Table 4. Ratio of data exchanging through only one server in nation wide Internet

# of users	Method 1	Method 2	Method 3
30	89.4%	92.6%	33.3%
60	84.0%	86.1%	15.6%
90	74.3%	80.2%	11.5%

– In the case of the network of world wide
  Fig. 2 (right) shows the average value of the response time of exchanging data among users on the network of world wide. Table 5 shows the ratio of exchanging data through only one server. Using the virtual space precedence method as well as the case of the network of nation wide, the ratio is the highest. When the network precedence method is used, most of the data are exchanged through several servers.

Table 5. Ratio of data exchanging through only one server in world wide Internet

# of users	Method 1	Method 2	method 3
30	91.5%	91.8%	28.9%
60	82.3%	84.2%	15.9%
90	75.8%	79.8%	12.3%

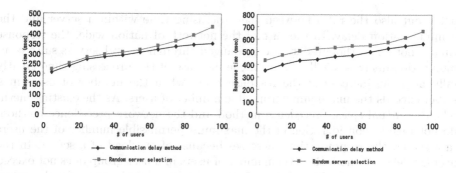

Fig. 3. Average response time of exchanging data in nation wide Internet (left) and in world wide Internet (right)

Verification of the Effectiveness of Server Selection.

- In the case of the network of nation wide
  Fig. 3 (left) shows the average value of the response time of exchanging data among users on the network of nation wide.
- In the case of the network of world wide
  Fig. 3 (right) shows the average value of the response time of exchanging data among users on the network of world wide.

Comparison with the Optimal Server Selection. Table 6 shows the average of the response time of using the average communication delay method (Method A), the linear programming method (Method B), and using the optimal server selection (Method C). The average communication delay method can serve as a few of increase as compared with the optimal server selection. Moreover, it seems that the response time of the linear programming method and the optimal server selection is almost the same, and this difference depends on the difference of the communication delay between users and servers and the difference of the communication delay among servers.

4.4 Consideration

It is thought that the difference between the network of nation wide and the network of world wide depends on not only the difference of the communication

Table 6. Comparison of response time between the proposed method and the optimal server selection

# of users	Method A	Method B	Method C
20	412.2msec	401.4msec	399.1msec
40	479.7msec	469.1msec	464.5msec

delay but also the ratio between the processing time within a server and the communication delay. In the case of the network of nation wide, the response time is not large, though data are exchanged through several servers since communication delay is small. However, the increase of the processing time greatly influences the increase of the response time, when the number of users in a server exceeds the maximum permissible number of users. As the existing methods, the virtual space precedence method and the network precedence method, do not take in consideration of the maximum permissible number of the users in a server, the response time increases because of overload of a server. In the average delay method, since the number of users in a user group does not exceed the maximum permissible number of users in a server in the case of making user groups, the response time can be small.

In the case of the network of world wide, since the processing time in a server is small compared with communication delay, the processing time does not influence the response time. Since communication delay is large, the time of exchanging data through several servers greatly influences the response time.

In Fig. 2 (right) and Fig. 3 (right), the difference of selecting servers using the average communication delay method and selecting servers at random becomes large as the number of users increases. If the number of users in a user group increases, it seems that the influence on the response time by selecting servers becomes large. Since the difference of the best values of the response time of selecting servers at random and the response time of selecting servers by the average communication delay method is large, it can be said about server selection that the selection technique is very effective.

When the response time of the optimal server selection is compared with the ones of the average communication delay method and the linear programming method as shown in Table 6, the difference is quite small. Therefore, it can be said that our proposed method is effective.

Now, we will compare the orders of calculation of the optimal server selection and the average communication delay method. Finding the optimal user group division is NP-complete problem [10]. Therefore, we compare the order of the average communication delay method with the order of the optimal server selection when the user groups are given. Here, let the number of users and the number of servers be N and S, respectively. The order of average communication delay method is $O(N)$. On the other hand, since all the combination of users and servers must be investigated in order to find the optimal server selection, the order becomes $O(NS^N)$. Therefore, it is possible in time when the calculation of the average communication delay method can be carried out in short time.

5   Conclusion

In this paper, we proposed a new server selection method for Net-VE systems based on client-server architecture with multiple servers. In order to exchange updates efficiently among users, our proposed method handles users who interact or recognize each other in a virtual space as a group, and selects the optimal server for the user group. Processing time will become large when group division is carried out by investigating the all combination of users. Therefore, the proposed method considered the frequency of data exchange among users from the position of users in a virtual space for making user groups. Moreover, if the communication delay between every server and every client would be calculated in the case of the server selection for a user group, the response time could be the minimum but it would take quite long time. In order to cope with such a problem, our proposed method selects a server for a user group based on the communication delay from the user in a group to a server. To evaluate our proposed method, we have done some simulations and showed the effectiveness of our proposed method. Furthermore, comparing our proposed method with the optimal server selection, the response time of our proposed method is almost the same as the one of the optimal server selection. Considering the time for calculation, it can be said that our proposed method is sufficiently effective.

As future works, we have to investigate how the size of user groups and the deployment of servers can influence Net-VE systems. Moreover, we should cope with how to change user groups and server selection when users move around in a large-scale virtual space.

Acknowledgment. This work was partly supported by Special Coordination Funds for promoting Science and Technology of the Ministry of Education, Culture, Sports, Science and Technology of Japan.

References

1. S. Benford, C. Greenhalgh, T. Rodden, and J. Pycock, "Collaborative Virtual Envrionments," *Commnications of the ACM*, pp.79-85, July 2001.
2. R. Fourer, D. M. Gay, and B. W. Kerinighan, *AMPLE A Modeling Language for Mathematical Programming.* boyd & fraser publishing company, 1993.
3. T.A. Funkhouser, "RING: A Client-Server System for Multi-user Virtual Environments," *Proceedings of ACM SIGGRAPH Special Issue on 1995 Symposium on Interactive 3D Graphics*, pp.85-92, 1995.
4. L. Gautier and C. Diot, "End-to-End Transmission Control Mechanisms for Multiparty Interactive Application on the Internet," *Proceedings of IEEE INFOCOM'99*, vol.3, pp.1470-1479, March 1999.
5. M. Hori, T. Iseri, K. Fujikawa, S. Shimojo, and H. Miyahara, "CittaTron: a Multiple-server Networked Game with Load Adjustment Mechanisms on the Internet," *Proceedings of the 2001 SCS Euromedia Conference*, pp.253-260, April, 2001.
6. B. Hulsebosch, "Content Distribution Networks," available at https://doc.telin.nl/dscgi/ds.py/Get/File-15534/cdnsota.pdf.

7. R. Lea, Y. Honda, and K. Matsuda, "Virtual Society: Collaboration in 3D Spaces on the Internet," *Computer Supported Cooperative Working*, vol.6, pp.227-250, 1997. available at `http://www.csl.sony.co.jp/person/rodger/CSCW/cscw.html`
8. M.R. Macedonia and M.J. Zyda, "A Taxonomy for Networked Virtual Environments," *IEEE MultiMedia*, vol.43, pp.48-56, January-March 1997.
9. L. Rosenblum adn M. Macedonia, "NPSNET-V A new Beginning for Dynamically Extensible Virtual Environments," *IEEE Computer Graphics and Applications*, pp.12-15, September-October, 2000.
10. O.K. So, *Partitioning Problem in a Very Large Scale Distrituted Virtual Environment*. Ph.D thesis, The Chinese University of Hong Kong. 1998.
11. "Butterfly.net: MMG technology platform for online games," available at `http://www.butterfly.net`.

Towards an Application-Aware Multicast Communication Framework for Computational Grids*

Moufida Maimour and CongDuc Pham

RESO/LIP - UCB Lyon - ENS Lyon
ENS, Bât. LR5, 46 allée d'Italie
69364 Lyon Cedex 07, France
Congduc.Pham@ens-lyon.fr

Abstract. With a logical view closer to a distributed operating system than a pure communication infrastructure, one might consider extending for computational grids the basic functionalities found in the *commodity Internet*'s network infrastructure to a higher level, thus offering higher value functionalities than the standard IP routing functionality that has basically remained unchanged for 2 decades. In this paper, we report on our early experiences in building application-aware components for a multicast communication protocol targeted for providing low latencies and low overheads for applications running on a computational grid. Performance results from both simulations and implementation prototypes confirm that introducing application-aware components at specific location in the network infrastructure can succeed in providing not only performances for the end-users but also new perspectives in building a communication framework for computational grids.

1 Introduction

The simplest perception one has of a computational grid [4] is a pool of geographically distributed computers that can be accessed and used in a structured manner to solve a given problem. Such grid infrastructures are foreseen to be one of the most critical yet challenging technologies to meet the exponentially growing demands for high-performance computing in a large variety of scientific disciplines: high energy physics, weather prediction, mathematics and combinatorial problems, genome exploration. . . . In the past few years, many software environments for gaining access to very large distributed computing resources have been made available (e.g. Condor [10], Globus [5], Legion [7] to name a few). National and international projects have been launched all around the world to investigate the potential of grid computing: DataGrid (www.eu-datagrid.org), EuroGrid (www.eurogrid.org), GriPhyn (www.gryphyn.org), PPDG (www.ppdg.net) to name some of them.

---

* This work is supported in part by the french ACI Grid program and by the E-Toile project.

A. Jean-Marie (Ed.): ASIAN 2002, LNCS 2550, pp. 140–152, 2002.

There are many possible utilizations of a grid, not only intensive computing but also on-line access to expensive scientific instruments or huge storage capacity for instance. However the very basic nature of a grid is to allow a large community of people to share information and resources across a network infrastructure. Moving, distributing data from one location to some other locations are operations common to most of grid applications. Today, most of these applications imply a rather small number of participants and it is not clear whether there is a real need for very large groups of users. However, even with a small number of participants, the amount of data can be so huge that the time to complete the transfers can rapidly become unmanageable! More complex, fine-grained applications could have complex message exchange patterns such as collective operations and synchronization barriers.

With a logical view closer to a distributed operating system than a pure communication infrastructure, one might consider extending for computational grids the basic functionalities found in the   's network infrastructure to a higher level, thus offering higher value functionalities than the standard IP routing functionality that has basically remained unchanged for 2 decades. In that sense, these ideas are very similar to those of the peer-to-peer (P2P) and overlay community and those of emerging P2P applications (such as Napster or Gnutella) and web services. Going a step further, we want to embed more generally in the network infrastructure some well identified, generic and basic functions for computational grids in the same manner IP routing is a well identified, generic and basic functionality in the commodity Internet. Therefore application-aware components (AAC) are introduced as opposed to traditional Internet routers although the practical realization of such components would certainly be based on "enhanced routers". We think this approach is highly justifiable since a grid, being a specialized subset of the Internet, should have a specialized set of network services for the data transported in the grid. At the moment, it is highly difficult, perhaps impossible, to know exactly what is a typical grid application, if any, but one might be able to exhibit high-level services that could be common to a large number of distributed applications or communication protocols: caching, filtering, interest management, reduction, election... The general description of such a programmable, configurable grid, view as a distributed system with AACs can be found in [9]. More information on P2P for the grids can be found at http://www.peer-to-peerwg.org and http://openp2p.com.

In this paper, we report on our early experiences in building such application-aware components for a multicast communication protocol targeted for providing low latencies and low overheads for applications running on a computational grid. The AACs are practically realized with the active networking technology as it will be described later on. The rest of the paper is organized as follows. Section 2 presents the AAC technologies and the active networking approach. Section 3 describes the reliable multicast case and Section 4 presents the performance results. Section 5 concludes.

2   Application-Aware Component Technology

The AACs concept calls for an infrastructure of network elements capable of executing specific processing functions, mostly on-the-fly, on data flows. It is possible to build such an infrastructure by involving only end-hosts: it is the peer-to-peer paradigm. However, although this scheme may work, even on large scale systems such as demonstrated by the recently general public P2P applications, there are a number of drawbacks to this approach: redundancy of functionalities, high end-host overhead, limited range of applications...

Recently, a disruptive technology called "active networking" proposes a new vision for the Internet that involves routers (so-called active routers) in the processing of data packets. In active networking [15], routers can execute, through an execution environment similar to an operating system (ANTS [16] for instance), application-dependent functions on incoming packet. With new perspectives both for telco operators and end-users, the use of active network concepts has been proposed in many research areas including multicast protocols [17,8,2], distributed interactive simulations [18] and network management [14]. There are many difficulties, however, for deploying in a large scale an active networking infrastructure. Security and performance are two main difficulties that are usually raised. However, active networking has the ability to provide a very general and flexible framework for customizing network functionalities in order to gracefully handle heterogeneity and dynamicity, key points in a computational grid.

In order to implement the AAC concepts, there is no need to go for a complete active networking scheme with an open architecture and the many security pitfalls. It is possible to adopt an operator's perspective which consists in deploying some well identified services (similar to any protocol supported by a router nowadays), chosen for their genericity. However this approach needs a high amount of standardization thus only very generic and core services are likely to be deployed.

3   Case Study: Reliable Multicast on a Grid

As a first illustration of a programmable grid infrastructure, we present the work we have done in providing an efficient framework for reliable multicast transfers on a computational grid. Multicast [3] is the process of sending every single packet from the source to multiple destinations in the same logical multicast group. Since most of communications occurring on a grid imply many participants that can be geographically spread over the entire planet, these data transfers could be gracefully and efficiently handled by multicast protocols provided that these protocols are well-designed to suit the grid requirements. Motivations behind multicast are to handle one-to-many communications in a wide-area network with the lowest network and end-system overheads while achieving scalability (end-system or application-multicast solutions can succeed in providing low complexity but lack scalability). In contrast to best-effort multicast, that typically tolerates some data losses and is more suited for real-time audio or video for instance, reliable multicast requires that all packets are safely delivered to the destinations. Desirable features of reliable multicast include, in addition to reliability, low end-to-end delays, high throughput and scalability. These characteristics fit perfectly the need of the grid computing and distributed computing communities. Embedding multicast support in a grid infrastructure would not only optimize the network resources in term of bandwidth saving, but mainly increase both performances for applications, and interactivity for end-users, thus bringing the usage of grids to a higher level than it is at the moment (mainly batch job submission).

3.1 The DyRAM Framework

DyRAM [11] is a reliable multicast protocol suite that uses active network technology to off-load basic functionalities traditionally performed by the end-hosts in the commodity Internet. Several high-level mechanisms have thus been identified to improve the performances (latency, scalability) of a multicast communication and have been separated as application-aware services (AAS) to be off-loaded in the network infrastructure (in active routers for the practical realization). Therefore the end-host part of the protocol is quite light and the main AAS consist in:

1. the early detection of packet losses and the emission of the corresponding NACKs.
2. the suppression of duplicated NACKs (from end-hosts) in order to limit the NACK implosion problem.
3. the subcast of the repair packets only to the relevant set of receivers that have experienced a loss. This service limits the scope of the repairs to the affected subtree.
4. the dynamic replier election which consists in choosing a link/host as a replier one to perform local recoveries. Dynamic election provides robustness to host and link failures.

DyRAM has been designed with the following motivations in mind: (*i*) to minimize AAC's load to make them supporting more sessions (mainly in unloading them from the cache of data) and (*ii*) to reduce the recovery latency. Avoiding cache in AACs is performed by a dynamic replier election service. The elected replier in our case is dynamically determined at each lost packet, and not determined at the beginning of the multicast session as in [13] which is only updated when the group membership changes, thus justifying the "dynamic replier" property of the protocol.

3.2 Application-Aware Components and Services

There can be a large variety of grid infrastructures but in most cases they use a similar network architecture: local computing resources are connected together using any kind of local/system area networks (Fast/Giga Ethernet, Fiber Channel, SCI, Myrinet...) and gain access to the rest of the world through one or more routers. So we will mainly assume that the computing resources are distributed across an Internet-based network with a high-speed backbone network in the core (typically the one provided by the telecommunication companies) and several lower-speed (up to 1Gbits/s) access networks at the edge, with respect to the throughput range found in the backbone. Figure 1 depicts such a typical grid infrastructure. For simplicity we represented an access network by a router but practically such networks would contain several routers.

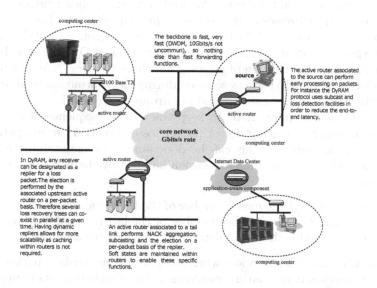

Fig. 1. DyRAM overview.

AACs could be hosted in Internet Data Center (deployed by an operator, difficult at this time) or in private domain, at the initiative of a computing center or a campus for example (very possible now, with AACs based on dedicated hardware such as powerful PC-based active routers). Within AACs, the early loss detection, the NACK suppression, the subcast and the replier election services can be implemented simply by maintaining information about the data packets and NACKs received. This set of information is uniquely identified by the session source and the multicast address. In principle, the nearest router to the backbone is a good location for installing the AAS. Also, in order to take advantage of the fast local recoveries with the replier election mechanism, it would be beneficial to have AACs close to the resource pools.

In the context of the DyRAM framework, all network elements at the edge are assumed to perform at least the NACK suppression and the subcast application-aware services. The AAC located at the sender's side, just before the core net-

work, is called the   . A preliminary study, detailed in [12], has shown
that the loss detection service is only beneficial if the loss detection capable
AAC is close enough to the source. Consequently the source AAC is the best
candidate to perform the loss detection service in addition to the two previous
services. The other AACs perform the replier election service.

NACK and data services. For each NACK received, the first upstream AAC
(either in Internet Data Center or in the private network) creates or simply
updates an existing NACK state (NS) structure which has a limited life time.
This structure maintains for every "nacked" packet, a subcast list (*subList*) that
contains the IP addresses of the receivers that experienced a loss.

On receipt of the first NACK packet for a data packet, the AAC would create
a corresponding NS structure, initialize a timer noted DTD (Delay To Decide)
that will trigger the election of a replier to whom this first NACK will be sent.
All subsequent NACK packets received during the timeout interval are used to
properly update the subcast list and are dropped afterward.

DyRAM also requires AAC to keep track of the sequence of received data
packets in order to quickly detect packet losses occurring from upstream and
affecting all its subtree. This can be done simply by maintaining a track list
structure (TL) for each multicast session handled by the AAC. A TL has three
components:

- *lastOrdered* is the sequence number of the last data packet received in order.
- *lastReceived* is the sequence number of the last received data packet.
- *lostList* contains the list of data packets not received by the router.

An AAC would detect a loss when a gap occurs in the data packet sequence.
The data service, in case no error occurred, then simply consists in updating the
track list. On a loss detection, the AAC would immediately generate a NACK
packet towards the source. If the AAC has already sent a similar NACK for a
lost packet then it would not send a NACK for a given amount of time (based
on a timer).

Dynamic replier election. Local recoveries, when possible, are performed
by elected receivers (repliers) that have correctly received the lost packet. The
replier election process executed by the first upstream AAC uses the *subList*
in the NS structure to determine which receiver can potentially be elected. The
algorithm basically works by comparing in the list of receivers which one does
not appear in the *subList* (there is no message exchanges during the election
process). However, the AAC does an on-the-fly election that consists in selecting
a default replier (the first receiver in the receiver list which is obtained during
the initialization session) when the first NACK arrives and updating the choice
of the replier at each NACK reception. The advantage of this approach is to
perform most of the election processing within the timer duration for gathering
NACK information. Once the election is completed, the AAC will forward the
NACK downstream toward the elected replier. This latter would then unicast

the repair packet to its upstream AAC which would in turn subcast the repair packet on all the links in the subcast list.

4   Performance Study

We implemented a simulation model of DyRAM (in the PARSEC language developed at UCLA [1]) and evaluated its performances on a network model. The network model considers one source that multicasts data packets to R receivers through a packet network composed of a fast core network and several slower edge access networks. AACs are located at the edge of the core network as described previously.

4.1   Local Recoveries and Replier Election

Figure 2a and 2b plot for DyRAM the number of retransmissions (M_S) from the source as a function of number the receivers and the completion time[1]. These results have been obtained from simulations of a multicast session with 48 receivers distributed among 12 local groups. The curves show that local recoveries decreases the load at the source as the number of receivers increases. This is especially true for high loss rates.

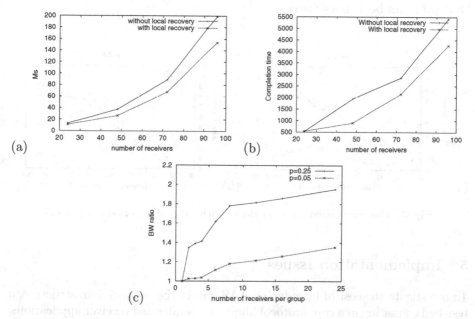

Fig. 2. (a) Load at the source, $p = 0.25$. (b) Completion time, $p = 0.25$. (c) Consumed bandwidth ratio.

---

[1] These 3 curves can be found in [11]. They are provided here for a better understanding of the paper.

Putting the recovery process in the receivers requires at least 2 receivers under a given AAC otherwise local recoveries can not be realized. Therefore the local group size (B) is an important parameter. In order to study the impact of B, simulations are performed with the 48 receivers distributed among groups of different sizes and figure 2c shows how much bandwidth (in ratio) can be saved with the local recovery mechanism. As the number of receivers per group increases, the consumed bandwidth is reduced by larger ratios for large loss rates. In fact, when the group size is larger it is more likely that the members of the group can recover from each other. For instance, figure 2c shows that with only 6 receivers per group and local recovery we can achieve a gain of 80%. This result is particularly interesting for distributed applications with many collective and reduction operations.

4.2 Early Loss Packet Detection

The next experiments show how the early loss detection service could decrease the delay of recovery. To do so, two cases noted DyRAM- and DyRAM+ are simulated. DyRAM- has no loss detection services whereas DyRAM+ benefits from the loss detection service in the source AAC. Figure 3 plots the recovery delay (normalized to the RTT) for the 2 cases as a function of the number of receivers. In general, the loss detection service allows DyRAM+ to complete the transfer faster than DyRAM-. For $p = 0.25$ and 96 receivers for instance, DyRAM+ can be 4 times faster.

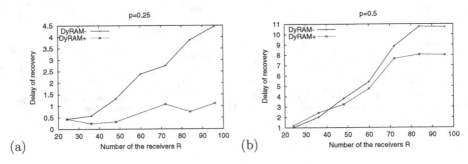

Fig. 3. The normalized recovery delay with (a) $p = 0.25$ and (b) $p = 0.5$

5 Implementation Issues

To investigate the cost of introducing AAS within the network infrastructure, a test-bed consisting in a core protocol library for sender and receiver applications, along with the previously described AAS has been developed in Java. The execution environment is Tamanoir [6]. Tamanoir can be installed on a linux-based PC and configured to act like a active router with dynamic download of user code into the execution environment.

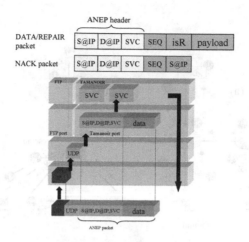

Fig. 4. Packet format and Tamanoir architecture.

5.1 Algorithms, Data Structures, and Packet Format

The track list (TL) is implemented as a double-linked list of bits (based on array implementation) that allows fast insertion/suppression of bits at the beginning/end of the list. The NS structure is handled with a hash table with the sequence number of the lost paper as the hash key. Each entry referred to a double-linked list of IP addresses (*subList*). In the current implementation, timers are handled by thread and a hash table of timer threads is used to maintain the list of timers. We will see later on that this approach may not be the best design choice.

Figure 4 depicts the data path of incoming messages. DyRAM packets used the ANEP [16] format and UDP is used for the transport as reliability is directly handle by DyRAM. We can see in the figure that incoming DyRAM packets are given to the Tamanoir execution environment (through the port number) which in turn selects the appropriate active service based on the SVC (service identifier) field.

5.2 Testbed and Scenario

The testbed consists in 2 PC-based AAC (Pentium II 400MHz, 512KByte cache, 128MByte RAM) running a Linux 2.4 kernel and a set of receivers. The Java version is 1.3.1.

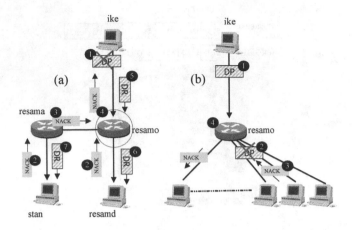

Fig. 5. (a) Topology 1: DP, NACK services and DR service. (b) Topology 2: replier election

2 configurations are used: topology 1, figure 5a, is used to measure the cost of packet services while topology 2, figure 5b is used to measure the cost of the dynamic replier election service. In the first configuration, the source `ike` multicasts packets to `stan` and `resamd` through 2 AACs. In order to measure the data services in this topology, one data packet is lost every 25 packets between the source and the first AAC `resamo`. Figure 5a shows the steps of the recovery process where the source is the replier: DP and DR refer respectively to Data Packet and Data Repair. The cost of the data packet service represents the processing time required to forward the packet to the destinations using the underlying IP multicast functionalities. Therefore, this cost is mainly an update of the track list when there is no sequence gap. In case of a gap sequence indicating a packet lost, the data service consists additionally in setting a timer for ignoring subsequent similar NACKs. The cost of the NACK service represents the processing time to update or create the NS. The cost of the data repair service represents the processing time of scanning the *subList* and to perform the subcast.

In topology 2, the source `ike` multicasts packets to a set of receivers through the AAC `resamo`. The cost of the replier election represents the processing time of comparing the *subList* list against the receiver list (obtained during the initialization session) in order to determine a replier for the lost data packet.

5.3 Cost of Active Services

Preliminary results on our testbed are illustrated in figure 6 and 7. Figure 6 shows the processing time in μs of a data packet, a repair packet and a NACK

packet at the `resamo` AAC. The x-axis shows the packet sequence number while
the y-axis shows the processing time. Data packet size is initially set to 4KByte.

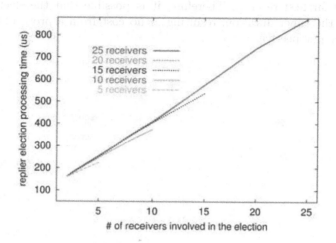

Fig. 6. Cost of packet services

We can see that, in the absence of packet losses, the processing time of a data
packet varies from $20\mu s$ to $40\mu s$. A gap in the x-axis represents a packet loss. For
instance, in our test scenario packet 49 is first lost thus making the processing
of packet 50 longer because of the loss detection and associated data structure
updates (track list, NS structures...). Figure 6 shows that each packet loss incur
an additional cost of about 12ms to 17ms for the next packet that corresponds
to the processing time for the data packet and the time for setting up a timer
thread for NACK discarding. It is worth to mention that the first overhead is only
about $250\mu s$! Several optimizations are possible for timer management (reuse of
old threads, only 1 thread with hash table for timer...) and we expect much
lower overheads in next implementations. The NACK packet and the repair
packet that follow the packet loss are processed in approximately $135\mu s$ and
$123\mu s$ respectively (for these packets, the x-axis indicates the current data packet
sequence number at the moment they are processed in order to respect the
chronological order). Varying the message size from 1KByte to 32KByte does
not change the results. To obtain the exact cost of introducing AAS, we must
add the cost for passing packet from the IP layer to the Tamanoir environment.
This cost is approximately of $460\mu s$ for a NACK and $640\mu s$ for a 1024-bytes
data packet. Finally, the data services on the test-bed introduce less than 1ms
of processing time per-packet.

Figure 7 shows the processing time to dynamically determine the replier. The
number of receivers under the AAC ranges from 5 to 25. The x-axis indicates how
many receivers are involved in the replier election process. For instance, if we
look at the 5-receivers curve, a number of 5 at the x-axis means that the correct

replier is found after having scanned 4 receivers. It must be noted that the replier election is performed on-the-fly during the time interval for gathering NACK information. In practice, this timer should be set to at least the propagation time to the farthest receiver. Therefore, it is possible that the election cost is masked by the timer duration, resulting in no cost from a protocol end-to-end performance perspective.

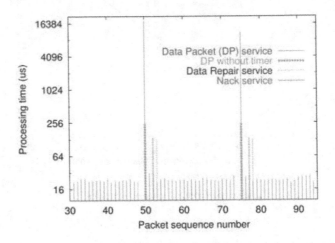

Fig. 7. Cost of replier election.

6   Conclusions

This paper reported on our experiments in implementing application-aware services for the grids, with a case study on the reliable multicast feature. Beyond the DyRAM protocol, the main contribution of this work is to show that application-aware components and services are viable concepts and bring more performance for the end-users. Enabling and generalizing the use of AAS on a grid infrastructure will provide a level of flexibility that have never been achieved in the Internet before and will certainly help for a massive usage of distributed computing.

The last part of the paper addresses the performance issues by measuring the processing cost of the AAS proposed in the DyRAM framework. The results are very encouraging as most processing costs range from tens of μs to hundreds of μs on a Pentium II 400MHz PC-based AAC. Given these results, we believe it is very possible to build AACs from regular PCs (using the most up-to-date processor and clock rate) and still get performances at high bit rates. This possibility, along with the possibility to perform application-level multicast within the DyRAM framework, would certainly help to disseminate the concept of application-aware components for computational grids by allowing local deployment of AACs, independently of carriers and ISP.

152   M. Maimour and C. Pham

References

1. R. B. et al. Parsec: A parallel simulation environment for complex systems. *Computer Magazine, 31(10), October 1998, pp77-85.*
2. M. Calderón, M. Sedano, A. Azcorra, C. Alonso. Active Networks Support for Multicast Applications. *IEEE Networks, May/June 1998.*
3. S. E. Deering and D. R. Cheriton. Multicast Routing in Datagram Internetworks and Extended LANs newblock In *ACM SIGCOMM'88* and *ACM Trans. on Comp. Sys., Vol. 8, No. 2.*
4. Foster, I., Kesselman, C. and Tuecke, S. The Anatomy of the Grid: Enabling Scalable Virtual Organizations. *International Journal of High Performance Computing Applications, 15 (3). 200-222. 2001.*
5. I. Foster and C. Kesselman. Globus: A metacomputing infrastructure toolkit. *Intl J. Supercomputing Applications, 11(2):115-128, 1997*
6. J.P. Gelas and L. Lefèvre. TAMANOIR : A High Performance Active Network Framework. *Workshop on Active Middleware Services 2000, 9th IEEE International HPDC, Pittsburgh.*
7. A. Grimshaw, A. Ferrari, F. Knabe and M. Humphrey. Legion: An Operating System for Wide-area computing. *IEEE Computer, 32(5):29-37, May 1999*
8. S. K. Kasera et al. Scalable fair reliable multicast using active services. *IEEE Networks, Special Issue on Multicast, 2000.*
9. L. Lefèvre, C. Pham, P. Primet, B. Tourancheau, B. Gaidioz, J. P. Gelas, M. Maimour. Active Networking Support for The Grid. *Proceedings of the third International Working Conference on Active Networks (IWAN'01), 2001.*
10. M. Litzkow and M. Livny. Experience With The Condor Distributed Batch System. In *IEEE Workshop on Experimental Distributed Systems, October 1990.*
11. M. Maimour and C. Pham. Dynamic Replier Active Reliable Multicast (DyRAM) *Proceedings of the 7th IEEE Symposium on Computers and Communications (ISCC 2002).*
12. M. Maimour and C. Pham. An analysis of a router-based loss detection service for active reliable multicast protocols. *Proceedings of the International Conference On Networks (ICON 2002), Singapore.*
13. Christos Papadopoulos, Guru M. Parulkar, and George Varghese. An error control scheme for large-scale multicast applications. In *IEEE INFOCOM'98*, pp1188–1996.
14. R. State, O. Festor, E. Nataf. A Programmable Network Based Approach for Managing Dynamic Virtual Private Networks In *Proceedings of PDPTA 2000*, Las Vegas, June 26-29.
15. D. L. Tennehouse et al. A survey of active network research. *IEEE Comm. Mag.*, pp80–86, January 1997.
16. D.J. Wetherall, J.V. Guttag and D.L. Tennehouse. ANTS: a Toolkit for Building and Dynamically Deploying Network Protocols. In *IEEE OPENARCH'98, San Francisco, April 1998.*
17. L. Wei, H. Lehman, S. J. Garland, and D. L. Tennenhouse. Active reliable multicast. In *IEEE INFOCOM'98.*
18. S. Zabele et al. Improving Distributed Simulation Performance Using Active Networks. In *World Multi Conference, 2000.*

Dynamic Resource Allocation in Core Routers of a Diffserv Network

Rares Serban, Chadi Barakat, and Walid Dabbous

PLANETE Project, INRIA Sophia Antipolis, France
{Rares.Serban,Chadi.Barakat,Walid.Dabbous}@sophia.inria.fr
http://www-sop.inria.fr/planete/index.html

Abstract. The Differentiated Services (DiffServ) architecture is receiving wide attention as a framework for providing different levels of service according to a Service Level Agreement (SLA) profile. The edge routers in a DiffServ network mark/shape/police flows based on their SLAs, and the core routers offer packets different treatments using the marks they carry. Core routers handle aggregates of flows instead of individual flows, which is known to considerably reduce the complexity of DiffServ. Tuning core routers is clearly an important issue to satisfy the needs of traffic marked at the edges. This tuning is actually characterized by extensive manual work, based on a trial-and-error process, which is often ineffective, time-consuming and costly to network managers. In this paper, we propose a dynamic, self-tuning mechanism for allocating resources in core routers among Diffserv services. Our mechanism is easy to implement, and does not require any particular signaling. It ensures that SLAs are respected, and allows at the same time an efficient utilization of network resources. We validate the performance of our mechanism by a campaign of experiments on a real network testbed.

1 Introduction

Network customers need guaranteed level of service from their Internet Service Providers (ISPs) to achieve their business objectives. Service Level Agreements (SLAs) between providers and customers define service level specifications [1] with traffic conditioning specification [2], monitoring service capabilities [3], service availability and the fees corresponding to each level. The traffic conditioning specification (TCS) defines service level parameters (bandwidth, packet loss, peak rate, etc.), offered traffic profiles and policies for excess traffic. Given the SLA of a stream of packets, the network has to allocate enough resources so that the service required by this stream is guaranteed. The allocation can be done in different ways, depending on the total amount of resources available in the network and the number of customers asking for a guaranteed service. One simple allocation is the one that uses the peak rate of traffic. This is the type of allocation supported by PSTNs (Public Switched Telephone Network). Another possible allocation is the one that uses the notion of effective bandwidth [4]. The effective bandwidth for traffic is the minimum bandwidth to be allo-

A. Jean-Marie (Ed.): ASIAN 2002, LNCS 2550, pp. 153-167, 2002.

cated in the network so that the probabilistic needs of the traffic (e.g., packet loss rate, tail of packet delay) are satisfied. In the effective bandwidth framework, the statistical multiplexing of the different streams of packets is used to minimize the total amount of resources to be allocated. Note that for any resource allocation scheme, there is always a maximum limit on the number of customers the network can support. When the number of customers approaches this limit, the resources start to be rare and the Quality of Service (QoS) required by customers cannot by realized. Thus, some kind of Call Admission Control (CAC) [5] has to be implemented by the network, to protect already accepted customers from newly arriving ones.

Differentiated Services (Diffserv) is an IETF framework for classifying network traffic into classes, with different service level for classes [6]. The edge routers in a DiffServ network mark/shape/police flows based on their SLAs, and the core routers offer packets belonging to these flows different treatments using the marks they carry. A flow is a stream of packets belonging to the same SLA. Core routers handle aggregates of flows instead of individual flows, which is known to considerably reduce the complexity of DiffServ, compared to its counterpart IntServ [7], where core routers allocate resources on a per-flow basis. The treatment a core router gives to packets from one service class is called PHB (Per Hop Behavior). The PHB classes (or service classes) defined in DiffServ are: Best Effort (BE), Assured Forwarding (AF) [8][9] and Expedited Forwarding (EF) [10][11]. The EF class is designed to support real time flows with hard delay and jitter constraints. The AF class is designed for flows only asking for bandwidth, mainly TCP flows. The AF has four (sub)classes, each one with three drop precedence [6]. At the onset of congestion, core routers start drop AF packets with the highest drop precedence, then those with the medium drop precedence, and finally if congestion persists, packets with the lowest drop precedence are dropped. Packets within a AF class are served in core routers in order. The different AF classes may differ in the applications and transport mechanisms they support. For example, TCP traffic can be protected from non-responsive UDP traffic by separating both types of traffic in two different AF classes. How to distribute traffic on the different service classes of DiffServ is out of the scope of this paper.

The performance of a DiffServ network is strongly dependent on how well edge and core routers work. Edge routers are responsible of marking/shaping/policing traffic. Core routers give packets different treatments based on the marks they carry. For example, EF packets are queued in a separate buffer and are served before packets of the other classes. Packets of the different AF classes are queued in separate buffers and are served using the CBQ mechanism [12]. We focus in this work on the tuning of core routers for AF traffic. This operation reflects the tuning of the weights of the CBQ buffer. The weights of CBQ control the way with which the available bandwidth at the output interface of the core router is distributed among the AF classes and the BE class. The weights do not have any control on the EF class, since EF packets are usually served with a strict priority over the other types of packets (AF and BE). The tuning has to be done so that each class of traffic realizes its needs, and the resources of the network are efficiently utilized. In particular, the tuning has to ensure that the BE traffic is not penalized by the AF traffic, and at the same time, that the BE traffic does not consume more than its fair share of the available bandwidth.

The tuning of core routers is actually characterized by extensive manual work, based on a trial-and-error process, which is often ineffective, time-consuming and costly to network managers. As we will explain later, a static tuning of core routers may result in an inefficient utilization of network resources, and a bias against one or more DiffServ classes. We believe that the tuning of core routers has to be dynamic, so that the available bandwidth is efficiently utilized and fairly shared among the different DiffServ classes (more details in Section 4). Moreover, the tuning has to be automatic, self-configurable, easy to deploy and to manage, without any additional signaling. In this paper, we motivate the dynamic tuning of core routers and we present a mechanism that respects the above rules. We implement our mechanism in Linux and we validate its performance by a campaign of experiments on a real network testbed.

While presenting our mechanism, we will make the assumption that the network is over-provisioned, i.e., there are enough resources in the core of the network to support the high priority traffic marked at the edge. On the other hand, the resources of the network may not be enough to support the total amount of traffic coming from the edge, i.e., the high priority plus the low priority traffic. The decision on whether to accept a new SLA is done at the edge of the network, and core routers dynamically tune their parameters so as to absorb the marked traffic and to utilize efficiently the network resources. Our mechanism can be easily extended to the under-provisioning case, by making some default assumption on the distribution of the bandwidth among the DiffServ classes. For example, a core router may give the highest priority to EF packets, and set equally the weights of the CBQ buffer for AF classes, with zero or a minimum amount of bandwidth to the BE class. We believe that the under-provisioning case is undesirable for the ISP and the customers and has to be avoided, which can be done by implementing CAC at the edge, or by renegotiating the SLAs of active customers.

We consider the allocation of bandwidth based on the average rate of high priority traffic of each DiffServ class. For simplicity of the analysis, we omit the EF service and we focus on AF and BE. EF is usually handled by a priority queue, without any special tuning to be done by the core router. Without loss of generality, we focus on a AF service with two drop precedence per-class. This latter service has been first introduced in [11]. At the edge, compliant packets of a AF class are marked with high priority (called IN packets), and non-compliant packets are injected into the network with low priority (called OUT packets). IN and OUT packets are buffered in the same queue in core routers, but are dropped differently at the onset of congestion. The idea is to start dropping OUT packets while protecting IN packets. When all OUT packets are dropped and the congestion persists, IN packets start to be discarded. The mechanism proposed in [11] to support such a preferential dropping is called RIO (RED IN/OUT).

In summary, our mechanism measures the rate of IN packets, and sets the parameters of the CBQ buffer so as to absorb all IN packets and to distribute fairly the rest of the bandwidth (called excess) among OUT and BE packets. As a case study, we consider a max-min fairness for the allocation of the excess bandwidth [13][14].

The remainder of this paper is organized as follows. The problem of tuning core routers is explained in Section 2. Section 3 presents our mechanism, which dynamically tunes core routers to allocate efficiently the available resources among DiffServ classes. Section 4 illustrates on some examples the drawback of static tuning, and motivates the dynamic tuning of core routers. Section 5 explains our experimental evaluation environment. Section 6 validates our mechanism with our experimental environment. Finally, Section 7 concludes the paper and gives some perspective on our future research activities in this direction.

2 Problem Description

The tuning of core routers in a Diffserv network is actually done in a static way by manual work based on a trial-and-error process. A static tuning is time-consuming and costly for network managers. Moreover, as we will see in Section 4, a static tuning may lead to an inefficient utilization of network resources and to an unfairness among the DiffServ classes. A dynamic tuning of core routers, or equivalently a dynamic allocation of resources in the core of the network, is needed to satisfy as much as possible all reservations of customers, and to fairly distribute the excess of bandwidth among them.

Consider a DiffServ network proposing to customers two AF services (AF1 and AF2), in addition to the classical BE service. This will be the type of networks we will consider throughout the paper. Our results hold in the case when more than two AF service classes are proposed. They also hold in the case when the network operator proposes the EF service to its customers.

A customer asks the network for some bandwidth of some class (AF1 or AF2). It may also ask the network for a simple BE service, with no bandwidth guarantee. As mentioned in Section 1, the difference between the two AF classes can be in the transport protocol used (TCP vs. UDP), in the number of customers authorized to join each class, in the policy applied to non-compliant packets, etc. The bandwidth allocated to a user of a AF class represents the maximum rate of IN packets the customer is allowed to inject into the network. All packets non compliant with the contract signed between the customer and the operator are marked as OUT at the edge. Some routers at the edge may choose to drop OUT packets instead of injecting them into the network. This is what we call shaping of flows.

Let $R_{AF1.1}$ (resp. $R_{AF2.1}$) denote the rate of data carried by IN packets of class AF1 (resp. AF2), which arrive at a core router and are destined to the same output interface. Let C be the total bandwidth available at the output interface of the core router. We are working in an over-provisioning case, which means that there is enough resources to absorb the high priority IN traffic. This can be written as,

$$R_{AF1.1} + R_{AF2.1} \leq C. \tag{1}$$

Now, denote by R_{AF1} (resp. R_{AF2}) the total rate of data carried by AF1 packets (resp. AF2 data) (IN + OUT). Denote by R_{BE} the data rate of the BE traffic arriving at the same core router and destined to the same output interface as the AF1 and AF2 traffic.

Dynamic tuning is only interesting in the case when the core router is congested. Core routers being work-conserving, the tuning of parameters does not impact the QoS perceived by customers in a non-congestion case. Our assumption is then,

$$R_{AF1} + R_{AF2} + R_{BE} \geq C. \qquad (2)$$

We consider that a customer is satisfied if its IN packets get through the network without being dropped. We also consider that it is in the interest of customers and operator that the excess of bandwidth in the network is fairly distributed among the three classes: AF1, AF2, and BE. The excess of bandwidth is equal to $C\text{-}R_{AF1.1}\text{-}R_{AF2.1}$. Given the variability of the traffic and the change in SLAs, it is very likely that a static tuning of core routers does not realize the above objectives. The problems that can be caused by a static tuning of weights at the output interface of a core router, can be summarized as:
- Unfairness in the distribution of the excess bandwidth;
- Bias against the IN packets of one or more AF classes.

We will study these problems of static tuning in Section 4 on some real scenarios. We will show the gain that a dynamic tuning of weights can bring. The comparison will be made between a stating tuning scheme, and our mechanism that dynamically adapts the weights at the output interface of routers, based on the incoming IN traffic. Our mechanism is designed with the main objective to realize the above objectives, that is, to accept the high priority IN traffic of the two AF classes, and to distribute the excess bandwidth fairly among the three classes we are considering: AF1, AF2, and BE. We start by explaining our mechanism in the next Section. In Section 4, we compare it to a static tuning scheme, and in Section 6 we validate its performance using our experimental network testbed (explained in Section 5).

3 Dynamic Resource Allocation Algorithm

Our algorithm has three parts: monitoring, excess bandwidth distribution rule and CBQ scheduler programming.

In the monitoring part, we measure the average data rate carried by IN packets for each one of the two classes AF1 and AF2. The interval over which the data rate is averaged is an important parameter of our mechanism. It must not be too small, since the system may become unstable, especially when we have a transport protocol like TCP, which adapts its rate as a function of the reaction of the network. A small averaging interval also results in high computational overhead. The averaging interval must not be very large too, since this slows the reaction of the mechanism to changes in traffic and SLAs. We will come later to the impact of this averaging interval on the efficiency of our mechanism with some experimental results.

The excess bandwidth distribution rule part forms the core of the algorithm. With no loss of generality, we use the following rule: the excess bandwidth is split into three parts and equally distributed among the three classes. We call this rule *fair division*. Other rules are also possible. For example, one can distribute the excess bandwidth among classes using non equal weights. The objective might be to give AF service classes bandwidth advantages over BE, or the opposite.

After the distribution of excess bandwidth, the algorithm computes the desired rates for CBQ classes (the optimal weights for each class), and programs the CBQ mechanism with these rates. The algorithm has the following description:

```
while(){
    -   Measure the throughput of IN-profile packets for
        both classes AF1 and AF2, and for each outgoing
        network interface: R_AF1.1, R_AF2.1;
    -   Compute the amount of excess bandwidth using
        measured values: Bw = C - (R_AF1.1 + R_AF2.1);
    -   Distribute the excess bandwidth following some
        rule. Ex: w = Bw/3;
    -   Program the CBQ scheduler using the computed op-
        timal rates: R_AF1 = R_AF1.1 + w, R_AF2 = R_AF2.1 + w,
        R_BE = w;
    -   Wait x seconds;
}
```

Let us illustrate the operation of our algorithm with the following example, taken from Section 4.2.2. We have a scenario where the AF1 service is used by a UDP traffic sending data at a constant rate 4Mbps, and the AF2 and BE services are used by TCP traffic. The TCP traffic is generated by means of long-lived TCP connections. For both service classes AF1 and AF2, the rate of IN-profile data is set to: $R_{AF1.1}$=2.5Mbps and $R_{AF2.1}$=2.5Mbps. The available bandwidth at the output interface of the core router is set to C=6Mbps. We start from a case where the bandwidth C is equally divided among the three service classes: R_{AF1}= R_{AF2}= R_{BE}=2Mbps. After the first iteration, our mechanism sets: R_{AF1}= 3Mbps, R_{AF2}= 2.5Mbps and R_{BE}= 0.5Mbps. The next iteration measures $R_{AF1.1}$= 2.5Mbps and $R_{AF2.1}$= 2.5Mbps. The algorithm stabilizes then with the following rates for the CBQ buffer: R_{AF1}= 2.8Mbps, R_{AF2}= 2.8Mbps and R_{BE}=0.3Mbps. The convergence is achieved in two steps. Clearly, this allocation of bandwidth C satisfies the two objectives of our mechanism. Indeed, $R_{AF1.1}$ and $R_{AF2.1}$ are satisfied, and the excess bandwidth $(C-R_{AF1.1}-R_{AF2.1})$=1Mbps is fairly divided among the three service classes.

4   Simple Scenarios to Compare Static and Dynamic Bandwidth Allocation Schemes

The goal of this section is to compare static and dynamic bandwidth allocation schemes using simple scenarios. We show how a static scheme results very likely in an efficient utilization of network resources, and a bias against one or more service classes. As a dynamic scheme, we use our mechanism, that we described in Section 3.

4.1 Unfairness in the Distribution of the Excess Bandwidth

Consider the case when we guarantee 2Mbps for the AF1 service, $R_{AF1.1} = 2$Mbps, and nothing for the AF2 service, $R_{AF2.1} = 0$. The CBQ scheduler in the core router statically limits each service class to 2Mbps. The link capacity is set to C=6Mbps. The traffic from one class cannot exceed 2Mbps, even if it is reserving much more bandwidth than the traffic in the other classes.

Suppose that the class AF1 wants to send more traffic than is guaranteed ($R_{AF1} = 4$Mbps), then this class will not obtain any share from the excess bandwidth, since the core router is limiting its maximum rate to 2Mbps. The other classes, which do not reserve any bandwidth, monopolize the excess bandwidth, which is completely unfair to class AF1. The weights of CBQ are clearly not adapted to this situation.

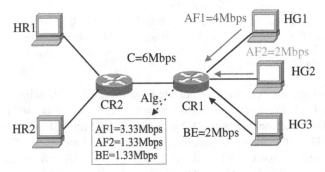

Fig.1. Unfairness in the distribution of the excess bandwidth case. HG - host generators and HR - host receivers. CR - core routers

Our mechanism solves this problem and allows a fair sharing of the excess bandwidth, which improves the AF1 service in this scenario. The rates allocated by our algorithm are shown in Fig.1. These rates are obtained with a fair division rule, which divides the excess bandwidth equally among the three service classes. Using this rule, we increase the AF1 bandwidth from 2Mbps to $R_{AF1}=3.33$Mbps, and we penalize the other services that do not ask for any guaranteed bandwidth, $R_{AF2}=R_{BE}=1.33$Mbps instead of 2Mbps in the static case.

4.2 Bias Against the IN Packets of One or More AF Classes

A customer is satisfied when the IN-profile packets it injects into the network succeed to get through. We recall that we are considering an over-provisioning case, otherwise this condition on satisfaction is not feasible. A static tuning of core routers may violate this condition, by penalizing a class sending only IN-profile packets, while accepting OUT-profile packets from another class, or accepting packets from the BE class. We illustrate this misbehavior with the following two scenarios. Our mechanism ensures a complete protection of IN-profile packets in an over-provisioning case. It does this by adapting the rates of CBQ to the rates of IN packets.

4.2.1 One Reservation Is Not Satisfied and One Is Satisfied

Consider the scenario where the AF1 class generates a total data rate of 4Mbps, and the AF2 class generates a total data rate of 0.5Mps: R_{AF1}=4Mbps and R_{AF2}=0.5Mbps. All packets of the AF2 class are marked as IN, $R_{AF2.1}$ = 0.5Mbps. The rate of data carried by IN packets of class AF1 is equal to $R_{AF1.1}$ = 3Mbps. In the static tuning case, the CBQ buffer is supposed to distribute the bandwidth C=6Mbps equally among the three classes. The BE traffic rate is set to 3Mbps.

In this scenario, class AF2 is satisfied since all its IN packets get through the network. However, class AF1 is not satisfied, since the CBQ buffer limits its rate to 2Mbps, whereas it is sending IN packets at a higher rate of 3Mbps. We are in a scenario where IN packets are dropped, and OUT/BE packets are served instead. The total rate of IN packets generated by the two classes is less than C, therefore it is possible to find another tuning that allows all IN packets to get through, and corrects the bias against class AF1. When running our mechanism, the rate allocated to AF1 increases to more than $R_{AF1.1}$, and the rate allocated to AF2 is kept larger than $R_{AF2.1}$ (Fig.2).

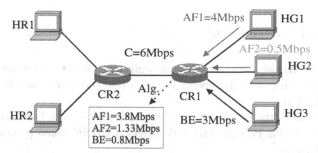

Fig.2. One reservation is satisfied from HG2. HG - Host Generator, HR - Host Receiver, CR - Core Router

Concerning the excess bandwidth (equal to 2.5Mbps in this scenario), our mechanism divides it equally among the three classes. So, the new distribution of the CBQ rates is: R_{AF1}= 3.8Mbps, R_{AF2}= 1.33Mbps and R_{BE}= 0.8Mbps.

4.2.2 All Reservations Are Not Satisfied

The last case we consider is when all reservations are not satisfied, due to an appropriate static tuning of CBQ weights. Suppose AF1 has a IN-profile traffic $R_{AF1.1}$=2.5Mbps and AF2 a IN-profile traffic $R_{AF2.1}$=2.5Mbps. If the CBQ limits the maximum rate of each class to 2Mbps, both classes AF1 and AF2 will not be satisfied since some of their IN packets will be dropped. On contrary, clients of the BE class are favored, since they obtain more than their fair share of the excess bandwidth (2Mbps instead of 0.33Mbps).

We apply our algorithm and we measure each class throughput at the output interface of the core router. The rule to divide the excess bandwidth is the same as that in the above sections. After a while, the rates allocated in the CBQ buffer to the different classes change: AF1 and AF2 receive $R_{AF1}=R_{AF2}=2.8$Mbps, and BE receives $R_{BE}=0.3$Mbps. This is exactly the desired allocation, that satisfies customers who ask for bandwidth, and distributes the excess bandwidth equally among the three classes.

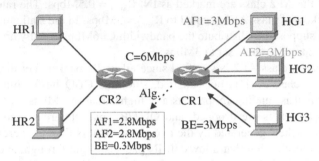

Fig.3. All reservations are not satisfied. HG - Host Generator, HR - Host Receiver, CR - Core Router

5 Evaluation Environment

The evaluation environment includes monitoring tools, traffic generator tools, traffic control tools and link emulator tools. The experimental results are based on cases presented in Section 4.

To validate our work, we use a test-bed network (Fig.4) with Linux Redhat 7.2 operating system. All the PC's are PIII with different clocks' speed processors and different network cards.

Our mechanism is implemented in the core router named Kisscool. Looking to Fig.4, each host at the right-hand side (Galak, Mnm, Raider) generates TCP or UDP traffic flows [15] to hosts at the left-hand side. The traffic is generated with the Iperf tool, and is marked at the output interfaces of the source hosts. The network bandwidth is 10Mbps. Using the NIST Net tool [16], we emulate a link with bandwidth 6Mbps between Kisscool and Kitkat routers.

The monitoring tool used is TCPSTAT [17]. It collects the throughput of each AF class at the incoming interfaces of the core router. To be effective, TCPSTAT works in Eth3, Eth2, Eth4 from Kisscool router.

We use the tc (traffic control) module implemented in the Linux Diffserv [18][19]. Traffic control can decide if packets are queued or if they are dropped (e.g., if the queue has reached some length limit or if the traffic exceeds some rate limit). It can decide in which order packets are sent (e.g. to give priority to certain flows). It can delay the sending of packets (e.g. to limit the rate of outbound traffic), etc. The traffic control code is implemented in Linux kernel and is configured with a command interface tc. The main components of Linux traffic control are filters, classes and queuing disciplines (e.g., qdisc).

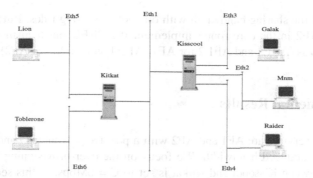

Fig. 4. Our test bed network. The core router is Kisscool host. Flow generators are instaled on Galak, Mnm and Raider.

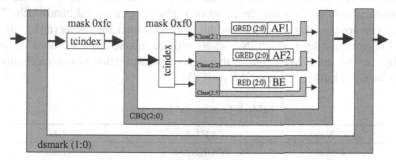

Fig. 5. Interior of core routers using dsmark, tcindex, CBQ, GRED and RED.

Packets are selected by the filters in classes (u32, fw, route, tcindex). Each class uses one of queuing disciplines (tbf, pfifo, red, gred). Schedulers used by tc are: CBQ (Class Based Queuing), PRIO (Priority queuing), HTB (Hierarchical Token Bucket). There are hierarchies of classes and filters.

Fig.5 shows the configuration of traffic control inside core router Kisscool. The queuing disciplines and classes reflect the usual Linux notation of displaying tree-based traffic control framework.

In order to use the DSCP to classify packets into the correct queue and class [20], we use two levels from a hierarchy of filters. The first level of filters is for parent dsmark(1:0) and the filter obtains DSCP from each packet. The filter is of type tcindex and it masks the TOS field with 0xfc to extract the DS filed and shift two bits to the right to get the DSCP. The second level of filters is for CBQ(2:0) (Class Based Queueing) scheduler and extracts the second digit from the classid of the packets. After masking with 0xf0 and shifting 4 bits to the right, the handle now corresponds to the correct class under the CBQ scheduler.

Finally, the last level is internal in the GRED (Generalized RED) implementation as it masks the packets with 0xf to extract the third digit of the classid and put them into their correct virtual queues under GRED [21].

The available bandwidth C at the output interface of the core router is divided by CBQ, which uses three classes with id: 2:1, 2:2 and 2:5. To avoid borrowing bandwidth from the ancestors and to block the bandwidth sharing of the same parent, we set the following parameters: isolated and bounded [16]. We need to set this parameters to control the sharing bandwidth with our policy sharing rules. Buffers associated to AF1 and AF2 in the core router implement the GRED mechanism with two drop precedence class (AF1.1 and AF1.2 for AF1, AF2.1 and AF2.2 for AF2).

6 Experimental Results

The proposed services are AF1 and AF2 with a positive guaranteed bandwidth and BE with a zero guaranteed bandwidth. We focus on the over-provisioning case. The link bandwidth between Kisscool and Kitkat is set to C = 6Mbps. In this section, we validate the scenarios studied in Section 4, where our mechanism is compared to a static bandwidth allocation scheme. We suppose that three customers located in the hosts at the right-hand side in Fig.4 ask the network for some guaranteed bandwidth. Table 1 gives an example on how much bandwidth each customer may reserve. In this example, the maximum rate at which IN packets will be injected into the network is equal to 2Mbps per AF class. We consider that before the activation of our mechanism, the rates in the CBQ buffer are set to 2Mbps (C/3).

Table 1. Guaranteed bandwidth

PC Name	AF1.1	AF2.1
Galak	650Kbit/s	550Kbit/s
Mnm	450Kbit/s	700Kbit/s
Raider	900Kbit/s	750Kbit/s
Total bw:	2000Kbit/s	2000Kbit/s

To simplify the experiment, we suppose that the traffic of each one of the three classes is generated by the same machine, e.g., Galak generates AF1 traffic, Mnm generates AF2 traffic, and Raider generates BE traffic. Then, if the traffic of a AF class is less than the guaranteed bandwidth, all packets of that class will be marked as IN-profile. The traffic of a AF class contains OUT-profile packets when its rate exceeds the guaranteed bandwidth for that class.

Figure 6 shows how our algorithm reacts to the unfairness in the distribution of the excess bandwidth (Section 4.1). We use UDP to generate the AF1 traffic (4Mbps) and multiple long-lived TCP flows to generate the AF2 and BE traffic. The AF2 traffic has only OUT-profile packets, which is realized by setting the guaranteed bandwidth of the AF2 class to 0.

The guaranteed profile for AF1 is $R_{AF1.1}$= 2Mbps, but the router receives more than this amount (it receives 4Mbps). After one iteration we observe that AF1 has R_{AF1}=3.33Mbps, AF2 has R_{AF2}=1.33Mbps and BE has R_{BE}= 1.33Mbps. AF1 realizes its guaranteed bandwidth $R_{AF1.1}$= 2Mbps, and is then satisfied. The AF2 class is penalized because it does not ask for any bandwidth in this scenario, so it gets approximately the same throughput as BE.

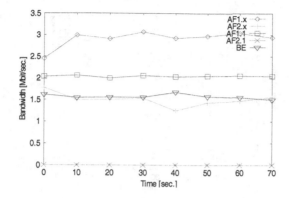

Fig. 6. Unfairness in the distribution of excess bandwidth (static case)

Table 2. Delay in AF1.1 service in the distribution of excess bandwidth case

	Min. [ms]	Avg. [ms]	Max.[ms]
Without alg.	2.108	23.799	68.891
With alg.	2.023	18.345	56.675

Table 2 shows the impact of our mechanism on the delay perceived by packets of class AF1. Our mechanism improves the quality perceived by this class by giving it a fair share of the excess bandwidth. This additional bandwidth is translated into a smaller end-to-end delay for packets of this class.

Figure 7 shows another case where one of the services (AF2) has low traffic, less than the guaranteed bandwidth, and another service (AF1) has more traffic than is guaranteed (Section 4.2.1). In this case, AF1 has UDP flows and AF2 and BE have long-lived TCP flows. The bandwidth guaranteed by the network to AF1 is set to 3Mbps, instead of 2Mbps as before (this follows a change in the contract according to a new agreement between customer and ISP). As expected, after two iterations AF1 gets R_{AF1}= 3.8Mbps, AF2 gets R_{AF2}= 1.33 and BE gets R_{BE}= 0.8Mbps. The priority traffic from each AF service class gets through the network. The two AF classes realize their desired rates. The BE service gets the smallest amount of bandwidth, since it has zero guarantee. In this case, the delay measured for AF2 has the same value with/without our algorithm (min.=1.772ms / avg.=19.708ms / max.=57.876ms).

The case when all service reservations are not satisfied is presented in Fig.8. We use for AF1 class UDP flows, and for AF2 and BE classes long-lived TCP flows. AF1 and AF2 classes ask the network for 2.5Mbps each (Section 4.2.2). In this case, we observe that our algorithm stabilizes the rates of the CBQ buffer after 20s.

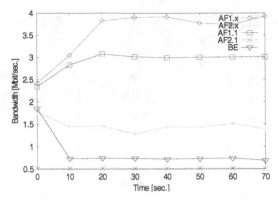

Fig. 7. One service reservation is not satisfied, one is satisfied (static case).

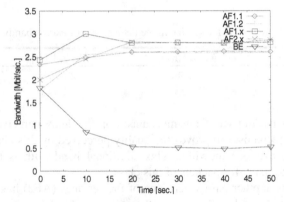

Fig. 8. All service reservations are not satisfied (static case).

Fig.9 shows how fast our algorithm should run. The speed of the algorithm is determined by the averaging interval. Every averaging interval, our algorithm passes once by the loop `while` described in Section 3. If it runs faster than 5 seconds, the system oscillates. We found the optimum value of the averaging interval to be 10 seconds, as shown in Fig.10. For this experiment, we use long-lived TCP flows for all the services. The dynamics of TCP congestion control is the reason for these oscillations of the system, when the averaging interval is small. One should expect that the instability of the system for small averaging interval does not exist in case of constant rate non-reactive UDP flows.

7 Conclusions and Future Work

Our mechanism is easy to implement and does not require any particular signaling. The bandwidth allocation is taken according to local decision rules. It ensures that SLAs are respected and allows at the same time an efficient utilization of network resources. It is flexible because it can use other division rules for excess bandwidth. Each ISP can define his own rules. The future work will be to test and to compare multiple excess bandwidth sharing rules. Another future work will be to test our mechanism with real applications like FTP, RealPlayer, and Web generators. In this paper, we only focused on constant rate UDP traffic and long-lived TCP flows.

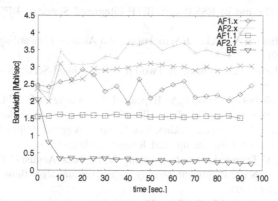

Fig. 9. The algorithm runs with a period of 5 seconds. In this case the TCP flows from AF services have no time to adapt their windows. So, this creates oscillations.

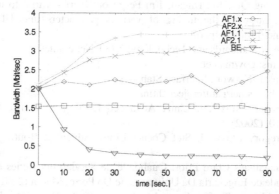

Fig. 10. The algorithm runs with a period of 10 seconds. In this case the TCP flows from AF services have time to adapt their windows. So, there are no oscillations.

References

1. R.J.Gibbens, S.K.Sargood, F.P.Kelly: An Approach to Service Level Agreements for IP networks with Differentiated Services, article submitted to Royal Engineering Society, January (2000)
2. D. Grossman: New Terminology and Clarifications for Diffserv, RFC 3260, April (2002)
3. A. Asgari, P. Trimintzios: A Monitoring and Measurement Architecture for Traffic Engineered IP Networks, IEEE/IFIP/IEE IST2001, Teheran, Iran, September (2001)
4. Jean Warland, G. Kesielis: Effective bandwidth for multiclass Markov fluids and other ATM sources, IEEE/ACM Tran. Networking, Vol.1, (1993) 424-428

5. H.G. Perros, K.M.Elsayed: Call Admission Control Schemes: A Review, IEEE Communications Mag., Vol. 34, No. 11, November (1996), 82-91.
6. S. Blake, D. Black, M. Carlson: An Architecture for Differentiated Services, RFC 2475, December (1998)
7. J. Wroclawski: The use of RSVP with IETF Integrated Services, RFC 2210, September (1997)
8. J. Heinanen, F. Baker, W. Weiss, J. Wroclawski: An Assured Forwarding PHB Group, RFC 2597, June (1999)
9. K. Nichols, V. Jacobson, L. Zhang: A Two-bit Differentiated Services Architecture for the Internet, April (1999)
10. V. Jacobson, K. Nichols, K. Poduri: An Expedited Forwarding PHB, RFC 2598, June (1999)
11. David D. Clark, Wenjia Fang: Explicit Allocation of Best-Effort Packet Delivery Servicc, IEEE/ACM Transactions on Networking, Vol. 6. No. 4, August (1998) 415–438
12. S. Floyd V. Jacobson: Link-sharing and Resource Management Models for Packet Networks, IEEE/ACM Transactions on Networking, Vol.3, No.4 August (1995)
13. L. Massoulie, J. Roberts: Bandwidth sharing: objectives and algorithms, IEEE Infocom'99, New York, March (1999)
14. Veselin Rakocevic, John M. Griffiths: Physical Separation of Bandwidth Resources for Differentiated TCP/IP Traffic, IEEE Infocom'99, New York, March (1999)
15. Ajay Tirumala, Feng Qin, Jon Dugan, Jim Ferguson: Iperf - a tool to measure maximum TCP bandwidth, allowing the tuning of various parameters and UDP characteristics, http://dast.nlanr.net/Projects/Iperf/
16. National Institute of Standards and Technology: NIST Net emulator, http://www.antd.nist.gov/nistnet
17. Paul Herman: tcpstat-Network Interface Statistics, http://www.frenchfries.net/paul/projects.html
18. Bert Hubert, Gregory Maxwell, Linux Advanced Routing & Traffic Control HOWTO, v0.9.0, January 10, (2002)
19. Bert Hubert, Gregory Maxwell, Stef Coene: Linux Advanced Routing&Traffic Control, http://lartc.org
20. Rui Pedro de Magalhaes Claro Prior: Qualidade de Servico em Redes des Comutacao de Pacotes, Faculdade de Engeharia Da Universidade Do Porto, March (2001)
21. W. Almesberger: Linux Traffic Control – Implemetation Overview, EPFL ICA Swiss, February (2001)
22. Randal L. Schwartz: Learning Perl, O'Reilly&Associates Inc. (1994)
23. Jerry Peek, Tim O'Reilly, Mike Loukides: Unix Power Tools, O'Reilly&Associates Inc. (1994)

Performance Analysis of Flow Loss Probability and Link Utilization in MPLS Networks for Traffic Engineering

Hitomi Tamura, Kenji Kawahara, and Yuji Oie

Department of Computer Science and Electronics, Kyushu Institute of Technology,
Iizuka, Fukuoka 820-8502, Japan
{tamu,kawahara,oie}@infonet.cse.kyutech.ac.jp

Abstract. As the Internet grows, various types of traffic, such as voice, video and data, have been transmitted. Therefore, the Internet should provide Quality of Service(QoS) required by each traffic as well as end-to-end connectivity, and routing decision should be based on the utilization of links/routers and/or application types of each traffic. This kind of routing is called Traffic Engineering (TE) and its objective is to improve performance for users, such as the flow loss probability, and for networks, such as the utilization of links, simultaneously, and some studies claim that MPLS(Multi-protocol Label Switching) technique can easily implement TE.

So far, there are some experimental results that showed how effective TE on MPLS network is, however, its performance would not be theoretically and quantitatively analyzed. Thus, in this paper, we will investigate basic and preliminary performance of MPLS networks for TE by analyzing flow loss probability and Smoothness index of link utilization in the queueing system.

Keywords: Traffic Engineering, MPLS, M/M/c/c queueing system, flow loss probability, link utilization, performance analysis

1 Introduction

As the Internet grows, the number of users is increasing, and various types of traffic, such as voice, video and data, have been transmitted. Therefore, the Internet should provide Quality of Service(QoS) required by each traffic. In order to transmit realtime traffic efficiently, the Internet guarantees the required bandwidth as well as its end-to-end connectivity. Hereafter, we will call this traffic *flow*. In the current Internet, IGP(Interior Gateway Protocol) is widely used for routing IP datagrams on some flow to their destination and it uses only hop count as the metric to set up the forwarding path during source-destination of the flow. However, this kind of routing decision would cause congestion at some intermediate link since there is a possibility that many flows of *minimum hop paths* concentrate there although traffic load in other links are relatively light. If these lightly loaded links could be used as *detoured paths*, it would be able to provide QoS for various types of flow and improve utilization of the network resources at the same time. For this purpose, routing decision should be based on QoS requirements of each flow and the available bandwidth of each links/routers in the network. This kind of routing is called Traffic Engineering(TE).

A. Jean-Marie (Ed.): ASIAN 2002, LNCS 2550, pp. 168–180, 2002.

Recently, MPLS(Multi-Protocol Label Switching) is suggested in MPLS Working Group, IETF(Internet Engineering Task Force)[1], as a new technology that improves the forwarding performance of IP routers on the Internet. MPLS is employed to combine Layer2 hardware switching technology and Layer3 routing one. Some IP flows are classified by FECs(Forwarding Equivalence Classes) on Ingress LSR(Label Switching Router) in MPLS network and each FEC is mapped to a fixed-size *label*. Routing decision from Ingress LSR to Egress one in MPLS networks is made based on the label that is an identifier of LSP(Label Switched Path) on Layer2. In addition to destination IP address, application types and these requirements are also mapped into some labels, so that MPLS will be useful technology for providing QoS. Furthermore, since LSPs can be explicitly (pre-)established according to these information, some studies claim that MPLS technique can easily implement Traffic Engineering(e.g. [2]).

So far, we have analyzed transmission delay and packet loss probability in *single* LSR for the purpose of resource management[3] and QoS provisioning[4], however they do not focus on performance of the whole MPLS network, e.g., the effectiveness of TE. In addition, although there are some experimental results(e.g. [5]) which show how effective TE in MPLS network is, its performance would not be analyzed theoretically and quantitatively. Thus, in this paper, we will investigate basic and preliminary performance of MPLS-TE network which is constructed by two Ingress LSRs and one Egress LSR. By modeling this network as the "Shared $2 \times$M/M/c/c" queueing system, we evaluate the flow loss probability and the Smoothness index of link utilization as performance measures.

This paper is organized as follows. In Section 2, we will describe the analytical model and analyze the flow loss probability and the Smoothness index of link utilization on MPLS-TE network. Section 3 provides numerical results and impacts of some traffic parameters on the performance. Finally, in Section 4, a brief conclusion is given.

2 Analysis

In this section, we describe an analytical model to investigate the performance of MPLS-TE network in which there are some routes from one Ingress LSR to the Egress LSR and derive the flow loss probability and the Smoothness index of resource utilization of each link as performance measures.

2.1 Analytical Model

As shown in Fig.1, we introduce the MPLS network model for our analysis. In this network, we assume that there are two Ingress LSRs and traffic flows arriving there, are basically transmitted to one Egress LSR via the link directly connected with each Ingress LSR. Furthermore, two Ingress LSRs also connect by a link. Here, we define Route_1E(2E) as an ordinary route for arrival flows at Ingress $LSR_{1(2)}$ to Egress LSR and Route_12E(21E) as a detoured via $LSR_{2(1)}$. We suppose that one flow is related to one LSP on each link, and that the maximum number of LSPs set on link $a(a = 1, 2)$ is c_a and that on the link between two Ingress LSRs is ∞. When a flow arrives at LSR_a, it is processed by the following policy:

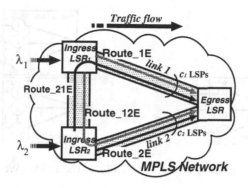

Fig. 1. Network Model

1. If the number of established LSPs on link1(2) $< c_{1(2)}$, then the flow is transmitted on Route_1E(2E),
2. If the number of established LSPs on link1(2) $= c_{1(2)}$ and
   a) if that on link2(1) $< c_{2(1)}$, then the flow is detoured on Route_12E(21E).
   b) if that on link2(1) $= c_{2(1)}$, then the flow is rejected to be transmitted.

In this model, we assume that traffic flows arrive at Ingress LSR$_a$ according to Poisson process with a parameter λ_a, and that the distribution of the transmission time on each LSP follows the exponential distribution with a parameter μ_a/c_a. When there is one Ingress LSR in the network, we can model it by the M/M/c/c queueing system as shown in Fig.2, and when there are two Ingress LSRs with no detoured route, it can be modeled as the 2×M/M/c/c queueing system as shown in Fig.3, namely, each Ingress LSR can be analyzed independently. However, in MPLS TE networks, arrival flows at Ingress LSR$_{1(2)}$ can be transmitted via link2(1), that is, they "share" links each other and this can not be modeled the 2×M/M/c/c queueing system. Therefore, we will call this model the "Shared 2×M/M/c/c" queueing system as shown in Fig.4. So far, the overflow call and its alternative routing have been treated in the traditional queueing theory. However, the concept that each overflow call at any overutilized links *shares* other underutilized ones would not be taken into account there, while this is acceptable to the Internet world. Thus, we shall analyze our proposed queueing system in the following subsections.

2.2 Definition of State Transition Matrix and Derivation of Steady State Probability

First, we focus on the M/M/c/c queueing system in which an LSP established for transmitting IP flow is defined as a customer, then give a state transition matrix of the 2×M/M/c/c queue. Finally, by modifying this matrix, we define that of the "Shared 2×M/M/c/c" queue and derive the steady state probability.

The M/M/c/c queueing system. Fig.2 illustrates the M/M/c/c queueing system. On LSR$_a$, since the maximum number of LSPs for transmitting IP flows is c_a, when a

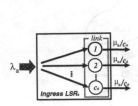

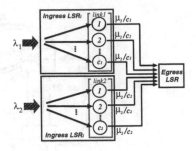

Fig. 2. The M/M/c/c queueing system   **Fig. 3.** The 2×M/M/c/c queueing system

flow arrives there and the number of established LSPs becomes equal to c_a, this flow is rejected. Here, we assume that IP flow arrives according to Poisson distribution with a parameter λ_a. Let $X_a(t)$ denote the number of established LSPs on Ingress LSR$_a$ at time t, and we define $p_a(i)$ as follows:

$$p_a(i) \overset{\triangle}{=} \lim_{t \to \infty} \Pr\{X_a(t) = i;\ 0 \le i \le c_a\}. \tag{1}$$

Then, we can give balance equations as

$$\left.\begin{aligned}
\lambda_a p_a(0) &= \frac{\mu_a}{c_a} p_a(1), \\
\left(\lambda_a + i\frac{\mu_a}{c_a}\right) p_a(i) &= \lambda_a p_a(i-1) + (i+1)\frac{\mu_a}{c_a} p_a(i+1), \quad \text{if } 0 < i < c_a, \\
\mu_a p_a(c_a) &= \lambda_a p_a(c_a - 1).
\end{aligned}\right\} \tag{2}$$

Therefore, let $\mathbf{Q_a} = [q_{a_{ij}} | 0 \le i \le c_a, 0 \le j \le c_a]$ denote the state transition matrix, and its elements are defined as follows:

$$q_{a_{ij}} = \begin{cases}
-\left(\lambda_a + i\dfrac{\mu_a}{c_a}\right), & \text{if } 0 \le i = j < c_a, \\
-\mu_a, & \text{if } i = j = c_a, \\
\lambda_a, & \text{if } 0 \le i < c_a, j = i+1, \\
\dfrac{\mu_a}{c_a}, & \text{if } 0 < i \le c_a, j = i-1, \\
0, & \text{otherwise.}
\end{cases} \tag{3}$$

The 2×M/M/c/c queueing system. In the previous subsection, we defined the state transition matrix of single M/M/c/c queueing system. In this subsection, we define that of the 2×M/M/c/c queueing system as shown in Fig.3 in which we deal with states of two M/M/c/c queueing systems simultaneously and derive the steady state probability. This system differs from the model for our analysis as shown in Fig.4. In this system, arrival flows at one Ingress LSR are never detoured via the other, namely, this model represents the current Internet without applying TE.

Here, we define $X_a(t)$ as the random variable which shows the number of LSPs established on link $a(a = 1, 2)$ at time t. The steady state probability of this system can be defined as

$$p(i, j) \overset{\triangle}{=} \lim_{t \to \infty} \Pr\{X_1(t) = i, X_2(t) = j;\ 0 \leq i \leq c_1, 0 \leq j \leq c_2\}, \qquad (4)$$

and then the balance equation for this system in steady state is as follows:

$$\left.\begin{array}{l} (\lambda_1 + \lambda_2)p(0,0) = \dfrac{\mu_1}{c_1}p(1,0) + \dfrac{\mu_2}{c_2}p(0,1), \\[2mm] \left(\lambda_1 + \lambda_2 + i\dfrac{\mu_1}{c_1} + j\dfrac{\mu_2}{c_2}\right)p(i,j) = \\[2mm] \qquad \lambda_1 p(i-1,j) + \lambda_2 p(i,j-1) + (i+1)\dfrac{\mu_1}{c_1}p(i+1,j) + (j+1)\dfrac{\mu_2}{c_2}p(i,j+1), \\[2mm] \qquad\qquad\qquad\qquad\qquad \text{if } 0 < i < c_1, 0 < j < c_2, \\[2mm] (\mu_1 + \mu_2)p(c_1,c_2) = \lambda_1 p(c_1-1,c_2) + \lambda_2 p(c_1,c_2-1). \end{array}\right\} \qquad (5)$$

Let $\mathbf{Q} = [q_{kl} \mid 0 \leq k, l = i(c_2 + 1) + j < (c_1 + 1)(c_2 + 1)]$ denote the state transition matrix, then we obtain $\mathbf{Q}$ as follows:

$$\mathbf{Q} = \mathbf{Q_1} \oplus \mathbf{Q_2}, \qquad (6)$$

where the operator $\oplus$ represents the Kronecker sum that is given by the following equation[6, pp. 168–169].

$$\mathbf{Q_1} \oplus \mathbf{Q_2} = (\mathbf{Q_1} \otimes \mathbf{I_{Q_2}}) + (\mathbf{I_{Q_1}} \otimes \mathbf{Q_2}), \qquad (7)$$

where $\mathbf{I_{Q_k}}$ is an identity matrix of dimension of $\dim(\mathbf{Q_k})$. Furthermore, the operator $\otimes$ represents the Kronecker product defined as the following equation using $\mathbf{A} = [a_{i,j}] \in {}^{m \times n}$ and $\mathbf{B} = [b_{i,j}] \in {}^{p \times q}$.

$$\mathbf{A} \otimes \mathbf{B} = \begin{pmatrix} a_{0,0}\mathbf{B} & a_{0,1}\mathbf{B} & \cdots & a_{0,n-1}\mathbf{B} \\ \vdots & \vdots & \cdots & \vdots \\ a_{m-1,0}\mathbf{B} & a_{m-1,1}\mathbf{B} & \cdots & a_{m-1,n-1}\mathbf{B} \end{pmatrix}. \qquad (8)$$

Hence, $\dim(\mathbf{Q}) = (c_1 + 1)(c_2 + 1)$.

Let $\mathbf{z} = [p(0,0), \cdots, p(0,c_2), p(1,0), \cdots, p(c_1,c_2)]$ denote the steady state probability vector, then $\mathbf{z}$ and the state transition matrix $\mathbf{Q}$ satisfy the following equation:

$$\mathbf{z}\mathbf{Q} = \mathbf{0}, \qquad \mathbf{z}e\left((c_1+1)(c_2+1)\right) = 1, \qquad (9)$$

where $e(m)$ represents a column vector of dimension m all of whose elements are equal to 1. Therefore, we can obtain the steady state probability of $2 \times$M/M/c/c queueing system by solving Eq. (9).

The Shared $2 \times$ M/M/c/c queueing system. In this subsection, we define the state transition matrix of the Shared $2 \times$ M/M/c/c queueing system as shown in Fig.4 by modifying

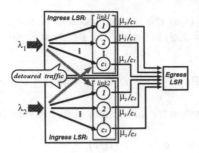

Fig. 4. The Shared $2 \times$ M/M/c/c queueing system

that obtained in the previous subsection. Let the random variable $Y_a(t) (a = 1, 2)$ denote the number of established LSPs at time t, and we define the steady state probability of the system as follows:

$$\pi(i, j) \triangleq \lim_{t \to \infty} \Pr\{Y_1(t) = i, Y_2(t) = j; \ 0 \leq i \leq c_1, 0 \leq j \leq c_2\}. \quad (10)$$

In the Shared $2 \times$ M/M/c/c queueing system, two Ingress LSRs share two links each other for transmitting flows. In this case, we define the state transition matrix $\mathbf{R} = [r_{kl} \mid 0 \leq k, l = i(c_2 + 1) + j < (c_1 + 1)(c_2 + 1)]$, and we can derive r_{kl} by using q_{kl} given by Eq.(6).

$$r_{kl} = \begin{cases} q_{kl} + \lambda_1, & \text{if } c_1(c_2 + 1) \leq k < (c_1 + 1)(c_2 + 1), l = k + 1, \\ q_{kl} - \lambda_1, & \text{if } c_1(c_2 + 1) \leq k = l < (c_1 + 1)(c_2 + 1), \\ q_{kl} + \lambda_2, & \text{if } k = m(c_2 + 1) - 1, l = (m + 1)(c_2 + 1) - 1, m = 1, 2, \ldots, c_1, \\ q_{kl} - \lambda_2, & \text{if } k = l = m(c_2 + 1) - 1, m = 1, \cdots, c_1, \\ q_{kl}, & \text{otherwise.} \end{cases} \quad (11)$$

Let $\boldsymbol{z_s} = [\pi(0, 0), \cdots, \pi(0, c_2), \pi(1, 0), \cdots, \pi(c_1, c_2)]$ be the steady state probability vector, then the following equation represents a relationship between the steady state probability vector $\boldsymbol{z_s}$ and the state transition matrix $\mathbf{R}$.

$$\boldsymbol{z_s}\mathbf{R} = \mathbf{0}, \qquad \boldsymbol{z_s}e\left((c_1 + 1)(c_2 + 1)\right) = 1. \quad (12)$$

Therefore, we can obtain the steady state probability of the Shared $2 \times$ M/M/c/c queueing system by solving Eq.(12).

2.3 Derivation of Performance Measures

By using the steady state probability of the $2 \times$ M/M/c/c queueing system and the Shared $2 \times$ M/M/c/c queueing system, we can derive some performance measures in case of non-TE networks and MPLS-TE ones, respectively. We first obtain the flow loss probability and the average number of established LSPs in links. Furthermore, we can derive the bandwidth utilization of each link by using the average number of established LSPs and define the Smoothness index of link utilization in the network.

Flow loss probability. In the $2 \times$M/M/c/c queueing system, an arrival flow at Ingress LSR_a is rejected when the number c_a LSPs are already used. Therefore, the flow loss probability P_{loss_a} is given as follows:

$$P_{loss_1} = \sum_{j=0}^{c_2} p(c_1, j), \quad P_{loss_2} = \sum_{i=0}^{c_1} p(i, c_2). \tag{13}$$

In the Shared $2 \times$M/M/c/c queueing system, an arrival flow at the system is rejected only when LSPs of both Ingress LSRs are fully used. Therefore, flow loss probability $P'_{loss} (= P'_{loss1} = P'_{loss2})$ is given by

$$P'_{loss} = \pi(c_1, c_2). \tag{14}$$

Smoothness Index of link utilization. Secondary, we obtain the average number of established LSPs in link $a (a = 1, 2)$. Let L_a denote the average number of LSPs established on Ingress LSR_a in the $2 \times$M/M/c/c queueing system and L'_a be that in the Shared $2 \times$M/M/c/c one, and they are given as follows:

$$L_1 = \sum_{i=0}^{c_1} i \sum_{j=0}^{c_2} p(i, j), \quad L_2 = \sum_{j=0}^{c_2} j \sum_{i=0}^{c_i} p(i, j). \tag{15}$$

$$L'_1 = \sum_{i=0}^{c_1} i \sum_{j=0}^{c_2} \pi(i, j), \quad L'_2 = \sum_{j=0}^{c_2} j \sum_{i=0}^{c_1} \pi(i, j). \tag{16}$$

By using L_a and L'_a, we can obtain the normalized bandwidth utilization of each link in $2 \times$M/M/c/c queueing system denoted by $u_a (a = 1, 2, 0 \leq u_a \leq 1)$ and that in Shared $2 \times$M/M/c/c queueing system denoted by u'_a. They are given as follows.

$$u_a = \frac{L_a}{c_a}. \tag{17}$$

$$u'_a = \frac{L'_a}{c_a}. \tag{18}$$

Here, by applying the definition of the Fairness Index[7], we shall define the Smoothness index S of link utilization. Let N denote the number of samples, which corresponds to the number of links directly connected between Ingress LSR and Egress one in this case, and let $u_i (1 \leq i \leq N)$ denote the sample value that is the normalized utilization of each link obtained by Eqs. (17) and (18), we can derive S are given as follows:

$$S = \frac{\left(\sum_{i=1}^{N} u_i \right)^2}{N \times \sum_{i=1}^{N} u_i^2}. \tag{19}$$

S satisfies that $\frac{1}{N} \leq S \leq 1$, and if the value of S gets closer to 1, then every links in networks are shared more equally.

3   Numerical Results and Discussions

In this section, we compare the performance of the MPLS-TE network with that of the non-TE network by showing impacts of two parameters, namely, the load of Ingress LSR$_a$($a = 1, 2$) ρ_a and the maximum number of LSPs c_a, on the flow loss probability and the Smoothness index of the normalized link utilization obtained in the previous section.

3.1   Homogeneous Case of Parameters in Terms of Ingress LSRs

In this subsection, we investigate the performance of MPLS-TE networks in the case when all parameters of two Ingress LSRs, namely, traffic load at each LSR and the maximum number of LSPs are homogeneous. Throughout this subsection, we assume that $\lambda_1 = \lambda_2 = \lambda$, $\mu_1 = \mu_2 = \mu$ and that $c_1 = c_2 = c$. Furthermore, we set μ to 1.0 and c to 10.

First, we show the impact of the traffic load ρ, which is equal to $\frac{\lambda}{\mu}$, on the flow loss probability of MPLS-TE network (labeled "TE" in Fig.5) and that without applying TE (labeled "non-TE" in Fig.5). Fig.5 illustrates the flow loss probability as a function of ρ. We first see from this figure that the flow loss probability at each Ingress LSR improves by TE. Furthermore, the rate of its improvement becomes larger when ρ is smaller, for example, TE succeeds in reducing flow loss probability two orders of magnitude when $\rho = 0.3$. This is because some flows are rejected at one Ingress LSR on non-TE network, while some of them can be detoured via the other Ingress LSR and be accepted in TE network.

In Fig.6, we show the normalized utilization of each link as a function of ρ. If ρ is small, the normalized utilization of each link on MPLS-TE network becomes almost equal to that on non-TE network. However, it is increasing as ρ because arrival flows detour more frequently. As mentioned above, it is clear that we can effectively use both links and can further reduce the flow loss probability by applying TE to MPLS network.

3.2   Heterogeneous Case of Parameters in Terms of Ingress LSRs

From now on, we investigate the impact of the traffic load of Ingress LSR$_1$ ρ_1 on the flow loss probability, the normalized utilization of each link and the Smoothness index when the traffic load of Ingress LSR$_2$ ρ_2 is fixed. We assume that $\mu_1 = \mu_2 = 1.0$ and $c_1 = c_2 = 10$.

If ρ_2 is relatively small. In Fig.7, we show the impact of ρ_1 on the flow loss probability of each LSR when ρ_2 fixed to 0.2. As shown in this figure, the flow loss probability of Ingress LSR$_1$ in TE network always improves if $\rho_1 \geq \rho_2$, since some of rejected flow at Ingress LSR$_1$ can be detoured via Ingress LSR$_2$. Therefore, it is intuitively found that the flow loss probability of Ingress LSR$_2$ in TE network degrades when ρ_1 is relatively large. However, if ρ_1 is below about 0.5, the flow loss probability at both Ingress LSRs in TE network can be reduced. Supposing that the loss probability of flows injected in Ingress LSR$_1$ is smaller than 10^{-3}. To achieve this requirement, ρ_1 should be less than

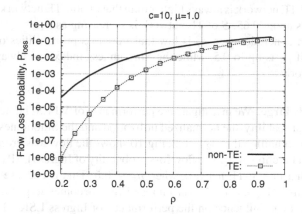

Fig. 5. Flow loss probability ($c = 10$).

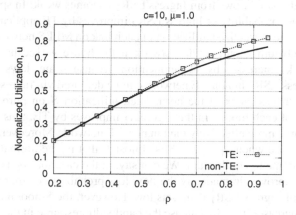

Fig. 6. Normalized Utilization ($c = 10$).

about 0.3 in non-TE network whereas TE network can accept ρ_1 more than two times as much as non-TE.

Secondly, we evaluate the effectiveness of TE from the point of view of bandwidth utilization on MPLS-TE network and we show the normalized utilization of each link in Fig.8. In non-TE network, the normalized utilization on link2 u_2 does not change even if ρ_1 increases. However, u_2 increases as ρ_1 on TE network. This is because the quantity of detoured traffic arriving at Ingress LSR_1 via Ingress LSR_2 increases as ρ_1 increases. Therefore, we can use the bandwidth resource of the whole MPLS network domain efficiently by applying TE.

Fig.9 shows the Smoothness index of the link utilization obtained by Eq.(19). From Fig.8, in non-TE network, since the normalized utilization of Ingress LSR_1 u_1 increase as ρ_1 while that of Ingress LSR_2 u_2 is fixed, the Smoothness index S becomes smaller when ρ_1 gets larger as shown in Fig.9. However, in TE network, both u_1 and u_2 increase as ρ_1 so that S of TE network is always higher than that of non-TE network. Furthermore, when ρ_1 exceeds about 0.65, S of TE network is increasing as ρ_1.

Thus we can conclude when ρ_2 is low that flow loss probabilities of both Ingress LSRs improve if ρ_1 is up to 0.5, while the Smoothness index can always increase on MPLS-TE networks.

If ρ_2 is relatively large. We investigate the performance of MPLS-TE network in terms of the flow loss probability, the normalized utilization and the Smoothness index of link utilization on the condition that $\rho_2 = 0.8$. Fig.10 shows the flow loss probability of each Ingress LSR as a function of ρ_1. The flow loss probability of Ingress LSR$_1$ in TE network is higher than that in non-TE network when $\rho_1 \leq 0.5$. This is because the number of detoured flows from Ingress LSR$_2$ via Ingress LSR$_1$ becomes larger if ρ_1 is smaller, that is, TE have a bad influence on the performance of Ingress LSR$_1$. However, TE is effective for reducing the flow loss probability of Ingress LSR$_1$ when $\rho_1 > 0.5$, since the influence of detoured flows from Ingress LSR$_2$ becomes weak. In spite of the value of ρ_1, the flow loss probability of Ingress LSR$_2$ improves by TE application.

Fig.11 shows the normalized utilization of each link on MPLS network for assessing the use of the bandwidth resource of the network. In this figure, we see that the normalized utilization of link1 increases by TE application because some flows that should be rejected on Ingress LSR$_2$ in non-TE network can be detoured via Ingress LSR$_1$. Fig.12 shows the Smoothness index of the normalized utilization S on purpose to evaluate how fair the use of each link is. In this figure, S improves by TE, thus we can use the bandwidth resource more effectively than in non-TE network. Moreover, S increases as ρ_1, especially in case when $\rho_1 \geq 0.7$, S is almost 1, that is, the normalized utilization of the both link come to equilibrium. We can say, in the case that ρ_2 is larger than ρ_1, TE application improves dramatically the flow loss probability of Ingress LSR$_2$ while it degrades that of Ingress LSR$_1$ if ρ_1 gets low. However, the Smoothness index of the link utilization increases, thus we can use the bandwidth resource in the MPLS network more efficiently by TE.

As mentioned above, we can see that the Smoothness index always improves by TE independent of the value of ρ_1 whereas the range of ρ_1 for improving the flow loss probability is limited, so we will show the range of ρ_1 for improving flow loss probability of both Ingress LSRs by TE in Fig.13, where the x-axis is ρ_2 fixed in the system and the y-axis indicates the range of ρ_1 in which the flow loss probability of both Ingress LSRs improves. For example, if ρ_2 is fixed to 0.2, the flow loss probability can be improved when ρ_1 ranges from 0.03 to 0.5. We can see from this figure that both the upper value and the lower one of range of ρ_1 increase as fixed ρ_2, and that when the difference between ρ_1 and ρ_2 is relatively small, both the flow loss probability and the Smoothness index can improve.

4   Conclusions

In this paper, we have quantitatively investigated the effectiveness of TE application to MPLS network. For this purpose, we modeled the "Shared 2×M/M/c/c" queueing system as MPLS network with applying TE and the "2×M/M/c/c" queueing system as

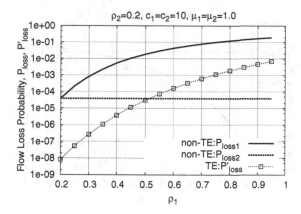

Fig. 7. Flow loss probability versus ρ_1 ($\rho_2 = 0.2$).

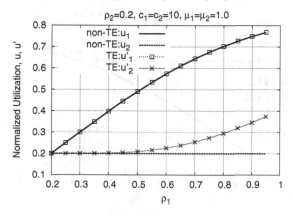

Fig. 8. Normalized utilization versus ρ_1 ($\rho_2 = 0.2$).

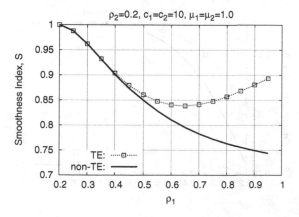

Fig. 9. Smoothness index versus ρ_1 ($\rho_2 = 0.2$).

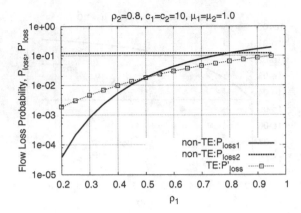

Fig. 10. Flow loss probability versus ρ_1 ($\rho_2 = 0.8$).

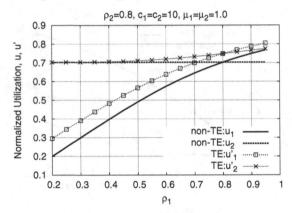

Fig. 11. Normalized utilization versus ρ_1 ($\rho_2 = 0.8$).

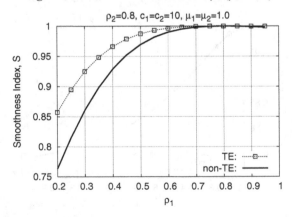

Fig. 12. Smoothness index versus ρ_1 ($\rho_2 = 0.8$).

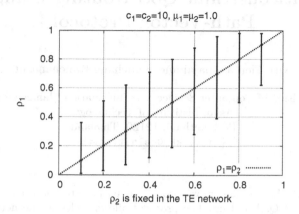

Fig. 13. The range of ρ_1 for improving P_{loss} by TE.

that without applying TE, and derived the flow loss probability of each Ingress LSR and the Smoothness index of each link utilization as performance measures.

Through some numerical results, in case that parameters of two Ingress-Egress LSR pairs are homogeneous, TE can improve both the flow loss probability and the normalized utilization of each link with any value of the input traffic load. When the load of one Ingress LSRs is different from the others, some IP flows on heavily loaded LSR are detoured via Ingress LSR with light load, so that the flow loss probability of Ingress LSR with light load degrades when the load difference between two Ingress LSRs is relatively large, while if it is relatively small the flow loss probability of both Ingress LSRs reduces considerably. Furthermore, the Smoothness Index always can be improved by TE regardless of the traffic load.

References

1. E. Rosen, A. Viswanathan, R. Callon, "Multiprotocol Label Switching Architecture," RFC3031, Jan. 2001.
2. D. Awduche, J. Mulcolm, J. Agogbua, M. O'Dell, J. McManus: "Requrements for Traffic Engineering Over MPLS," RFC2702, Sep. 1999.
3. S. Nakazawa, H. Tamura, K. Kawahara, Y. Oie, "Performance Analysis of IP Datagram Transmission Delay in MPLS: Impact of Both Number and Bandwidth of LSPs of Layer 2," IEICE Trans. Commun., vol.E85-B, no.1, pp.165–171, Jan. 2002.
4. S. Nakazawa, H. Tamura, K. Kawahara, Y.Oie, "Performance Analysis for QoS Provisioning in MPLS Networks," to appear in Proc. The 10th International Conference on Telecommunication Systems, Modeling and Analysis(ICTSM10), Oct. 2002.
5. T. Bayle, R. Aibara, K. Nishimura, "Performance Measurements of MPLS Traffic Engineering and QoS," *Proc. ISOC INET2001*, June 2001.
6. W. Fischer and K. Meier-Hellstern, "The Markov-modulated Poisson process (MMPP) cookbook," Performance Evaluation, vol. 18 , pp.149-171, 1993.
7. R. Jain, *The art of computer systems performance analysis*, John Wiley & Sons, 1991.

Multiconstraint QoS Routing Using a Path-Vector Protocol

Kitt Tientanopajai and Kanchana Kanchanasut

Division of Computer Science and Information Management
Asian Institute of Technology
Pathumthani, 12120, Thailand
{kitt, kk}@cs.ait.ac.th

Abstract. In this paper, we propose a path-vector protocol for multiconstraint QoS routing. The protocol allows nodes in the network to exchange paths, and constructs new paths using our distributed algorithm. Explicit paths provided by the protocol could be used for both multiconstraint QoS and best-effort services. To deal with scalability, we introduce an algorithm to reduce the number of paths by using a clustering method. The method searches and removes paths based on similarity of measurements of path metrics. Simulation results show that our path-vector protocol is scalable and capable to provide explicit paths for multiconstraint QoS routing. Success rate of QoS path setup in simulated heterogeneous networks could be as high as 92 percents.

1 Introduction

QoS-based routing has been developed to provide services that could not be achieved by the Internet's best-effort routing. With QoS-based routing, rate of transmission, delay, reliability, and other traffic characteristics of paths between two nodes can predicted, and guaranteed in advance. One basic problem of QoS-based routing is to find the paths that satisfy a set of QoS constraints. Many studies proposed to solve the problem by extending the existing best-effort protocol. For instance, SMM-DV [1] uses the single-mixed metric scheme on a distance-vector protocol. The RFC2676 [2] provides a framework for OSPF to enable QoS functionality. However, a distance-vector-based protocol is capable to distribute only one metric, i.e., the distance, and it pre-computes only one optimal path for each destination. The protocols could not preserve all metrics required in QoS path computation, and thus it fails to provide the path that satisfy multiple QoS constraints. A link-state protocol can be designed to provide multiple metrics but Wang and Crowcroft [3] proved that the algorithm for multiconstraint path computation are NP-complete when it algorithm involves two or more additive and/or multiplicative metrics. Still, many of the studies use the link-state approach, and attempts to reduce complexity of the algorithm by deploying heuristics.

Instead of distributing distances or link-state information, our path-vector protocol, named QoSPV, distributes a set of paths to neighbors. The protocol

A. Jean-Marie (Ed.): ASIAN 2002, LNCS 2550, pp. 181–194, 2002.

selects paths to be distributed based on similarity of the path metrics. With this technique, only paths to the same destination but different path metrics are distributed to neighbors. The neighbors keep all the paths in its path table, which is used to provide paths for both QoS and best-effort routing. Finding paths that satisfy multiple QoS constraints could simply be done by searching the feasible paths from the path table. The result from simulations shows that QoSPV allows nodes to learn multiple paths to each destination. The protocol scales well to the size of the network and finds the path that satisfies multiple QoS requirements in polynomial time. The success rate of path setup is as high as 92 percents in random heterogeneous networks.

The rest of this paper is organized as follows. In Sect. 2, we provide a description and basic operations of QoSPV routing protocol. The section 3, and 4 describes the algorithm for path construction and advertisement construction, respectively. The section 5 provides related works. The results from simulation are presented in section 6, and we give our conclusion in the last section.

2 Description of QoSPV Routing Protocol

In QoSPV, every node requires to maintain a   , which is a data structure to keep all paths that the node recognized. Basically, QoSPV is a protocol to update the path table by exchanging a set of paths called an   . The Fig.1 shows the main components of QoSPV.

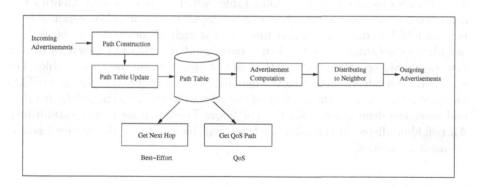

Fig. 1. Components of QoSPV routing protocol

2.1 Advertisement

The advertisement can be constructed by carefully selecting a set of paths from the path table. The node distributes an advertisement to its neighbors during neighbor establishment and path update process. The neighbors construct and learn new paths from the advertisement received using the algorithm described in Sect. 3. After constructing new paths, the neighbors keep all the paths in its path table.

Constructing advertisement is one of our primary concern since the advertisement affects to scalability of the protocol and success rate of QoS path setup. An advertisement that contains more alternative paths allows QoSPV to achieve a higher success rate of QoS path setup. However, such the advertisement also increases the size of the path table, which limits scalability of the protocol. Ideally, an advertisement should be small but still provides paths that satisfy different QoS constraints. We have found that it is possible to construct such advertisement by carefully selecting paths based on the path metrics. First, all paths that reach to the same destination are partitioned based on their measurements of metrics. Paths with the same or similar measurements of metrics are put into the same partition. Each partition would contain paths that provide the same or similar characteristics. Thus, we select only one path, the path with minimal hop count, from every partition to be included in an advertisement. By this method, an advertisement would contain only paths with significantly different path metrics. The actual algorithm for advertisement construction and an example of advertisement construction are described in Sect. 4.

2.2   Neighbor Establishment

QoSPV uses a mechanism similar to those of the Hello protocol described in the OSPF [4] to discover new neighbors and maintain neighbor relationships. Every node requires to maintain a neighbor table, which is used to store identity and dead interval of every established neighbor. All nodes are also responsible to periodically broadcast a HELLO message through all network interfaces. The neighbor establishment starts when a node receive a HELLO messages from a new neighbor, i.e., the neighbor that is not listed in the neighbor table. The node sends an advertisement to the new neighbor in order to reply the HELLO message received, adds the identity of the new neighbor into the neighbor table, and reset the dead interval for the neighbor. The neighbor is now established. All neighbors listed in the neighbor table will be notified if the received advertisement is changed.

2.3   Path Updates

In QoSPV, every node needs to keep the advertisement it distributed to its neighbors so that it can recall the paths that have already been distributed. Each node also requires to monitor local paths to its neighbors, and updates the path table if any of them have been changed significantly. Since the path table is updated, the advertisement may also be changed, and the node must construct a new advertisement. The new advertisement must be compared with the one that has been distributed to its neighbors. If there are any differences, the node must distribute the new advertisement to neighbors in order to notify the changes of the paths.

2.4   Multiple Constraints

For each path, QoSPV provides the measurements of available bandwidth, available buffer, propagation delay, jitter, loss rate, cost, and hop count. Thus, it is possible to specify one or more constraints on the metrics. In general, the constraints are specified in the form of the flow specification [5]. A flow specification consists of two parts: TSpec and RSpec. The TSpec describes characteristics of traffic while the RSpec describes the reservation characteristics. With the flow specification, it is possible to compute end-to-end delay, D_{e2e}, by the following equation.

$$D_{e2e} = D_{queueing} + D_{transmission} + D_{propagation} \tag{1}$$

RFC 2212 [6] describes that,

$$D_{queueing} = \frac{(b-M)}{R} + \frac{(p-R)}{(p-r)} + \frac{M+C_{tot}}{R} + D_{tot} \tag{2}$$

where b, r, p, m, and M are parameters specified in the TSpec. They are bucket depth, bucket rate, peak rate, minimal policed unit, and maximum datagram size, respectively. R is the data rate, which is a part of the RSpec. C_{tot} and D_{tot} is rate-dependent error term, and rate-independent error term, respectively. In this paper, we assume that C_{tot} and D_{tot} are all zero, and $p = \infty$. Thus, $D_{queueing}$ is simplified to

$$D_{queueing} = \frac{b}{R} + \frac{C_{tot}}{R} + D_{tot}$$
$$= \frac{b}{R} \tag{3}$$

Therefore,

$$D_{e2e} = \frac{b}{R} + D_{transmission} + D_{propagation}$$
$$= \frac{b}{R} + \frac{M}{R} + D_{propagation}$$
$$= \frac{b+M}{R} + D_{propagation} \tag{4}$$

Since $D_{propagation}$ is already provided by the protocol, D_{e2e} can be computed. This means that, the protocol could also find the path with an end-to-end delay constraint. When a delay constraint, $D_{request}$, is specified along with a flow specification, the protocol computes D_{e2e} from the flow specification. The QoS request can be provided if there exists the path that satisfies the flow specification e.g., available bandwidth $\geq R \geq r$, available buffer $\geq b$, and $D_{request} \geq D_{e2e}$.

3   Algorithm for Path Construction

Basically, a path is a set of links that serially connect one node to another. A path connecting from node N_1 to node N_n, denoted $P(N_1, N_n)$, could be expressed as

$$P(N_1, N_n) = \langle L(N_1, N_2), L(N_2, N_3), \dots, L(N_{n-1}, N_n) \rangle \tag{5}$$

where $L(N_1, N_2), L(N_2, N_3), \dots, L(N_{n-1}, N_n)$ are the links that form the path $P(N_1, N_n)$. Suppose there exists a bidirectional link $L(N_0, N_1)$ that directly connects between node N_0 and N_1 (i.e., N_0 is a neighbor of N_1) then N_0 could also reach to N_n using the path

$$
\begin{aligned}
P(N_0, N_n) &= \langle L(N_0, N_1) \rangle \parallel P(N_1, N_n) \\
&= \langle L(N_0, N_1) \rangle \parallel \langle L(N_1, N_2), L(N_2, N_3), \dots, L(N_{n-1}, N_n) \rangle \\
&= \langle L(N_0, N_1), L(N_1, N_2), L(N_2, N_3), \dots, L(N_{n-1}, N_n) \rangle
\end{aligned} \tag{6}
$$

Since link $L(N_0, N_1)$ is bi-directional, then there exists the link $L(N_1, N_0)$ that is identical to $L(N_0, N_1)$ but transmits data in the opposite direction. Therefore, node N_1 can distribute the path $P(N_1, N_n)$ to node N_0. Node N_0 then recognizes that there exists the link $L(N_0, N_1)$ as well as the path $P(N_0, N_n) = L(N_0, N_1) \parallel P(N_1, N_n)$. This implies that node N_0 could learn new paths from all the paths that have already been recognized by N_1. However, to avoid loop, node N_0 must ensure that $P(N_1, N_n)$ does not list N_0 in its sequence. Finally, we could establish a theorem that describes a relationship of information stored in the path table as showed in Theorem 1, and then define the path construction algorithm as showed in Algorithm 1.

Theorem 1. $\Pi(N_1)$ $\qquad\qquad\qquad\qquad\qquad\qquad\qquad$ N_1 $\qquad$ $\Pi'(N_1)$
$\qquad\qquad\qquad\qquad\qquad\qquad$ $\Pi(N_1)$ $\qquad$ $\Pi'(N_1) \subset \Pi(N_1)$
$\qquad\qquad\qquad L(N_1, N_0)$ $\qquad\qquad\qquad\qquad\qquad$ N_0 $\;\Pi(N_0)$

$$
\begin{aligned}
\Pi(N_0) &= \Pi(N_0) \cup \{\langle L(N_0, N_1)\rangle\} \\
&\cup \{P : \Pi'(N_1) \mid N_0 \notin P \cdot \langle L(N_0, N_1)\rangle \parallel P\}
\end{aligned}
$$

The proof is straightforward. From Eq. 6, if there exists a set of path $\Pi'(N_1) \subset \Pi(N_1)$ and $\langle L(N_0, N_1)\rangle$, then the set $\{P : \Pi'(N_1) \cdot \langle L(N_0, N_1)\rangle \parallel P\}$ must also exist. The condition $N_0 \notin P$ is set to avoid loop. $\square$

Because the path sequence is changed when applying the path construction algorithm, the path metrics must be recomputed. The computation depends on the class of the metric: whether it is　　　　　　　,　　　　　　　, or　　　　　. The general definition of these three classes of metrics according to [7] is showed in Definition. 1.

Algorithm 1 QoSPV path construction algorithm

Require:
  N: the node that receive $\Pi'(M)$
  $\Pi(N)$: the set of all path N recognized
  $\Pi'(M)$: the advertisement distributed by M
  $L(M, N)$: the link that N receives $\Pi'(M)$
Ensure:
  Updated $\Pi(N)$
1: **for all** P in $\Pi'(M)$ **do**
2:   **if** N is not listed in P **then**
3:     $\Pi(N) = \Pi(N) \cup \{\langle L(N, M) \rangle \parallel P\}$
4:   **end if**
5: **end for**
6: $\Pi(N) = \Pi(N) \cup \{\langle L(N, M) \rangle\}$

Definition 1.
$$P(N_0, N_n) = \langle L(N_0, N_1), L(N_1, N_2), \ldots, L(N_{n-1}, N_n) \rangle$$
$$M$$

$$M(P(N_0, N_1)) = M(L(N_0, N_1)) + M(L(N_0, N_1)) + \ldots + M(L(N_{n-1}, N_n))$$

$$M(P(N_0, N_1)) = M(L(N_0, N_1)) * M(L(N_0, N_1)) * \ldots * M(L(N_{n-1}, N_n))$$

$$M(P(N_0, N_1)) = \min(M(L(N_0, N_1)), M(L(N_0, N_1)), \ldots, M(L(N_{n-1}, N_n)))$$

According to the definition, delay, jitter, and cost are additive. Reliability, i.e. (1 - loss rate), is multiplicative. Available bandwidth and available buffer are concave. Therefore, given a path $P \in \Pi'(N_1)$ and the link $L(N_0, N_1)$, the metrics of path $Q = L(N_0, N_1) \parallel P$ could computed as follows.

$$M_d(Q) = M_d(P) + M_d(L(N_0, N_1))$$
$$M_j(Q) = M_j(P) + M_j(L(N_0, N_1))$$
$$M_c(Q) = M_c(P) + M_c(L(N_0, N_1))$$
$$M_l(Q) = 1 - [(1 - M_l(P) * (1 - M_c(L(N_0, N_1))))]$$
$$M_{bw}(Q) = \min(M_{bw}(P), M_{bw}(L(N_0, N_1)))$$
$$M_{bf}(Q) = \min(M_{bf}(P), M_{bf}(L(N_0, N_1)))$$

where M_d, M_j, M_c, M_l, M_{bw}, and M_{bf} are the measurement of propagation delay, jitter, cost, loss rate, available bandwidth, and available buffer, respectively. If $\Pi'(N_1) = \oslash$, then the sequence of Q contains only $L(N_0, N_1)$ and the metrics of Q are set to those of the link $L(N_0, N_1)$.

4   Advertisement Construction Algorithm

The advertisement construction algorithm is described in Algorithm 2. Basically, the algorithm is an implementation of a clustering method [8]. Applying the algorithm to a set of paths causes the paths to be partitioned based on measurements of metrics.

Algorithm 2 Clustering method of path partition

Require:
  P: all paths in the path table
  t: threshold distance
Ensure:
  A: advertisement

1: $A \leftarrow \oslash$
2: **for** each destination D **do**
3:    $P^D \leftarrow$ a set of path to destination D
4:    $n \leftarrow$ the number of members in P^D
5:    $G \leftarrow \oslash$
6:    **for** $i = 0$ to $n - 1$ **do**
7:      $G \leftarrow G \cup \{P_i^D\}$
8:    **end for**
9:    $distance \leftarrow 0$
10:   **while** $distance < t$ **do**
11:     $distance \leftarrow \propto$
12:     $x \leftarrow \propto$
13:     $y \leftarrow \propto$
14:     $n \leftarrow$ the number of members in G
15:     **for** $i, j = 0$ to $n - 1; i \neq j$ **do**
16:       $d_{i,j} \leftarrow \max(p : G_i, q : G_j \cdot |pq|)$
17:       **if** $d_{i,j} < distance$ **then**
18:         $distance \leftarrow d_{i,j}$
19:         $x \leftarrow i$
20:         $y \leftarrow j$
21:       **end if**
22:     **end for**
23:     **if** $distance < t$ **then**
24:       $G_x \leftarrow G_x \cup G_y$
25:       $G \leftarrow G - G_y$
26:     **end if**
27:   **end while**
28:   $n \leftarrow$ the number of members in G
29:   **for** $i = 0$ to $n - 1$ **do**
30:     $sp \leftarrow$ the minimal hop count path in G_i
31:     $A \leftarrow A \cup \{sp\}$
32:   **end for**
33: **end for**

There are many clustering methods available, e.g., the single-link method, the completed-link method, and the Ward's method. We choose to implement the completed-link method in QoSPV because it generally outperforms the others [9]. The completed-link method requires distances or similarity coefficients to partition data. We represent path metrics as a point in n-dimension Euclidean vector space, where n is the number of metric considered in QoS path computation. The Euclidean distance of n-dimensional vector space could be computed by the equation

$$d_{P,Q} = \sqrt{\sum_{i=0}^{n}(P_i - Q_i)^2} \tag{7}$$

where P_i and Q_i is a measurement of the i-th dimension of the point representing path P and Q, respectively. Initially, the method assigns one path to one partition. Then, for each iteration, the clustering method merges two partitions that the maximum distance between them is the minimum. The process is repeated until the distance is greater than the threshold. Thus, for the threshold value of zero, all paths would be included in a advertisement. If the threshold is set to one, all paths to the destination will be merged into one group, and an advertisement would contain only the shortest path. Fig. 2 shows an example of advertisement construction.

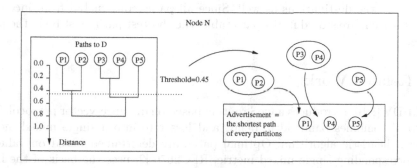

Fig. 2. An example of path partition

From the example, path $P1$, $P2$, $P3$, $P4$, and $P5$ are paths from node N to destination D, with hop count of 1, 4, 3, 2, 2, respectively. The path $P3$ and $P4$ are merged at distance of 0.2, creating a partition of $\{P3, P4\}$. $P1$ and $P2$ are merged at 0.4. With the threshold of 0.45, the algorithm produces three partitions: $\{P3, P4\}$, $\{P1, P2\}$, and $P5$. The shortest path, i.e. the path with minimal hop count, from these three partition, $P1$, $P4$, and $P5$ is selected to be an alternative path for the destination D. Node N applies the same method to every destination, and combines all the alternative paths to create an advertisement.

Because the algorithm selects the path with minimal hop count from every partition, the shortest path to the destination is always included in the advertisement constructed. All neighbors that receive the advertisement learn not only a set of paths, but also the shortest path to each destination.

Proposition 1. N

N

Let P_D be a set of path from N to destination D, and sp_D be the shortest path from N to D, then we know that $sp_D \in P_D$, and no path $p \in P_D$ is shorter than sp_d. Applying algorithm 2, after line 27, P_D would be partitioned into, says, j partitions ($1 \le j \le n$ is the number of paths in P_d) and sp_D must be located in one of the j partitions because $sp_D \in P_D$. At the line 30-31, regardless of which partition contains sp_D, the path sp_D would always be included in an advertisement because the partition is a subset of P_D and no path $p \in P_D$ is shorter than sp_d. $\square$

Proposition 2. N

Let M be a neighbor of node N, and D be a destination, the shortest path from N to D can either be the link $L(N, D)$ if D is a neighbor of N, or the path $\langle L(N, M) \rangle \parallel$ (the shortest path from M to D). Because all advertisements sent to N contain the shortest path for each destinations (Proposition 1), the set of paths constructed from the advertisements must contain the shortest path from N to the destinations as well. Since all paths constructed from incoming advertisement are stored in the path table, the shortest path must be in the path table. $\square$

5   Related Work

SMM-DV [1,10] introduces a QoS routing based on distance-vector protocol. The protocol combines bandwidth, delay, and loss rate into a single mixed metric using a heuristic algorithm. Optimal paths are determined based on value of the corresponding single mixed metric. RFC2676 [2] uses the basis of the link-state protocol. Paths are pre-computed using an algorithm that chooses minimal hop-count path that has the widest bandwidth. This algorithm is referred to as a widest-shortest path algorithm. Wang and Crowcroft [3], proposed another algorithm referred to as a shortest-widest path algorithm. The algorithm searches for path with widest bandwidth, and if there is more than one path available, the one with the minimal delay is chosen. Widyono [11] proposed another algorithm called Constrained Bellman-Ford (CBF) that provides the minimum cost paths with optimal delay constrained.

6   Simulation Results

We wrote a QoSPV simulation program in Java. The program was run on 1 GHz Pentium III PC with 256 MB of memory. We simulated networks with

size between 10 and 50 nodes. The network larger than 50 nodes could not
be simulated due to limitations of speed and memory of the PC we used. For
each size of networks, 20 topologies are randomly generated with at least node
degree of 2, and average node degree of 4, which is the average node degree
of the Internet [12]. Links are randomly chosen among T1, T3, and OC3 with
characteristics showed in Table 1. Loss rate of every link is set to zero. The
threshold used in Algorithm 2 is varied from 0.00001 to 1.

Table 1. Simulated link characteristics

Link	Rate (Kbit/sec)	Delay (msec)	Jitter (msec)	Buffer (Kbyte)	Cost
T1	1544	50	10	256	64
T3	44736	5	5	512	2
OC3	155000	1	1	1024	1

For every network, the simulation program randomly chooses 1,000 pairs
of sources and destinations to setup paths with multiple constraints of end-
to-end delay, data rate, and buffer space. The end-to-end delay constraint is
varied between 10 and 60 msec. For each delay constraint, the program sets
data rate between the value of 128 Kbit/sec and 4,096 Kbit/sec, which may
cause bandwidth bottlenecks in T1 links. The buffer space is a random value
between 8 Kbyte and 64 Kbyte.

6.1   Average Number of Paths

We measure size of every advertisement distributed across networks as well as
size of the path table. Fig. 3 and 4 shows the average number of paths of advertisement and path table, respectively.

For every threshold value, Fig. 3 shows that the size of advertisement is
increased by the size of the network. It also indicates that smaller threshold
values produce a larger advertisement. This is because Algorithm 2 generates
more partitions of paths when specifying smaller values of threshold. Fig. 4 shows
the same shape of curves as Fig.3, but in different scale. The reason is that the
path table is a collection of paths constructed from all incoming advertisements.
These two figures confirm that the size of the path table can be controlled by
the threshold value.

6.2   Average Success Rate

On all simulations, we determined how often QoSPV could find and setup the
path that satisfy the QoS requirement. Then, we calculated the success rate of
path set up to compare among networks with different sizes. Fig. 5 shows what
we have found.

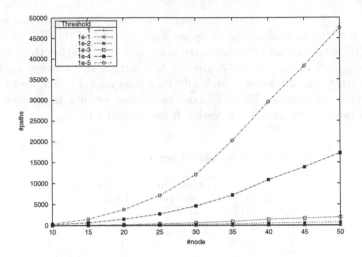

Fig. 3. Average number of paths in advertisement

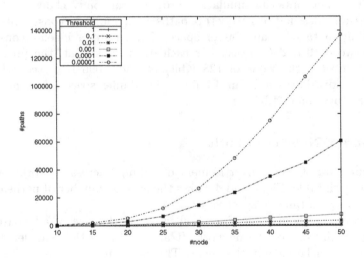

Fig. 4. Average number of paths in path table

From the Fig. 5, smaller networks achieve higher success rate than larger networks. The reason is quite straightforward. In a large networks, sources and destinations are usually apart by a large number hops. Thus, the end-to-end delay of paths between them are relatively higher than those in small networks that sources and destinations are mostly neighbors. This means that the paths between a source and a destination in a large network would hardly satisfy the low end-to-end delay constraints.

Fig. 6 also shows averages success rate of QoSPV but plots against the threshold values. The figure indicates that higher threshold values cause lower success

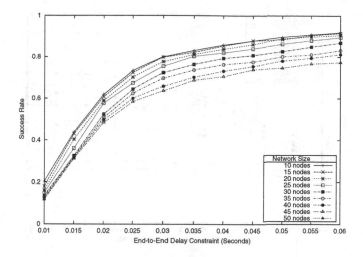

Fig. 5. Average success rate on networks with different size

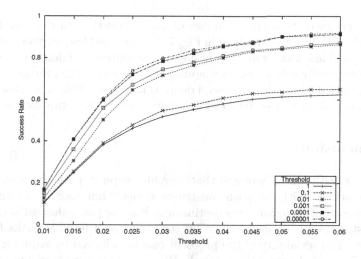

Fig. 6. Average success rate of different threshold values

rate of the routing. This is because a higher value of the threshold produces smaller advertisements, providing smaller number of alternative paths, and decreasing the possibility to find paths that satisfy QoS requirements.

To compare between the size of advertisement (Fig. 4) and the success rate (Fig. 6), the figures indicate that increasing the threshold value of 0.0001 to 0.001 slightly reduces the success rate of QoS path setup, but dramatically reduces the size of advertisement as well as the size of path table. This threshold value of 0.001 might not be the optimal value for the system but it can be used as a guideline to fine-tune the protocol to deliver at optimal performance.

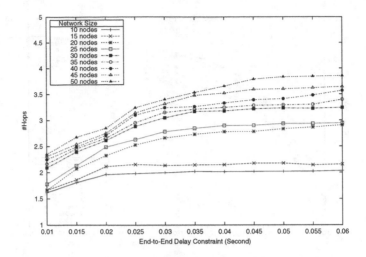

Fig. 7. Average number of hops

We determined the average number of hops of every path that can be setup successfully. The result is provided in Fig. 7. It indicates that, on average, smaller networks provide a smaller number of hops since sources and destinations in such network are usually neighbors. The figure also shows that the average number of hops is increased when the end-to-end delay is increased. This is because a larger end-to-end delay increases chances for longer paths to be setup successfully.

7   Conclusion

QoSPV is a path-vector protocol that provides explicit paths between sources and destinations. With our path construction algorithm, QoSPV automatically constructs a set of paths for every destination. Finding paths that satisfy multiple QoS constraints can easily be done by searching such feasible paths from the path table. The scalability of the protocol can be achieved by reducing number of paths distributed across the network. We show that our algorithm is capable to reduce the number of paths by using a clustering method to search for paths that measurements of path metrics are similar.

Results from simulation indicate that QoSPV achieves high success rate of QoS path setup, and scales quite well to the size of the network. The results also indicate that both success rate of path setup and scalability of the protocol depend on the threshold value used in the algorithm for clustering. Therefore, the performance of the protocol could be controlled by adjusting the threshold value.

References

1. L. H. Costa, S. Fdida, and O. C. Duarte, "Distance-vector QoS-based Routing with Three Metrics" in IFIP Networking'2000/HPN. (2000) 847–858.
2. G. Apostolopoulos, D. William, S. Kamat, R. Guerin, A. Orda, and T. Przygienda, RFC 2676 - QoS Routing Mechanisms and OSPF Extension, IBM, Lucent, Upenn, Technion, and Siara System (1999)
3. Z. Wang, and J. Crowcroft, "Quality-of-Service Routing for Supporting Multimedia Applications" in IEEE Journal on Selected Areas in Communications, Vol. 14, No. 7. (1996)
4. J. Moy, RFC 2328 - OSPF version 2, Ascend Communications. (1998)
5. C. Partridge, RFC 1363 - A Proposed Flow Specification, BBN. (1992)
6. S. Shenker, C. Partridge, and R. Guerin,
RFC 2212 - Specification of Guaranteed Quality of Service, Xerox, BBN, and IBM. (1997)
7. X. Xiao, and L. M. Ni, "Internet QoS: A Big Picture" in IEEE Network. (1999)
8. M. R. Anderberg, Cluster analysis for applications.
Academic Press. (1973)
9. G. Milligan, and P. Isaac, "The Validation of Four Ultrametric Clustering Algorithms" in Pattern Recognition, vol. 12. (1980) 41–50.
10. L. H. Costa, and O. C. Duarte, "A Scalable QoS-based routing mechanism for supporting multimedia applications" in IEEE International Conference on Multimedia Computing and Systems, vol. 2. (1999) 346–351.
11. R. Widyono "The design and evalulation of routing algorithms for real-time channels" in Technical Report TR-94-024, UC Berkeley. (1994)
12. H. F. Salama, D. S. Reeves, and Y. Viniotis, "A distributed algorithm for delay-constrained unicast routing" in Proc. of IEEE INFOCOM'97. (1997)

Design and Implementation of a Web-Based Internet Broadcasting System on QoS Multicast Routers

Masatsugu Tonoike[1], Takaaki Komura[2], Kenji Fujikawa[1],
Yasuo Okabe[1], and Katsuo Ikeda[3]

[1] Graduate School of Informatics, Kyoto University
[2] ASTEM RI
[3] Osaka Institute of Technology

Abstract. We have designed and implemented an Internet broadcasting system using QoS multicast routers. The routers has been developed as a prototype of our research project and that are equipped with SRSVP as a resource reservation and multicast signaling protocol. The system we have designed here can broadcast input video streams, and can also relay and edit video streams transmitted by other stations. We have defined "ibcast URI," which describes parameters required for receiving broadcast streams as an URI on the Web. A receiver can start to watch any program by only clicking its URI on the time table on his Web browser.

1 Introduction

Recently broadcasting has begun to converge into internetworking, as the rapid deployment of web-based real-time video broadcasting system like RealPlayers and Windows MediaPlayers. The slow dial-up access via analog PSTN or ISDN is now being replaced by broadband access like cable modems, ADSL or FTTH. Internet broadcasting systems currently used have, however, weak points that prevent the systems from being deployed in commercial use. One is that the stream is sent as unicast; those systems have no scalability in the number of receivers. In other words, the broadcast station must prepare so many servers as in proportional to the number of receivers. Another point is that there is no guarantee of quality of service (QoS) on the network layer. Thus the application must do explicit congestion control, which cause considerable delay by buffering, and still not enough stable over congested network.

We, the Real Internet Consortium[14], have been developing a QoS multicast routing protocol called SRSVP[7]. SRSVP is an integration of RSVP and PIM-SM[4,5], and supports both multicast and QoS guarantee simultaneously[15]. The protocol has been implemented as free software and we are now distributing it. There has been shipped routers that are equipped with SRSVP as a commercial product[1].

---

[1] The Furukawa Electric FITELnet-G series, http://www.furukawa.co.jp/fitelnet/g/

A. Jean-Marie (Ed.): ASIAN 2002, LNCS 2550, pp. 195–205, 2002.

In this research, we have designed and implemented an Internet broadcasting system using the routers equipped with SRSVP. The system fully utilizes IP multicast, and thus you can send a video stream to a great number of receivers from your own small PC. The stream is QoS guaranteed; receivers can watch a program without any interference of other flows like web access.

The system we have designed here can also edit and relay video streams transmitted by other stations We can easily add a voice or a telop of the mother tongue to a video stream from another country.

We have defined "ibcast URI," which describes parameters required for receiving broadcast streams. A receiver can start to watch any program by only clicking its URI embedded in the time table on the Web.

In Section 2, we will show requirements to implement an Internet broadcasting system, and in Section 3, we will describe SRSVP, the QoS multicast routing and resource reservation. We will give the design of our system in Section 4 and describe the details of its implementation in Section 5. In Section 6, we will show the evaluation results of some preliminary experiments of our system.

2   Requirements for Internet Broadcasting System

2.1   IP Multicasting

IP multicast is a mechanism that makes copies of a packet on a router and send them to multiple receivers or next-hop routers. A sender has to send only one packet to a specified multicast IP address for a stream. There is no need of sending the same streams multiply at a time in IP multicasting, even when there are many receivers. The load of a multicasting server is quite the same as that of a server for a unicast stream. IP multicast is the mechanism exactly for scalable (and possibly global) broadcasting.

However, IP multicast might have so many receivers and hence we do not have any scalable mechanism of explicit congestion control or packet retransmit used in TCP. Instead, we need some QoS guarantee mechanism at the network layer.

2.2   QoS Guarantee on the Internet

QoS (Quality of Service) on the Internet here stands bandwidth, delay (jitter) and packet-loss ratio. Mechanism for QoS on the Internet is implemented on each router. Each router has a queue on it, and when it receives a packet it first puts the packet into the queue and sends packets from the queue according to its scheduling algorithm. If the queue overflows, some packets are lost. WFQ (Weighted Fair Queuing), which is a conventional technique for QoS on the Internet and utilized in the IntServ framework, guarantees QoS by using queues per flows each and excluding interference from other flows. But preparing as many queues in proportion to flows on a router is a costly solution and very difficult to implement on high-speed hardware routers. On the other hand, there has been proposed another framework for QoS: DiffServ[2]. The routers have only two queues; a queue for QoS flows and a queue for best-effort traffic. The hardware architecture is simple and easy to be implemented, but DiffServ can guarantee no explicit quality of service in, e.g., the packet-loss ratio.

Here we utilize routers based on PPQ (Policed Priority Queuing)[3,6]. PPQ is a scheduling algorithm that has only two queues like DiffServ EF routers. The routers do not have per-flow queues and hence do not do per-flow shaping but do per-flow policing. Packets that overflow the prescribed bandwidth for the QoS flow are discarded before put into the queue. PPQ assumes flows that have little burstiness, and can assures a specified packet loss ratio, like 10^{-5} at each router. Our prototype PPQ router can deal with more than 1,000 flows on a $1Gbps$ high-speed link.

3   QoS Multicast Routing Protocol SRSVP

3.1   Overview

SRSVP (Simple Resource ReSerVation Protocol)[7] is proposed by Real Internet Consortium as a QoS multicast routing protocol on the Internet. SRSVP integrates the features of RSVP[1] and PIM-SM[2].

On SRSVP, each multicast tree has a rendezvous point at its root, like PIM-SM. Rendezvous point receives a unicast stream from senders and relay it as a multicast stream to receivers. The sender itself may be a rendezvous point. Resource reservation is done dynamically in the receiver initiated manner. But QoS parameters are specified by the rendezvous point and receivers must follow them.

3.2   Rendezvous Point

A rendezvous point receives a unicast stream from senders and relay it as a multicast stream to receivers. A rendezvous point also responds resource reservation messages from receivers. In our SRSVP implementation, rendezvous points are not simple routers but rather application gateways; they can do authentication of senders, start and stop of relaying streams, resource reservation to senders, etc. We utilize these features in specifying the IP address and the port number of the sender, specifying the IP address and the port number of the broadcast server, and controlling the start and stop of streams.

3.3   Resource Reservation

Resource reservation is done in the receiver initiated manner. Figure 1 shows the behavior how resource reservation and receiving a stream are done. The resource reservation mechanism is invoked when a receiver send a resource reservation message to a rendezvous point (Fig. 1). Here the sender sends the stream not

---

[2] Here we are mentioning mainly on DiffServ EF (Expedited Forwarding) class

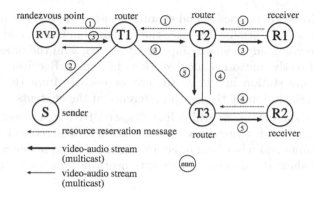

Fig. 1. SRSVP multicast resource reservation

directly to the multicast IP address but to the rendezvous point (Fig. 1). The rendezvous point that receives the stream from the sender resents the stream to multicast address (Fig. 1). When another receiver makes resource reservation for the stream (Fig. 1), the reservation is merged at a router and the multicast stream will reach to the receiver (Fig. 1). In this example, there is not enough bandwidth between T1 and T3, so a route between T1 and T2 is chosen by the QoS routing feature of SRSVP.

4 Design of the Internet Broadcasting System

4.1 Overview

An example configuration of Internet broadcasting is shown in Fig. 2.

We have in mind a live relay broadcast of a 2002 FIFA worldcup soccer game which will be held in Korea. First a broadcast station will send a stream to

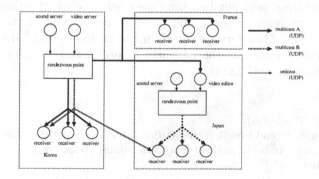

Fig. 2. Overview of Internet broadcasting

audience in Korea via multicast, and simultaneously send the stream to stations in other countries. A station will receive the stream from Korea, add commentary in Japanese to voice, add telops in Japanese to video, send the processed stream to audience directly and other local stations in Japan. Receivers can watch a stream from any station in the world, not necessarily from the nearest one. They can choose station by their own preference of the contents.

In the next subsection, we will define "ibcast URI", which describes parameters needed in broadcasting. Next we will show how a receiver can watch a program he wants and what kind of actions are needed on a viewer application. Then we will show the detailed configuration of the broadcast station and its components.

4.2   ibcast URI

We define here "ibcast URI (Internet BroadCAST Uniform Resource Identifier)," which describes parameters needed in receiving an Internet broadcast stream. Broadcast programs might be done in various format and quality, to be suited to the contents and available bandwidth. Receivers must know the parameters beforehand, at least before they set their video recorder to record a program. Receivers must also know the start time and the end time of the program. SAP (Session Announcement Protocol)[8] is an experimental standard to announce parameters of a multicast session, but SAP has poor scalability in the number of broadcast sessions. In broadcasting system, we do not have to announce the parameters periodically; only the receivers who want to watch the program have need to get the parameters. Thus in our system, the parameters are announced on the Web, just as a time table, so that receivers can get them on demand.

We have designed the ibcast URI, referring to the parameters specified in SDP (Session Description Protocol)[8]. We omit probably useless fields like "phone number to contact", which can be announced by original HTML, and add some fields needed in SRSVP. Session description in ibcast URI consists of multicast address, port number, time the session becomes active and time it becomes inactive, repeat interval and repeat times, format of the stream, parameters and QoS. The syntax is shown in Fig. 3. Here [and] stands optional fields, * stands repetition of the item just before more than zero time, and + stands repetition more than once.

```
ibcast://(IP address)/
[t=(start time):(end time)& [r=(repetition interval):(repetition times)&]* ]
[m=rtp:(port number):(payload type):(encoding) :(clock rate)
 [:(parameters)]* ]+
```

Fig. 3. The syntax of ibcast URI

The following example ibcast URI in Fig. 4 indicates that a 2-ch CD-quality audio stream is broadcasted on multicast address 224.130.54.22 with port 9000, and a 30fps motion JPEG steam is on the same address with port 9001.

```
ibcast://224.130.54.22/m=rtp:9000:96:X-S16LE:
44100:2&m=rtp:9001:97:JPEG:30
```

Fig. 4. An example ibcast URI

4.3   Receiver Application

We have designed a receiver application so that any user can watch programs just like ordinary TV or radio sets on his PC, without any knowledge of the underlying protocols. The usage is very simple. Just browsing a program time table on the Web, and when he or she clicks the URI of a program that is now, the receiver application is invoked. When he clicked URI of the program that is to be broadcasted later, the program is reserved to be recorded and at the start time of the program notification message of resource reservation is indicated.

Fig. 5. Receiver application

4.4   Broadcasting Stations and Rendezvous Points

Internet broadcasting stations are composed of sound servers, video servers and a rendezvous point.

The contents that video servers and sound servers send to the rendezvous point are either streams the servers captures in real time, streams stored on the disks of the servers, or streams received from other servers in real time.

The rendezvous point receives streams and relay them to the specified multicast address with specified port number. The rendezvous point also receives resource reservation messages and send reply messages that establish the reservation.

The rendezvous point has features of live-relaying programs, i.e., receiving, decoding, postprocessing, reencoding and resending streams. We may use this in synthesizing multiple streams into one, imposing telops, and recompressing the video rate.

5   Implementation of the System

We have implemented a prototype Internet broadcasting system based on the design described in the previous section. We adopt Motion JPEG as video format. Motion JPEG is in frame-by-frame manner and is suitable for frame-level postprocessing at a rendezvous point.

5.1   Specification

- Video
  - 320×240 JPEG stream, 30 frame per second. The bandwidth consumed is about $4Mbps$.
  - Compression is done in real time.
- Audio
  - 16bit, $44100Hz$, sampled stereo audio stream without compression.
  - The bandwidth consumed is about $1400kbps$.

5.2   Modules

The component modules implemented are listed in Table 1.

Servers and clients are implemented on FreeBSD 4.3[12]. We have utilized the SDL library [9] in video drawing and the libjpeg library [10] in JPEG compression.

5.3   Controling Burstiness

Our QoS router is based on PPQ described in Section 2.2. The router polices flows and discards packets that overflow the prescribed bandwidth and burstiness.

Table 1. component modules implemented

Sender	Receiver
Audio server	Audio client
Video server	Video client
Rendezvous point	ibcast URI parser

Our early implementation of a video server captures a frame of video, compresses it, and then sends packets for one frame at once. But this causes more burstiness than PPQ expects, so some packets are discarded at routers.

Thus we have added a shaper, which controls intervals among sent packets almost evenly, on video servers. Even a video server sends packets with little burstiness, there is a possibility that the arriving packets at a rendezvous point may have illegal burstiness by jitter on data-link layer. So we have also added shaping feature on rendezvous points.

5.4   Encoding and Decoding

Before implementation, we have investigated the speed of encoding of MMX JPEG 0.1.2[13], a libjpeg variant which supports MMX features of Intel Pentiums The library is compiled by pgcc (Pentium GNU C Compiler) 2.95.2[11] with -O6 -march=pentiumpro options. We have measured 1000 times the time in compressing a 320×240 RGB image stored on a buffer on the main memory and storing the compressed image in JPEG format on another buffer. The average of the gotten result is shown in Table 2.

Table 2. Time needed in JPEG encoding and decoding

machine specification	JPEG encode	JPEG decode
Pentium III $750MHz \times 2$	17,932 μsec	7,864 μsec
Athlon $850MHz$	18,591 μsec	7,852 μsec
Pentium II $333MHz$	33,289 μsec	18,185 μsec

In order to encode a video stream with rate of 30 frames per second, process for a frame must be done in $33msec$. Indeed, this is possible on recent CPUs like Pentium III $750MHz$ in real time. And a machine that has dual Pentium III $750MHz$ on it can do both encoding and decoding simultaneously, in almost the same speed when either of encoding or decoding is executed. Namely we can do decoding and encoding on the same host; we can receive a video stream, decode it, do some processing, re-encode and redistribute.

As a simple example of such a processing, we have implemented a relay server which receives an input Motion JPEG stream, decodes it, imposes a telop on it, re-encodes and sends.

The hardware is based on dual Pentium III $750MHz$, and we execute two processes on it as Fig. 7.

The first process receives the input stream, decodes and imposes a telop. The second process does encode and resend. Stream data is passed between the two process via a pair of sockets.

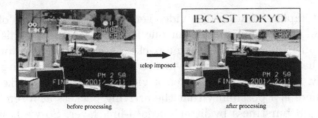

before processing   after processing

Fig. 6. Imposing a telop

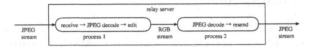

Fig. 7. Flow on a relay server

6   Experiment and Evaluation

6.1   Environment

We have done an experiment broadcasting video streams as shown in Fig. 8[3].
All clients can receive any program of any area. In SEOUL area, the video and
audio streams are mixed at the rendezvous point and sent as multicast streams.
In TOKYO area, two streams are sent. One is a audio and video stream at
the area. The other is a processed video and audio stream. The video stream
is originally multicasted at the SEOUL station and caption is imposed on it at
TOKYO. The voice is replaced in Japanese one, which is sent from SEOUL via
unicast. In KYOTO area, a VoD (Video on Demand) stream is multicasted, but
some audience are watching the program sent from SEOUL and processed at
TOKYO.

   We have confirmed that the system works well as follows. First we invoked
a video server and an audio server at the sender side using the controller, and
then set up the rendezvous point for broadcasting.

   Next we accessed the Web page of the program time table, invoking the
receiver application by clicking the ibcast URI and confirmed that we could
correctly start to watch the program. We have also confirmed that the feature of
relaying works well by receiving a live-relay stream, as is shown in Fig. 8. Here
a stream from SEOUL is received at TOKYO station, a telop is imposed in real
time, and the processed stream is re-broadcasted.

---

[3] The experiment is done actually in our local site. The labels of the areas like TOKYO
and SEOUL are fiction.

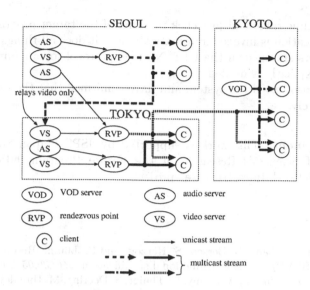

Fig. 8. Overview of our experiment environment

6.2   Effectiveness of QoS Guarantee

We have done an experiment that assures that the stream which has reserved QoS by SRSVP does not get any affect from other flows, by comparing a stream without QoS reservation. We had prepared two receiver hosts, one station host, and 15 VoD servers that generates a number of streams. The station started a program via multicast, one receiver host received it with QoS reservation, and the other host received it without reservation. The VoD servers sent a number of video streams to both of the receiver hosts as jamming.

As we had expected, intolerable loss of frames and voice is observed at the receiver host without reservation, while the host with reservation can receive the stream without any awarable interference of the streams from VOD servers.

7   Concluding Remarks

We have designed and implemented a scalable and high-quality Internet broadcasting system based on QoS multicast routers. The system works on ordinary PC, and this means that any person can have his own broadcast station with almost the same quality as current TV broadcasting system, if we have the next-generation Internet infrastructure with QoS multicasting. The system has also a capability of live relaying. Anyone can receive a program, edit it in real time and resend to the world.

The system is designed on full utilization of Web technology. All parameters required in receiving (or making reservation for recording) and resource reservation are embedded in newly defined "ibcast URI". All the receiver has to do is brows the time table and just click the URI of the target program. Then the receiver application is invoked automatically and it does all things according to the parameters specified in the URI. No new protocol for announcing of such parameters explicitly is needed.

We have also tested the system and have confirmed that the QoS guarantee works effectively.

Acknowledgment. This work is supported by JSPS (Japan Society for the Promotion of Science)'s Research for the Future Program 99P01301, "Self-Organizing Network Infrastructure" project.

References

1. R. Braden, L. Zhang, S. Berson, S. Herzog, and S. Jamin. Resource reservation protocol (RSVP) – version 1 functional specification. *RFC2205*, 1997.
2. D. Estrin, D. Farinacci, A. Helmy, D. Thaler, S. Deering, M. Handley, V. Jacobson, C. Liu, P. Sharma, and L. Wei. Protocol independent multicast-sparse mode (pim-sm): Protocol specification. *RFC2362*, 1998.
3. K. Fujikawa, Y. Fujimoto, K. Ikeda, N. Matsufuru, and M. Ohata. Comfortable service: A new type of integrated services based on policed priority queuing. *Tech. report IPSJ 2000-DPS-98*, pages pp.25–30, June 2000.
4. K. Fujikawa and K. Ikeda. RSVP integrated multicast (RIM). *INET'99*, June 1999.
5. K. Fujikawa, M. Ohta, and K. Ikeda. Integration of multicast routing and QoS routing. *Proc. of INET2000*, July 2000.
6. K. Fujikawa and Y. Okabe. Comfortable service based on policed priority queuing for per-flow QoS guarantee. *DIMACS Mini-Workshop on Quality of Service Issues in the Internet*, February 2001.
7. K. Fujikawa and W. Sheng. Simple resource reservation protocol (SRSVP). Internet Draft, draft-fujikawa-ric-srsvp-01.txt, 2001.
8. M. Handley and V. Jacobson. SDP: Session description protocol [RFC 2327], April 1998.
9. S. Lantinga. Simple directmedia layer (SDL). *http://libsdl.org/*.
10. Independent JPEG Group. (libjpeg). *http://www.ijg.org/*.
11. Pentium Compiler Group. (PGCC). *http://www.goof.com/pcg/*.
12. The FreeBSD Project. (FreeBSD). *htp://www.freebsd.org*.
13. The MJPEG/Linux square. (MMX Jpeg). *http://sourceforge.net/projects/mjpeg/*.
14. The Real Internet Consortium. (RIC). *http://real-internet.org/*.
15. T. Sekiguchi, Y. Koyama, K. Fujikawa, Y. Okabe, and K. Iwama. Hierarchical path QoS on a QoS-based multicast protocol SRSVP. *Proc. 2002 Workshop on High Performance Switching and Routing (HPSR 2002)*, May 2002.

Web-Based Middleware for Home Entertainment

Daiki Ueno[1], Tatsuo Nakajima[1], Ichiro Satoh[2], and Kouta Soejima[3]

[1] Department of Information and Computer Science, Waseda University
[2] National Institute of Informatics, Japan Science and Technology Corporation
[3] Fujitsu LSI Solution Limited

Abstract. In future domestic environments, we will have various home appliances that are connected to home networks. Connecting these appliances requires middleware for providing high level functionalities that hides details of complex issues about respective home appliances. The middleware should be simple and extensible. Also, the middleware needs to access various services on the Internet in an easy way because it is very important to provide future home entertainments that access Internet services.

In this paper, we show our Web-based middleware for home computing environments. Recently, many companies have announced to sell Web-based home appliances. Our middleware enables us to integrate these appliances without their modifications. Also, our middleware allows us to build attractive future home applications that are connected to the Internet. We also show some experiences with our current prototypes and describe current ongoing work to improve the current system.

1 Introduction

Our future life will be augmented by embedding processors in our environments. Analog wireless circuits and various sensors will be integrated with a processor and a memory[11,19], and a variety of computing functionalities will be embedded in our surrounding environments[3]. A vision of [4,5,23] can be soon realized from the hardware point of view.

In ubiquitous computing environments, our home will be augmented by various embedded processors[9,13]. Thus, it is possible to control a variety of home appliances, and various our own information can be retrieved to adapt actions of appliances according to our preference and environmental information. For example, audio and visual appliances like televisions will be connected by standard high speed networks such as IEEE 1394. Also, lights and air conditioners in our rooms are controlled by cellular phones or PDA devices via wireless networks, and our furniture may embed processors to provide various context information to appliances[21]. Finally, these networks are integrated by a home gateway.

However, from the software point of view, a middleware component is necessary to integrate various home appliances to enhance our life. Currently, it is not easy to build middleware components that will be widely used. For example, Jini[22] and Universal Plug and Play(UPnP)[7] are very popular, but a few appliance has adopted these middleware components. On the other hand,

A. Jean-Marie (Ed.): ASIAN 2002, LNCS 2550, pp. 206–219, 2002.

the HTTP protocol will be widely embedded in various appliances in the near future, and it is very cheap to implement the Internet protocol in a processor now[19]. Therefore, most of future appliances will embed HTTP servers to allow us to access the appliances from any places on the Internet.

The serious problem of the current HTTP protocol is that the protocol does not provide important functions such as a directory service and an automatic configuration management that are necessary to build sophisticated home computing environments. In this paper, we propose a new approach to incorporate these services in the Web based home computing environments without modifying traditional Web servers. In the traditional approaches such as HAVi and Jini, supports of integrating with Internet services is very weak because they have been developed before the Internet was widely used in domestic domains. Also, the traditional middleware specifications are too heavy for embedded devices. On the other hand, our system is based on Web based protocols. Thus, it is easy to be integrated with various Internet services. Also, our middleware is very light-weighted due to the adoption of simple Web-based protocols.

The remainder of this paper is structured as follows. Section 2 presents some requirements for middleware for home computing. In Section 3, we describe home computing environments that consist of various appliances containing Web servers. In Section 4, we propose our approach to integrate home appliances. We also present our system to provide a directory service and an automatic configuration management in Web based systems. Section 5 presents several discussions and the current status of our system. In Section 6, we show some experiences with our current system, and describe future work. Finally, Section 7 concludes the paper.

2   Middleware for Home Computing

Our current home appliances now embed very powerful processors to make our life smarter, and software on the appliances may provide various services for home entertainments. Future home computing applications require high level abstraction to build them in an easy way. The software providing high level abstraction is called   . For example, HAVi[6] offers high level abstraction to control various audio and visual home appliances such as TV and VCR. The middleware allows us to build attractive home computing applications without taking into account the differences among vendors.

We have also implemented HAVi on Java and Linux, and shown the effectiveness to provide high level abstraction to build home computing applications[20]. However, we found that the middleware is too complex and big for usual home appliances. For example, in our implementation, HAVi is written in Java, and the amount of bytecodes is about 1Mbytes. Also, using mobile codes makes robust implementation hard.

Currently, the Internet is ubiquitous, and we believe that home appliances will be connected via the Internet in the near future to access various services on the Internet. Thus, we need middleware to make it easy to integrate various home appliances for realizing attractive home entertainments. Some Japanese companies have announced to sell home appliances that contain Web servers[1]. However, it is not easy to integrate these appliances with services on the Internet because there is no high level support to integrate them.

We believe that future middleware for home computing should be simple and enable home appliances to be integrated with various services on the Internet. In the following sections, we show the advantages of Web-based middleware for home computing environments, and present our Web-based middleware.

3   Web-Based Home Computing Environments

Our future home will embed a variety of processors for controlling home appliances and retrieving the current status of the appliances as describing in the previous section. In the near future, a processor will contain a hardware accelerator to implement the Internet protocol, and implement Web servers at the very low price. Web servers are embedded in various appliances[2], and a variety of our surrounding physical objects may contain URLs to attach information to physical objects[10][2]. These system will augment our physical objects or integrate physical world and virtual world[4,8,17]. Also, commercial products that have adopted Web technologies like the Emit technology[1] appears. Thus, we believe that an appliance embedding a Web server will be found in the near future anywhere.

Home computing environments that we assume contain various appliances such as televisions, video cassette recorders, lights, and microwaves that embed Web servers. These appliances can be controlled from any Web browsers, or an application program that speaks the HTTP protocol. For example, a television embedding a Web server allows a vendor to diagnosis it from his Web browser. Therefore, it is easy to maintain home appliances remotely. Also, it is possible to control lights in a room from a Web browser. This situation makes us to build cheap home automation systems.

However, the current HTTP protocol does not provide necessary functions to integrate appliances. We think that the following functionalities are necessary to use appliances containing Web servers in future home computing environments.

- Context-aware device control
- Directory service
- Automatic configuration management

The context-aware device control should make it possible to control appliances using the HTTP protocol, and the action should be changed according to the user's situation. A directory service provides a way to access the target

---

[1] Toshiba has started to sell Web-based microwaves, refrigerators, and washing machines.
[2] In [18], they have proposed the Websign markup Language which contains URL for returning information about the physical object sending a Websign document. Also, the document includes some additional information such as location information to customize the query or control.

appliances. An automatic configuration management maintains the currently available appliances.

Our system provides the above functionalities without modifying home appliances containing Web servers. Therefore, our approach is very practical because it is easy to adopt commercial appliances containing Web servers.

4   Implementing a Web-Based Home Appliance Middleware

This section presents our Web-based home computing system. Web-based means that users can access home appliances from standard Web browsers via the HTTP protocol. Therefore, the access to home appliances becomes uniform and easy due to the Web-based operations. Also, our system can connect appliances that support various protocols for home computing such as Jini, UPnP(Universal Plug and Play) and HAVi by converting the protocols to the HTTP protocol.

The following goals are important to design our system.

- Our system should be simple. Especially, it should avoid to make appliances too complex.
- Our system should be integrated with various services on the Internet.
- Our system should support context-awareness.

Our system can realize the first goal to adopt the Web-based protocol. The appliances in our system are assumed to support a subset of the HTTP protocol or the UPnP protocol, that can be implemented as a small size of programs. The commands to control appliances are delivered on HTTP or SOAP. The second goal can also be achieved by adopting the Web-based protocol because there are many services on the Internet, and the number of the service will be dramatically increased in the near future according to the popularity of Web services. The third goal can be realized by the URL based naming scheme presented in Section 4.2. The section presents our prototype system of Web-based home computing middleware.

4.1   Web-Based Home Appliances

Our middleware component allows users to access Web-based home appliances from standard Web browsers. Our system consists of a directory server and Web-based home appliances. The directory server knows all IP addresses of Web-based home appliances. Also, the server allows users to access the appliances by using the intuitive names. Since the directory server is described in Section 4.3, the section focuses on our Web-based home appliances. Currently, our Web-based home appliances allow us to control X10-based devices[24].

Our Web-based home appliance consists of three components. The first component is the X10 server, the second component is the X10 interface device, and the last component is X10 modules. The X10 server consists of the HTTP component and the X10 component. The HTTP component accepts HTTP requests for controlling X10 modules over the Internet. Also, our extension allows the component to accept commands for controlling X10 modules by using the special expression described in the next section. The X10 component connects to a X10 interface device via a serial line, and executes the X10 protocol. In our implementation, the HTTP component has been implemented in Java, but the X10 component module has been implemented in the C language and it runs on Linux directly because processing the X10 protocol is timing critical. On the other hand, the HTTP component can be easily implemented in Java since Java provides very high level HTTP supports.

The X10 interface device is a module sending signals to other X10 modules over AC power lines. The X10 protocol is defined for sending commands between a traditional computer and an X10 interface device.

There are several types of X10 modules. For example, the appliance modules turn AC power on and off. The lamp modules turn the power of a light on and off, and also adjust the brightness gradually. The radio modules receive radio signals from sensors or remote controllers that transmit commands. These modules are controlled by a computer through an X10 interface device. Also, the modules can be controlled by remote controllers or sensor modules through radio modules.

Currently, we have developed X10 based home appliances, but our system can support various home appliances if the appliances support either the HTTP/SOAP protocol or the UPnP protocol. In the near future, we have a plan to develop other appliances such as a Web-based television and VCR for validating the effectiveness of our approach. Also, some companies have announced to sell various products that support the HTTP/SOAP or UPnP. We believe that the appliances can be used in our system without modifying them, and the appliances can be accessed in a higher level way by using the functionalities provided by our system.

4.2   Accessing Home Appliances via the HTTP Protocol

The HTTP component is a part of the X10 server, thus our system enables us to control X10 modules via the HTTP protocol from Web browsers. In our approach, commands to control the X10 modules are encoded in URLs to transmit HTTP requests.

The Web-based approach enables us to control home appliances easily and naturally. Our system accepts a query request using the standard HTTP GET requests proposed in [15]. The request expression is designed based on the URL expression.

Two examples are shown below. In both examples, x10server.com indicates the host computer's name that implements X10-based home appliances. In the first example, "house=A" and "device=4" means that the module's house code is 'A' and device code is '4' respectively[3]. Also, "power=on" means a command to turn a module to be connected to a light 'on'. Therefore, the expression means turning on module A4 connected to x10server.com. Similarly, in the second ex-

---

[3] The house code and the device code are used as an address to identify each X10 module.

ample, the expression indicates the brightness of module C2 to be connected to a light is up 10 degrees.

(1) http://x10server.com/?house=a&device=4/!power=on/

(2) http://x10server.com/?house=c&device=2/!bright=10/

The URL-based expression can be used for controlling a variety of appliances. Therefore, clients are able to utilize the Web-based home appliances in a seamless way. Also, the expression makes it possible to convert various plug and play protocols for home computing such as Jini, UPnP, and HAVi since the expression enables us to specify target appliances via function names[14]. Our approach enables us to compose appliances by transmitting HTTP requests from an application program since both the name of appliances and the commands to control the appliances are encoded in URLs.

The example shows that our naming scheme can support to control appliances. However, our scheme can support higher level control. For example, http://gw/?func=TV/ identifies an appliance which has a function of a television. Also, http://gw/?func=TV&place=Living-Room/ identifies the television in my living room. The example shows that our naming scheme is very powerful. Especially, our naming scheme can support the context-aware selection of an appliance and forwarding requests to an appropriate appliance in a context-aware way, and these features are very important for future home computing middleware. Although traditional home computing middleware such as HAVi, Jini, or UPnP do not support context-awareness. Our system's powerful naming scheme provides various naming conventions.

4.3   Web-Based Home Computing System

The most important requirement for designing our Web-based home computing system is that an appliance containing a Web server should not be modified. Because commercial appliances that contain Web servers do not allow us to modify their Web servers, but developing a new plug and play protocol is not easy since it is very hard to standardize the new protocol. However, automatic configuration that can be found in Jini or UPnP must be supported for building home computing environments because usual people does not know how to configure home networks.

In traditional Web-based environments, a client needs to know the URL of each appliance before accessing it. However, it is not easy to know the URL if there is no directory service to find the URL for an appliance that a user wants to access. Automatic configuration requires a directory service to register URLs for respective appliances.

Our home computing system provides a Jini like directory server, and it makes it possible to integrate Web-based home appliances[15]. However, our system does not assume the extension of the Web server to use commercial products that contains Web servers. Therefore, our directory server finds all connected Web-based appliances proactively. This means that the server contacts a DHCP server and retrieves IP addresses leased for all appliances connected to a network. Then, the directory server transmits HTTP requests to all appliances whose IP addresses are retrieved by the DHCP server. If a file describing the specification of services provided by each appliance is returned to the directory server, the information is stored in the database on the directory server that is used for forwarding HTTP requests received from clients to target appliances.

Also, our system can use UPnP as a low level protocol. When a directory server receives an advertisement from an appliance, the directory server sends a HTTP GET request to the appliance to retrieve a file describing the service specification provided by the appliance. In this case, UPnP based appliances can be also used without modifying their programs.

4.4   A Sample Scenario

In this section, we describe a sample scenario that shows how our system works. In the scenario, a user has a PDA device for controlling appliances. These appliances contain Web servers, and a directory server collects information about the currently available appliances as described in the previous section. In the current example, the database converts a function name to a house code and a device code of a X10 module connected to an appliance indicated by the function name.

When a PDA device opens a Web browser in our home, the first HTTP GET request is snooped by a gateway Web server running on a router. The server returns a HTML page containing a list of appliances that are currently available in our house. The page is automatically generated by the directory server using information collected from Web-based appliances. In our example, we assume that the page contains a link to http://www.home.tokyo.jp/TV/!power=on/ that means to turn a TV appliance on in our house.

Let us assume that a user sends a command to turn on the TV appliance that is connected to a X10 module by clicking the above URL. The browser of the PDA device transmits a GET command with http://www.home.tokyo.jp/TV/ !power=on/. The URL is translated to http://tv.home.tokyo.jp/?house=a &device=4/!power=on/ on the directory server, and forwards the URL to the Web server of the TV appliance. This means that a user accesses the television of our home without knowing the IP address or the host name of the directory server since the address is automatically searched by the system. Also, "http://www.home.tokyo.jp/TV/" is translated to "http://tv.home.tokyo.jp/". This means that the user needs not to know the actual IP address or the host name of our television. Finally, when the Web server of the TV appliance receives the URL, the server turns the power switch of the TV appliance on by sending a X10 command to turn on a X10 module to be connected to the TV appliance.

The framework is very powerful and can be extended to connect various home computing protocols such as Jini, HAVi, and UPnP.

4.5   Integrating Home Networks

Our middleware has a lot of advantages over traditional home computing middleware such as HAVi, Jini, and UPnP, but these standard middlewares will be widely used for various home appliances. Thus, it is important to support to interoperate between these middlewares. The section shows that our middleware also can be used to ontegrate these middlewares in a systematic way. We show how our middleware connect HAVi, Jini, and UPnP in this section.

As shown in Figure 1, we assume that there are three home networks that are connected to the Internet via respective application-level gateways. These home networks respectively support UPnP, HAVi, and Jini protocols. Application level gateways support our URL-based naming scheme and communicate with other gateways by using the HTTP protocol.

Application-level gateways in our system consist four components. The first component implements home network protocols such as HAVi, Jini, or UPnP. The component behaves as one of home network devices. For example, if a component implements the Jini protocol, it behaves as a Jini device. The second component implements HTTP. The component behaves as a Web server.

The third component implements a protocol translator. The translator converts between the HTTP transaction described in the previous section and home network protocols. For example, the HAVi translator converts both from HTTP to the HAVi protocol and from the HAVi protocol to HTTP. We have also implemented the Jini translator and the UPnP translator in our current prototype

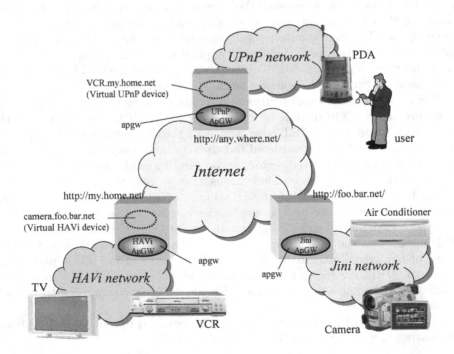

Fig. 1. Connecting Home Networks

implementation. The most important role of the component is to connect a protocol specific naming scheme to our URL-based naming scheme.

The last component is the registration manager. The registration manager can be accessed by HTTP from a Web browser or a home network protocol from some appliances that implement the protocol. If an appliance on a home network likes to be accessed from my home network, the name of the appliance that we like to access should be registered on my application-level gateway. The name can be registered via either HTTP or a home network protocol. After the registration, a new pseudo home network device is created in the application-level gateway. The pseudo device registers its name in a lookup service. The role of the pseudo device is to covert control commands that are delivered on the home network as HTTP messages.

For example, let us assume that we like to control a VCR device on a HAVi network from a PDA connecting to a UPnP network. In the HAVi network, the VCR device is registered as "VCR", and its application-level gateway(HAVi ApGW) is registered as "apgw" in the HAVi lookup service. In the UPnP network, the PDA devices is registered as "PDA" and its application-level gateway(UPnP ApGW) is registered as "apgw" in the UPnP lookup service. However, the registration is necessary only if the PDA device is accessed from other devices.

Now, we like to register the HAVi VCR device in the UPnP network for controlling the HAVi VCR device from the UPnP PDA device. From the PDA device, a user registers the HAVi VCR device in UPnP ApGW as a pair of "VCR" and "http://my.home.net/VCR" from the Web browser on the PDA device. UPnP ApGW creates a pseudo UPnP device on UPnP ApGW, and registers "VCR" in the UPnP lookup service. When the PDA device likes to control the HAVi VCR device, the PDA device tries to find the VCR device via the UPnP lookup service. The lookup service returns a reference to the pseudo device that is created on UPnP ApGW. Then, a control command is delivered to the pseudo device via the UPnP protocol. The pseudo device converts the UPnP request to HTTP , and forwards the request to HAVi ApGW according to the host name part of "http://my.home.net/VCR/". HAVi ApGW receives the HTTP request, and finds the VCR device with the name "VCR" that is specified in the file name part of the URL via the HAVi lookup service. Finally, the command is converted to the HAVi command, and it is delivered to the target VCR device.

Also, let us assume that we like to control a Jini camera device from a HAVi TV device. In this case, a user registers a pair of "Camera" and "http://foo.bar.net/Camera/" on HAVi ApGW using the HAVi protocol, where the TV device finds HAVi ApGW via the HAVi lookup service with the name "apgw". Similar to the previous example, a HAVi command is converted to a HTTP command at HAVi ApGW, and the HTTP command is converted to a Jini command at Jini ApGW.

There is a proposal to connect HAVi and Jini via the HAVi-Jini bridge. However, the approach needs to implement a lot of bridges if there are several home network protocols. Moreover, when a new home network is proposed, it is not realistic to create a lot of bridges to convert among protocols. In our approach, a new home network protocol requires to implement a converter to translate between HTTP and the new home network protocol.

5   Current Status and Discussion

5.1   Current Status

Our Web-based home computing system allows us to control several appliances like lights, televisions, and video casette recorders. Also, our middleware can integrate several home computing protocols. Currently UPnP-based appliances and Jini-based appliances can be connected. We are also working on integrating HAVi-based appliances in our system. The system makes our labolatory smart, and we can use any devices to control various appliances in our labolatory.

Figure 2 shows our X10-based home computing system that enables us to control lights from a Web browser running on a PDA. In the scenario, the browser transmits the URL, http://gw.home.net/Light/!power=on/ to turn the lights on. Also, Figure 3 is a photo showing our system that enables several appliances supporting different protocols for home computing to be integrated. The system allows us to transmit a signal from a X10 remote controller to a X10 server. The server sends a command to a home gateway by using the HTTP protocol. Lastly, the gateway delivers a request via the Jini protocol to control a Jini-based laser disc. The system currently runs on a standard PC and a StrongARM

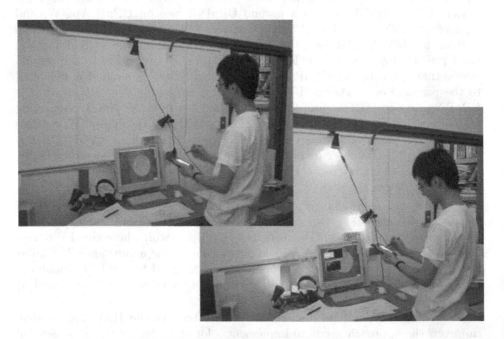

Fig. 2. Web-based Home Computing System

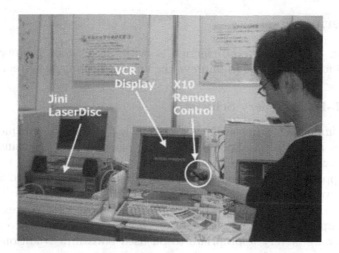

Fig. 3. Connecting Jini and Web-based appliances

based embedded device where embedded Linux runs. The same software can be executed on both hardware platforms without modifying it.

5.2 Discussion

Our approach makes it possible to realize the location-aware appliance control as described in the following way. When a user connects his client device to the Internet, all packets will be forwarded to the nearest router. A gateway server runs on the router, and any HTTP requests are snooped by the gateway server. The gateway server may return a page to the browser when the first HTTP request is snooped. The page can be customized according to the location of the server because the nearest gateway server returns the page. This means that a user knows the currently available appliances near him/her. For example, the scenario described in the previous section is able to show a list of available appliances near the user. By deploying multiple directory servers in a house, a user's action can be adapted according to his/her location.

Our system is desirable as an infrastructure for realizing ambient displays [26] or calm technologies[25]. For example, let us assume that a URL that controls a television is clicked. When a user sends a HTTP POST request to control the television to the gateway server. The server may return a page containing a IMG tag that contains a URL to turn on a light. Thus, the light on the appliance is also turned on because the URL in the IMG tag is automatically accessed[4]. This is an example of an ambient display so our system is very attractive as an experimental infrastructures for ubiquitous computing researches.

---

[4] The approach requires to modify the Web server because the command part needs to be process in a HTTP GET request.

6   Experiences

The section describes several experiences with our current prototype system, and show future directions to improve the current prototype system.

6.1   URL-Based Query Scheme

The most important proposal in our system is the URL-based query scheme. This makes it possible to specify the name of appliances by using the name of their functionalities. The approach is very powerful because it is possible to select appliances, or to transmit commands in a context-aware fashion. For example, if you specify a television, the directory server can forward commands according to your location and preference. We believe that context-awareness is a very important topic to realize future home computing environments, and our middleware is very appropriate to be used both in a traditional domestic environment and in a future ubiquitous environment.

6.2   Commodity Software

We believe that using commodity software is very important to reduce the development cost of home appliances. In our case, our software has been developed in Java and runs on Linux. Currently, Linux and Java have became popular to be used in embedded systems. By adopting Linux, it is easy to develop various Internet-based software since there are many open sources. Also, Java provides automatic memory management and rich class libraries. Thus, the combination of Linux and Java makes the development cost dramatically cheap.

However, we found that there are several problems to adopt Java for developing home appliances. The first problem is that software does not take into account remaining memory capacity. To build robust software, resource-awareness is very important. We hope that future Java virtual machine should support resource-awareness.

The second problem is that most of libraries are too generic for home appliances. For example, if we like to adopt SOAP to receive commands, we use a standard XML parser and a SOAP library, but the appliances receives only fixed commands. We are considering to use a partial evaluator to reduce the unused codes in a systematic way.

6.3   Web-Based Home Appliances

Currently, we are focusing on traditional home appliances such as televisions and microwaves to control from our middleware. However, in the future domestic environments, various objects will become smart by embedding processors. For example, my sweater will have a sensor to monitor my feeling, and our table may change its color by receiving a command from my sweater when my feeling is changed.

We believe that everything in our domestic environments will be smart and may contains Web servers. Moreover, future materials will become intelligent to make our future life smarter. Our middleware can be used to control them in an integrated way. The combination of these smart daily objects created by using the smart materials, and Web services will provide us very attractive new entertainments that may change our daily life significantly.

7 Conclusion

This paper has described Web-based middleware for home entertainment. The middleware has been designed from our experiences with building HAVi-based home computing systems[16], and allow various home appliances to be integrated in a uniform way.

Currently, we are designing a new version of Web-based middleware for home computing The middleware is based on SOAP and WSDL. Thus, it is easy to integrate future Web services. Also, the middleware provides context-aware appliances selection and command execution in a more systematic way. The characteristics is very important to realize the vision of ubiquitous computing that makes our life smarter.

Also, we are discussing with several companies to make our middleware de facto standard for home computing environments. In the near future, we hope that various companies sell Web-based appliances. Also, Web-based objects that are everyday computational things such as smart shoes, cups, or tables may be available. Our middleware makes it possible to integrate the appliances with various services on the Internet, and enables us to build future advanced applications.

References

1. emWare's EMIT Technologies, http://www.emware.com/
2. Gaetano Borriello and Roy Want, "Embedded Computation Meets the World-Wide-Web", Communications of the ACM, Vol. 43 No.5. 2000.
3. H.-W.Gellersen. A.Schmidt, and M.Beigl, "Adding Some Smartness tp Devices and Everyday Things", In Proceedings of the Third Workshop on Mobile Computing System and Applications, 2000.
4. N. Gershenfeld, "When Things Start to Think", Owl Books, 2000.
5. Andy Harter, Andy Hopper, Pete Steggles, Andy Ward, Paul Webster, "The Anatomy of a Context-Aware Application", In Proceedings of the 5th Annual ACM/IEEE International Conference on Mobile Computing and Networking, 1999.
6. HAVi Consortium, "HAVi Home Page", http://www.havi.org/.
7. Intel(R) UPnP Software Development Kit V1.0 for Linux, http://www.intel.com/ial/upnp/tech.htm.
8. H. Ishii, B.Ullmer, "Tangible Bits: Towards Seamless Interfaces between People, Bits and Atoms", In Proceedings of Conference on Human Factors in Computing Systems,1997.
9. C.D. Kidd, et. al., "The Aware Home: A Living Laboratory for Ubiquitous Computing Research", In Proceedings of the Second International Workshop on Cooperative Buildings, 1999.

10. T. Kindberg, et. al., "People, Places, Things: Web Presence for the Real World", In Proceedings of the Third Workshop on Mobile Computing System and Applications, 2000.

11. J. M. Kahn, R. H. Katz and K. S. J. Pister, "Mobile Networking for Smart Dust", ACM/IEEE Intl. Conf. on Mobile Computing and Networking (MobiCom 99), 1999.

12. T. Nakajima, "Towards Universal Software Substrate for Distributed Embedded Systems", In Proceedings of the International Workshop on Real-Time Dependable Systems, 2001.

13. T. Nakajima, et. al., "Technology Challenges for Building Internet-Scale Ubiquitous Computing", In Proceedings of the Seventh IEEE International Workshop on Object-oriented Real-time Dependable Systems, 2002.

14. T.Nakajima, D.Ueno, I.Satoh, H.Aizu, "A Virtual Overlay Network for Integrating Home Appliances", In the Proceedings of the 2nd International Symposium on Applications and the Internet, 2002.

15. T.Nakajima and I.Satoh, "Naming Management in a Web-based Home Computing System", In Proceedings of the 20th IASTED International Multi-Conference on Applied Informatics, 2002.

16. T.Nakajima, "Experiences with Building Middleware for Audio and Visual Networked Home Appliances on Commodity Software", In Proceedings of ACM Multimedia 2002, 2002.

17. Joseph Newman, David Ingram, Andy Hopper, "Augmented Reality in a Wide Area Sentient Environment", In the Proceedings of the 2nd International Symposium on Augmented Reality (ISAR 2001).

18. S.Pradhan, C.Brignone, J.H.Cui, A.McRenolds, M.T.Smith, "Websigns: Hyperlinking Physical Locations to the Web", IEE Computer, Vol.34, No.8, 2001.

19. Seiko iChip, http://www.seiko-usa-ecd.com/intcir/html/assp/s7600a.html

20. K.Soejima, M.Matsuda, T.Iino, T.Hayashi, and T.Nakajima, "Building Audio and Visual Home Applications on Commodity Software", IEEE Transactions on Consumer Electronics, Vol.47, No.3, 2001.

21. N.A. Streitz, J.Geibler, T.Holmer, "Roomware for Cooperative Buildings: Integrated Design of Architectural Spaces and Information Spaces", In Proceedings of the First International Workshop on Cooperative Buildings, 1998.

22. Sun Microsystems, "Jini Technology"

23. Mark Weiser, "The Computer for the 21st Century", Scientific American, Vol. 265, No.3, 1991.

24. X10.org, "X10 technology", http://www.x10.org.

25. M. Weiser, J.S. Browns, "Designing Calm Technology", http://www.fxpal.xerox.com/chi97/white-papers/Mark%20Weiser.html.

26. G. Wisneski, H. Ishii, et. al. "Ambient Display: Turning Architecture Space into an Interface between People and Digital Information", In Proceedings of the First International Workshop on Cooperative Buildings, 1998.

MicroBill: An Efficient Secure System for Subscription Based Services*

R.K. Shyamasundar and Siddharth B. Deshmukh

School of Technology and Computer Science
Tata Institute of Fundamental Research
Homi Bhabha Road, Mumbai 400005, India
{shyam,siddharth@tcs.tifr.res.in}

Abstract. In this paper, we describe the design and development of a microtransaction system to provide an efficient, secure and flexible subscription based solution to e-commerce for digital goods and services. The system is integrated with a multi-instrument payment system as well as a role based PKI system. This has enabled us to support various privacy and authentication aspects of microtransactions.

1 Introduction

The enormous growth in the number of people connected to the Internet over recent years is starting to be mirrored by an equally rapid increase in the value of business transactions carried out over the World Wide Web. From digital deliverables such as software, encoded music and video to a wide range of physical products and services, from books to flowers, banking services to travel bookings, the volume and value of commerce over the Internet (referred to as e-commerce) has shot up almost exponentially over the last few years[1]. A good percentage of the transactions over the Internet is accounted for by digital goods and services. In general, e-commerce covers a broad spectrum of transactions varying from   to   . In   , the need is to cater to a large volume of transactions of low intrinsic financial value. The main challenge of management here, is to keep the cost of each transaction to a minimum possible value over aggregates so that the overhead cost of each e-transaction can be proportionately reduced. As the intrinsic value of each   is very high, the challenge lies in providing a high level of authentication, security and non-repudiation. The selling of digital goods (video, music, software) would in near future surpass the selling of physical goods (books,CDs) over the Internet. Many believe that traditional entertainment, such as new movies and Bonanza reruns, will be bought and delivered digitally in the future to your

---

* The work was done under the project *Design and Implementation of Secure Systems for E-Commerce*, supported from MIT, New Delhi.
[1] Forrester estimates that e-commerce will account for 8.6 % of worldwide sales of goods and services by 2004.

A. Jean-Marie (Ed.): ASIAN 2002, LNCS 2550, pp. 220–232, 2002.

TV/Computer. Vendors and Merchants should be able to sell contents, information, and services over the Internet for a very small charge (a fraction of a dollar). Users may be charged a periodic – daily, monthly or annual – fee to subscribe to a service. There is therefore an overwhelming need for a subscription based service model to cater to these needs.

Another business model which shows much prominence in the e-commerce arena pertaining to digital goods, and services, is the utility model. The utility model is based on metering usage, or a "pay as you go" approach. Unlike subscriber services, metered services are based on actual usage rates. Traditionally, metering has been used for essential services (e.g., electricity, water, long-distance telephone services etc.). Internet service providers (ISPs) in some parts of the world operate as utilities, charging customers for connection minutes. Also, there are services such as chat and online gaming services which require the user to pay on a usage basis.

The development of flexible, secure microtransaction systems has been a priority area for research and development as it has direct bearing on the acceptance and promotion of e-commerce. Some of the prominent efforts in the development of microtransaction systems have been addressed in NetBill [4], Payword [10], MicroMint [10], and MiniPay [6].

The development of NetBill [4] demonstrated how properties such as   , and   are important in the development of such systems. The NetBill system is essentially a trusted-third party system with accounts of its users. Under such a scenario, NetBill supports the important feature of non-repudiation of transactions. Payword [10] is a credit based protocol. It is extremely efficient when a user makes repeated requests to the same vendor. It uses hashing techniques in a major way as a way of authentication; public key operations are used essentially for signature verifications, which are relatively efficient. Micromint [10] is designed to provide reasonable security at very low costs, and is optimized for unrelated low-value payments. They don't have public key operations at all, and are hence extremely efficient. However, the system suffers from drawbacks related to the generation and storage of   . MiniPay [6] was designed to support 'click and pay' applications, where the user buys the information or service as a part of the browsing process. It is a natural extension of the familiar web surfing interface: to buy information or service, the user just clicks on a MiniPay link, much like clicking a normal hyperlink. However, it has the disadvantage of having no support for macrotransactions, and for transactions dealing with non-digital goods and services. It is also not suited for transactions in digital goods, such as software downloads, etc. as the transactions are non-atomic in nature. This may lead to at times the user being not able to download the full software even after making the payments, due to several reasons such as network failure, etc. Apart from NetBill [4] all the other protocols fail in providing the user with a certified delivery mechanism which is of prime importance when it comes to transacting in digital goods and services. It too is however plagued with drawbacks that even the transactions involving zero-priced goods need to be logged at the centralized NetBill server, resulting in all the load getting focused at just one point.

In this paper, we describe the design and development of a microtransaction system to provide an efficient, secure and flexible subscription based solution to e-commerce for digital goods and services. We have developed a suite of protocols called   , on top of the Multi-Instrument E-Commerce System (MIES) [12] built at T.I.F.R. An overall structure depicting the integration of MicroBill with the MIES [12] system is shown in Figure 1. The MicroBill System offers the following advantages:

1. Suitable for setting up Micro-Transaction systems.
2. It does not require any additional accounting and billing system to be installed.
3. It uses a role based PKI system, and hence, also provides support for authenticated group memberships, tokenized or voucher based payments/subscriptions etc.
4. It supports privacy, as it is possible to subscribe anonymously with proper authentication through the underlying PKI system.
5. As it has been built over MIES, that provides support for macrotransactions, it is possible to take advantage of the macrotransactions periodically or sporadically through a spectrum of payment instruments.
6. It inherits properties such as money atomicity, goods atomicity, non-repudiation of transactions from the underlying MIES payment architecture.

Rest of the paper is organized as follows: section 2, gives a brief introduction to the software architecture of MIES, as also discusses its unique features, followed by section 3 which gives a brief operational overview of the MicroBill set of protocols. Section 4 describes the various MicroBill protocols for subscription based services followed by discussions in section 5.

2   Overview of MIES

As mentioned already, our MicroBill system is integrated with the MIES [12] system as shown in Figure 1. The software components over which the MicroBill suite of protocols is built is shown encompassed in a dotted box at the top of the figure.

Let us first note down some of the distinctive features of the MIES system that will benefit the MicroBill system. Some of the key features of MIES are:

1. It is integrated with a PKI system, ROADS [13] built at TIFR; ROADS is based on SPKI/SDSI's [9] and supports role based authentication certificates. This will be of vital importance in achieving various aspects of privacy.
2. It uses an XML-based message passing protocol; this ensures that the system does not have the constraints of proprietary data formats, allowing systems to communicate using standard means of data representation.

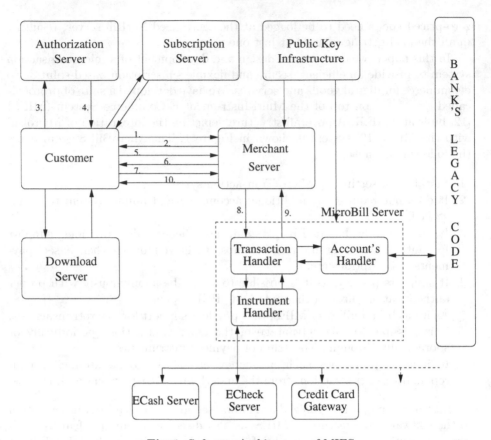

Fig. 1. Software Architecture of MIES

3. It has a distributed architecture, and supports a wide variety of payment instruments such as ECash, ECheck, Credit Cards, etc. This leads to the much needed flexibility in e-commerce.

For further details of MIES reference is made to [12].

3   Operational Overview of the MicroBill System

Before we go into the operational overview of the MicroBill, let us look at the structure of the software components such as merchant server, subscription server, and download server that makeup the MicroBill system (Figure 1).

A : Merchant Server

These are service providers providing a variety of services such as digital downloads (software, music, video, etc.), information browsing, etc. They also act as front offices for displaying and selling commodities, over the web. They act as intelligent price negotiators, and in case the deal is struck, they provide the necessary support for completion of the transaction with the help of the MIES server. The Merchant has also the task of interacting with the digital wallet of the customers towards selection of the transaction protocol, cryptographic protocol, the payment instrument to be used, etc.

B : **Subscription Servers**

Subscription Servers are trusted servers that can also be implemented by third parties as services. These servers have the following roles to perform:

1. As a repository of its clients subscription certificates.
2. Issuer of authorization tokens to gain access to services from the download server, information services, accessing paid services, etc.

C : **Download Servers**

Download Servers are trusted servers that can also be implemented by third parties as a service. They provide a service of high bandwidth download capable of handling several downloads simultaneously. They respond to requests of users only against authorization tokens granted by trusted subscription servers, merchant servers, etc.

Broadly speaking the functioning of the Microbill system can be described as follows:

1. Aid the user in obtaining (or purchasing) a subscription certificate: This could be done in two ways through the MIES server:
   a) Buy the subscription certificate from the respective merchant through the MIES server using the MIES protocol.
   b) If the user has an account with MIES, he could get a credit voucher directly from MIES server for submission to the subscription server.
2. Use the subscription certificate provided by the user to provide the services through the subscription servers as per the certificate.

The suite of protocols of the MicroBill system have to address the following transactions:

1. Transaction where the Customer logs into the Merchant's website to subscribe to its' services. It corresponds to fi
               . For this purpose, we make use of the MIES transaction protocol in our system.
2. Transactions for accessing the pre-subscribed digital goods and services as per the provisions of the subscription certificate.

In this section, we describe the transaction protocol used to procure the subscription certificate. The protocol for realizing the subscription services are described in the next section.

3.1   Procuring a Subscription Certificate

For this purpose, we use basically the MIES protocol. The steps adapted are described below informally. For formal details, the reader is referred to [12].

A subscription certificate can be obtained by the user using the protocol described below:

0. **Initialization Phase:** The user logs on to the merchant's web site and opts to subscribe himself to an electronic service, say e-magazine. The Merchant Server prompts the user to invoke its digital wallet to complete the transaction. The customer now invokes the digital wallet, a handshake takes place between the Digital Wallet and the Merchant Server; through the handshake parameters for the transaction protocol, and the payment instrument are decided between the two as appropriate.

I. **Price Request Phase:** This phase is basically concerned with the price negotiations like mode of delivery, time, and destination if the goods are of non-digital format. This phase is also used to inform the customer of the requisite authorization and discount coupons, to be submitted along with the request. This phase corresponds to messages labelled 1 and 2 in Figure 1.

II. **Transaction Authorization Phase:** This phase is used by the Customer to obtain the requisite credentials, required by the Merchant Server to process the transaction further. The Customer gets these credential certificates through his local Authorization Server. The Authorization server checks if the customer has the requisite permissions to conduct the transaction and in case found eligible, provides the customer with an authorization certificate to be sent to the merchant for processing the transaction. This step corresponds to messages labelled 3 and 4 shown in Figure 1.

III. **Download-Authorization Token Delivery Phase:** Once the customer has obtained the requisite authorization certificate the customer directs the merchant to deliver the Download-authorization token by supplying the authorization certificates as well as the identity generated by the customer for reference during the price negotiation phase that was used during the price request phase. This step corresponds to messages labelled 5 and 6 as shown in Figure 1.

It must be noted that:

  a. Download-authorization tokens delivered in this phase are of encrypted nature, and hence, of no use to the customer; the key for decrypting the goods are delivered only at the end of the Payment Phase.

  b. Download-authorization tokens contain a reference to the subscription server entitled to store the certificates. Note that this is at the users discretion so as to prevent the user from placing the certificate with multiple subscription servers and thereby using the service, more than it is authorized to.

IV. **Payment Phase:** After the encrypted goods are delivered, the customer submits payment to the merchant in the form of a signed Electronic[2] Payment Order (EPO). At any time before the signed EPO is submitted, a customer may abort the transaction and be in no danger of its being completed against his will. The submission of the signed EPO marks a point of no return for the customer.

After the customer presents the signed EPO to the Merchant, the Merchant endorses the EPO and sends it to the MIES Server. The Endorsed EPO adds the merchant's account number, the merchant's memo field, and the decryption key of the goods along with the merchant's signature.

At any time before the endorsed EPO is submitted to the MIES server, the Merchant may abort the transaction and be in no danger of its being completed against his will. The submission of the Endorsed EPO marks the 'point of no return' for the merchant.

On receipt of the endorsed EPO the MicroBill Server, verifies the signatures of the parties involved, the contents of the transaction, and then caries out the transaction on behalf of the customer. In case the transaction completes successfully, it prepares the digitally signed Receipt for the same that includes the symmetric key used to decipher the encrypted Subscription Certificate.

The receipt is returned to the merchant, along with an indication of the customers new account balance (encrypted so that only he may read it). The EPOID of the EPO is repeated in the customer specific data to ensure that the merchant cannot replay data from an earlier transaction.

The merchant provides the receipt details as provided by the MIES server on being probed by the customer for the same. On receipt of the Symmetric key, the Customer deciphers the encrypted text to retrieve the Subscription Certificate.

The Subscription Certificate is now deposited with the Customer's Subscription Server which at a later point provides the Customer with appropriate tokens to access the subscribed goods/services.

Before we go into the protocols for subscription based services, let us look at some of the properties satisfied by the above setup. The MIES protocol satisfies the following properties.

1. **Secure Transaction:** By secure payment transaction, we mean that no third party can make either a passive or an active attack on the transaction (such as tampering the data, corrupting it, or forcing abnormal termination), as also prevent the third party intrusions into getting access to the customers private information such as e-cash , Credit Card No., etc. sent over the network. This is partly achieved through the usage of SSL, amongst communicating parties, as also through encryption of the payment related information using public key cryptography.

---

[2] In order to maintain a proper account of all the transactions in its database, a globally unique identifier called EPOID is assigned for each EPO.

2. **Privacy:** Privacy implies freedom from unauthorized intrusion into ones' personal affairs. It is brought about in the MIES transaction through the usage (optional) of the SSL protocol for sending the messages across the network and also through the integration of the system with the SDSI/SPKI certification provided through ROADS [13] system.

3. **Optional Anonymity:** The protocol provides for anonymity through the usage of the role based SPKI/SDSI [9] certification of the ROADS [13] system.

4. **Non-Repudiation:** Non-repudiation is achieved through the usage of the digitally signed messages, in the communication between the parties involved in the transaction.

5. **Dispute Resolution:** The system maintains a log of all the transaction receipts in its database, this would act as evidence in case of non delivery or fraud on the part of the Merchant, it would also act as a dissuader for false claims from the customers.

6. **Server Load Balancing:** The system delegates the product download functionality to the Download servers, in the process relieves the merchant servers from the extra load of sending in the encrypted software to the customers; this results in a reduction of the overall cost associated with the merchant servers, and thereby acts as an incentive to small merchants who can't afford the heavy costs associated with the setting up of the required infrastructure.

7. **Low Cost per Transaction:** The MIES transaction protocol results in the MIES server acting as an aggregator of the small payments made per transaction, converting it into one large transaction over the traditional financial network using payment instruments such as Credit Cards, etc. Thus, there is an overall reduction in transaction costs, resulting in a low per transaction cost.

4 Protocols for Subscription Based Services

The primary transaction protocol described in the previous section allows us to get a subscription certificate. For completing such a transaction, it goes through the MIES server's authentication server, payment gateway, etc. In other words, this is a macro transaction and the cost of the transaction is not negligible. Thus, if we require repeated (periodic or sporadic) services, it will not be convenient to use the above protocol as the overhead cost will be considerable. Protocols required for getting the subscription services after purchasing the subscription certificate, need to cater to the following roles:

1. Secure protocol for submission of subscription certificates; in other words, the certificate obtained (purchased) is deposited with the subscription server.
2. A secure protocol for using (or getting) the pre-subscribed services (or goods) after depositing the certificate with the subscription server.

The above protocols are described in the following sections. For the sake of ease of understanding, we have repeated some aspects of negotiations; this will be clear from the context.

4.1   Subscription Certificate Deposit Protocol

The Subscription Certificate Deposit protocol is used to securely deposit the subscription certificate, received by the user at the end of the MIES transaction protocol. The protocol assures a secure and certified deposit of the subscription certificate with the subscription server.

It assures a secure and certified deposit of the subscription certificate, through an adaptation of the SPEKE [7] protocol. It maintains in its database a record for every user, containing the following attributes: username, W=h(pwd), and 'B' a random value. Here, 'h' is a one time hash function (such as SHA1, MD5), 'pwd' is the password of the user, B is a random value which is computed at the time of generation of the users account, and is stored in the users database.

Notation: In the following, we use C, and S to denote Customer, and the Subscription Server respectively.

The protocol is described below:

1. C $\longrightarrow$ S (Request for submitting a Subscription certificate made by the Customer to the Subscription server).
   The user makes a request to the subscription server, for submitting a subscription certificate, the XML format request is given below (here, A is the random number chosen by the user while sending the request):

   ```
   <Request>
           <UserID>XYZ< /UserID>
           <publicKey>W^A modp < /publicKey>
           <EncryptedText>
               <RequestType>Certificate Submission< /RequestType>
               <SubscriptionCert>Certificates< /SubscriptionCert>
               <HandshakeSecret>Secret< /HandshakeSecret>
           < /EncryptedText>
   < /Request>
   ```

2. S $\longrightarrow$ C (Signed confirmation of the submission sent by the Subscription server to the Customer). On receipt of the submission request, the subscription server deciphers the encrypted part of text using the hash 'W' stored against the users' account. It retrieves the subscription certificate meant to be deposited and stores it in its repository. After storing the certificate, the subscription server sends a confirmation of the same back to the user. The XML format for the confirmation, is as shown below.

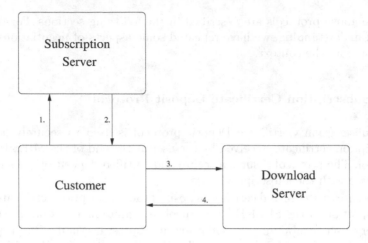

Fig. 2. Pre-Subscribed Goods Download sequence

```
<Confirmation>
        <publicKey>W^B modp < /publicKey>
        <EncryptedText>
                <Result> ... < /Result>
                <TimeStamp> ... < /TimeStamp>
                <HandshakeSecret>Secret< /HandshakeSecret>
        < /EncryptedText>
< /Confirmation>
```

On receiving the confirmation from the subscription server, the user computes key k through the equation $k = W^{AB}$ mod p. This key is used to decipher the encrypted text. On deciphering, the confirmation of the transaction is done by comparing the HandshakeSecret sent by the subscription server, to that sent earlier by the user.

4.2   Secure Protocol for Accessing Pre-subscribed Goods

Pre-subscribed goods/services are primarily of two types, first being the periodicals such as e-magazines, etc. and second being services such as chat, online games, as also paid browsing sites, etc. The protocol followed for each of these two types are almost the same except the fact that the authorization tokens granted in each type differs.

A typical access scenario, is described below:

1. C $\longrightarrow$ S (Request for Authorization token.)
   Before accessing any digital download the customer has to first get the requisite authorization token for the same from the subscription server. The XML

format for the request made by the Customer to the Subscription Server for a subscription token is as shown below.

```
<Request>
        <UserID>XYZ< /UserID>
        <Key>W^A modp < /Key>
        <timestamp>2000082400:00:00< /timestamp>
        <expirydate>2000082900:00:00< /expirydate>
        <EncryptedText>
                <RequestType>Token Request< /RequestType>
                <SubscriptionID>..< /SubscriptionID>
                <SubscriptionIssueNo>..< /SubscriptionIssueNo>
                <HandshakeSecret>Secret< /HandshakeSecret>
        < /EncryptedText>
< /Request>
```

2. S ⟶ C (Authorization Token Granted.)
On receiving a request from the user, the subscription server searches in its repository, if there is an appropriate subscription certificate issued against the user's name, he grants the user an authorization token against it. The XML format subscription servers reply is as shown below.

```
<Reply>
        <Key>W^B modp < /Key>
        <EncryptedText>
                <AuthorizationToken> ... < /AuthorizationToken>
                <TimeStamp> ... < /TimeStamp>
                <expirydate>...< /expirydate>
                <HandshakeSecret>Secret< /HandshakeSecret>
        < /EncryptedText>
< /Reply>
```

3. C ⟶ D (Download Request.)
After receiving the authorization token from the subscription server, the user approaches the download server with the authorization token for downloading the digital goods. The XML format of the download request is as shown below.

```
<DownloadRequest>
        <UserID>XYZ< /UserID>
        <publicKey>..< /publicKey>
        <timestamp>2000082400:00:00< /timestamp>
        <expirydate>2000082900:00:00< /expirydate>
        <AuthorizationToken> ... < /AuthorizationToken>
< /DownloadRequest>
```

4. D ⟶ C (Digital Download) The download server responds to the customers request by checking the authentication token; after the verification of the token, it sends the requested software in an encrypted manner using the user's public key. The XML format of the download servers response is shown below.

```
<Download>
        <EncryptedDownload>..< /EncryptedDownload>
< /Download>
```

The authentication token sent by the subscription server to the user has the following format:
[tokenNo, SubscriptionServerID, UserID, IPAddress, PublicKey,TimeStamp, ExpiryDate, MerchantID, SubscriptionNo, SubscriptionIssue]S-priv
where, S-priv is the private key of the subscription server, used to clear sign the authentication token sent to the user.

However, in this sort of software architecture there is always a risk of a replay attack where in the same authorization token is submitted by the user more than once to the download server for access. This kind of replay attack is avoided through the usage of timestamps and expiry dates in the authorization tokens, along with some kind of small duration catching mechanisms at the server end.

5   Discussion

In this paper, we have described a set of protocols for getting services/goods through subscription. As these subscription based protocols don't have to go through the authorization servers, payment gateways, etc. result in an overall reduction of overhead without foregoing security. These aspects make it ideally suited for real time applications such as video games, online chats, search engines, etc. They also find applications where online discounts are offered on one time purchases, etc. The above protocols have been implemented as part of MIES at TIFR and are undergoing tests. Work is also under progress in the development of highly efficient protocols for access to pre-subscribed sites for services based on role based certificates such as SPKI/SDSI.

References

1. Stefan A. Brands. *Rethinking Public Key Infrastructures and Digital Certificates: Building in Privacy.* MIT Press, Cambridge, Mass., 2000.
2. D. Chaum, A. Fiat, and M. Naor. Offline electronic cash. In *Proceedings of CRYPTO'88*, 1988.
3. David Chaum. Online ecash checks. *Advances in Cryptology EUROCRYPT '89*, 1989.
4. Benjamin Cox, J. D. Tygar, and Marvin Sirbu. Netbill security and transactiion protocol. *Proceedings of the first USENIX Workshop on Electronic Commerce*, 1995.

5. N. Daswani, D. Boneh, H. Garcia-Molina, S. Ketchpel, and A. Paepcke. Swaperoo: A simple wallet architecture for payments, exchanges, refunds, and other operations, 1998.
6. Amir Herzberg and Hilik Yochai. Minipay : Charging per click on the web. *Computer Networks*, 29:939–951, 1997.
7. David P. Jablon. Strong password only-authenticated key exchange. september 25, 1996.
8. Radia Perlman and Charlie Kaufman. Secure password-based protocol for downloading a private key. *Proceedings of the 1999 Network and Distributed System Security*, 1999.
9. Ronald L. Rivest and Butler Lampson. SDSI – A simple distributed security infrastructure. Presented at CRYPTO'96 Rumpsession, 1996.
10. Ronald L. Rivest and Adi Shamir. Payword and MicroMint: Two simple micropayment schemes. In *Security Protocols Workshop*, pages 69–87, 1996.
11. Adi Shamir. Fast signature screening. Presented at CRYPTO'95 Rumpsession; to appear in RSA Laboratories CryptoBytes, 1995.
12. R. K. Shyamsundar and S. B. Deshmukh. MIES: A multi instrument ecommerce system. TR, TIFR, May 2002.
13. R. K. Shyamsundar and Vishwas Patil. ROADS: Role based authorization and delegation system. TR, TIFR, May 2002.

Author Index